YO-ABK-896

YOUR MOST COMPREHENSIVE AND
REVEALING INDIVIDUAL FORECAST

SUPER HOROSCOPE

GEMINI

19 99

May 21 - June 20

BERKLEY BOOKS, NEW YORK

The publishers regret that they cannot answer
individual letters requesting personal horoscope information.

1999 SUPER HOROSCOPE GEMINI

PRINTING HISTORY
Berkley Trade Edition / August 1998

All rights reserved.
Copyright © 1974, 1978, 1979, 1980, 1981, 1982
by Grosset & Dunlap, Inc.
Copyright © 1983, 1984 by Charter Communications, Inc.
Copyright © 1985, 1986, 1987, 1988, 1989, 1990, 1991, 1992, 1993, 1994, 1995,
1996, 1997, 1998
by The Berkley Publishing Group.
This book may not be reproduced in whole or in part, by
mimeograph or any other means, without permission.
For information address: The Berkley Publishing Group,
a member of Penguin Putnam Inc.,
200 Madison Avenue, New York, New York 10016.

The Penguin Putnam Inc. World Wide Web site address is
http://www.penguinputnam.com

ISBN: 0-425-16326-1

BERKLEY®
Berkley Books are published by The Berkley Publishing Group,
a member of Penguin Putnam Inc.,
200 Madison Avenue, New York, New York 10016.
"BERKLEY" and the "B" logo
are trademarks belonging to Berkley Publishing Corporation.

PRINTED IN THE UNITED STATES OF AMERICA

10 9 8 7 6 5 4 3 2 1

CONTENTS

THE CUSP-BORN GEMINI

Are you *really* a Gemini? If your birthday falls during the third week of May, at the beginning of Gemini, will you still retain the traits of Taurus, the sign of the Zodiac before Gemini? And what if you were born late in June—are you more Cancer than Gemini? Many people born at the edge, or cusp, of a sign have difficulty determining exactly what sign they are. If you are one of these people, here's how you can figure it out, once and for all.

Consult the cusp table on the facing page, then locate the year of your birth. The table will tell you the precise days on which the Sun entered and left your sign for the year of your birth. In that way you can determine if you are a true Gemini—or whether you are a Taurus or Cancer—according to the variations in cusp dates from year to year (see also page 17).

If you were born at the beginning or end of Gemini, yours is a lifetime reflecting a process of subtle transformation. Your life on Earth will symbolize a significant change in consciousness, for you are either about to enter a whole new way of living or are leaving one behind.

If you were born during the third week of May, you may want to read the horoscope book for Taurus as well as for Gemini, for Taurus holds the key to a hidden and often perplexing side of your personality—yet one that is the seed of your cosmic uplift and unfolding.

Mobility is your aim and variety your purpose. Yet you are drawn again and again to fixed, immobile Taurus. Your compulsion to settle down, find stability, wealth, and constancy attracts you to Taurus, and this attraction is a dilemma. For where is your true commitment? To variety—that old spice of life—or to the solid, substantial promise of Taurus?

At best, you symbolize the birth of perception, the capacity of the mind to know and communicate information.

If you were born during the fourth week of June, you may want to read the horoscope book for Cancer, as well as Gemini, for in Cancer you find not only financial security but a way of making all your assets grow.

4

You are about to settle down, about to dock your ship in a port and stay awhile; but there is a restlessness in you that is irrepressible. You are preparing to make yourself secure. You can be shrewd, money-minded, and practical despite your moodiness, naivete, and sometimes irksome adolescent approach to life.

Above all, you are a skilled manipulator of language and design and your powers of reason lie behind everything you think and do.

THE CUSPS OF GEMINI

DATES SUN ENTERS GEMINI (LEAVES TAURUS)

May 21 every year from 1900 to 2000, except for the following:

	May 20		May 22
1948	1972	1988	1903
52	76	89	07
56	80	92	11
60	81	93	19
64	84	96	
68	85	97	

DATES SUN LEAVES GEMINI (ENTERS CANCER)

June 21 every year from 1900 to 2000, except for the following:

June 20		June 22	
1988	1902	1915	1931
92	03	18	35
96	06	19	39
	07	22	43
	10	23	47
	11	26	51
	14	27	55

THE ASCENDANT: GEMINI RISING

Could you be a "double" Gemini? That is, could you have Gemini as your Rising sign as well as your Sun sign? The tables on pages 8–9 will tell you Geminis what your Rising sign happens to be. Just find the hour of your birth, then find the day of your birth, and you will see which sign of the Zodiac is your Ascendant, as the Rising sign is called. The Ascendant is called that because it is the sign rising on the eastern horizon at the time of your birth. For a more detailed discussion of the Rising sign and the twelve houses of the Zodiac, see pages 17–20.

The Ascendant, or Rising sign, is placed on the 1st house in a horoscope, of which there are twelve houses. The 1st house represents your response to the environment—your unique response. Call it identity, personality, ego, self-image, facade, come-on, body-mind-spirit—whatever term best conveys to you the meaning of the you that acts and reacts in the world. It is a you that is always changing, discovering a new you. Your identity started with birth and early environment, over which you had little conscious control, and continues to experience, to adjust, to express itself. The 1st house also represents how others see you. Has anyone ever guessed your sign to be your Rising sign? People may respond to that personality, that facade, that body type governed by your Rising sign.

Your Ascendant, or Rising sign, modifies your basic Sun sign personality, and it affects the way you act out the daily predictions for your Sun sign. If your Rising sign indeed is Gemini, what follows is a description of its effect on your horoscope. If your Rising sign is not Gemini, but some other sign of the Zodiac, you may wish to read the horoscope book for that sign as well.

With Gemini on the Ascendant, that is, in the 1st house, your ruling planet Mercury is therefore in the 1st house. Mercury in this position gives you a restless spirit, pushing you on a constant search for knowledge. You are always alert for new information, and your quest may take you far afield to explore unfamiliar subjects and even foreign lands. Mercury confers a subtle wariness that could be your best defense when people try to fool you or cheat you. On the other hand, that trait could be aggressively used as a weapon against people, giving rise to unworthy actions, tricks, or disputes.

The desire to express yourself will be very strong in your personality. You tend to rely on logic rather than intuition, and you could go to great lengths to prove to yourself and to others the validity of your ideas. This need for expression combined with an equal need for variety gives your life a lot of surface drama: you are endlessly changing your focus of experience. In your lifetime you may hold a series of seemingly unrelated jobs; move frequently to new residences in unusual surroundings; make friends, drop them, pick them up again; change your world view often. Although other people may judge you to lack seriousness, that is not really so. You seek ideas and experience to help you understand and order your environment because you want from it maximal comfort and constant ego satisfaction.

Human contact is another large need for Gemini Rising individuals. It gives your desire to express yourself an audience. Yours is the sign of brothers and sisters, relatives, family. If you do not have a closely knit blood family, you will create a familylike network among friends, workmates, neighbors, and community contacts. You like to keep up with distant acquaintances, even ex-lovers, just so you can invite them to participate in one of your shindigs. And of course your home will be the center of attraction. For you are more than just tidy and fashionable; you know how to arrange a setting and accommodate people in order to stimulate the greatest communication between them.

Your youthful appearance and pleasing speaking voice attract people to you, and you know it. You are not above heightening the effect of these natural assets. You have been known to adapt your costuming to suit the occasion, and you sometimes manipulate your speech patterns to display emotions you don't feel or to invoke emotions in other people. As a result, you can be accused of self-centeredness.

Charm is your great natural talent; you do it with words, words, words. Gemini teachers can fascinate bored students into enjoying, let alone learning, a boring subject. Gemini adults can sweet-talk unruly youngsters into rational behavior. Gemini people in general lighten the lives of their friends with endless small talk about clothes, things, events, places, other people. You also enlighten your friends when you talk on that deeper, more sophisticated level of patterns of experience and cause and effect.

Writing and public speaking are arts that you with Gemini Rising can rely on consistently. Scholarly work is a possibility in your lifetime. Intellect is the key word that will allow you to understand any environment. Although your financial fortunes may change, your mercurial talents will deepen and survive.

RISING SIGNS FOR GEMINI

Hour of Birth*	Day of Birth		
	May 21–25	**May 26–30**	**May 31–June 4**
Midnight	Aquarius	Aquarius	Aquarius; Pisces 6/3
1 AM	Pisces	Pisces	Pisces
2 AM	Pisces; Aries 5/23	Aries	Aries
3 AM	Aries	Taurus	Taurus
4 AM	Taurus	Taurus	Taurus; Gemini 6/3
5 AM	Gemini	Gemini	Gemini
6 AM	Gemini	Gemini	Gemini; Cancer 6/2
7 AM	Cancer	Cancer	Cancer
8 AM	Cancer	Cancer	Cancer
9 AM	Cancer; Leo 5/24	Leo	Leo
10 AM	Leo	Leo	Leo
11 AM	Leo	Leo	Virgo
Noon	Virgo	Virgo	Virgo
1 PM	Virgo	Virgo	Virgo
2 PM	Virgo	Libra	Libra
3 PM	Libra	Libra	Libra
4 PM	Libra	Libra; Scorpio 5/25	Scorpio
5 PM	Scorpio	Scorpio	Scorpio
6 PM	Scorpio	Scorpio	Scorpio
7 PM	Scorpio; Sagittarius 5/23	Sagittarius	Sagittarius
8 PM	Sagittarius	Sagittarius	Sagittarius
9 PM	Sagittarius	Sagittarius; Capricorn 5/28	Capricorn
10 PM	Capricorn	Capricorn	Capricorn
11 PM	Capricorn	Aquarius	Aquarius

*Hour of birth given here is for Standard Time in any time zone. If your hour of birth was recorded in Daylight Saving Time, subtract one hour from it and consult that hour in the table above. For example, if you were born at 7 AM. D.S.T., see 6 AM above.

Hour of Birth	Day of Birth		
	June 5–10	June 11–15	June 16–21
Midnight	Pisces	Pisces	Pisces
1 AM	Pisces; Aries 6/7	Aries	Aries
2 AM	Aries	Taurus	Taurus
3 AM	Taurus	Taurus	Taurus; Gemini 6/18
4 AM	Gemini	Gemini	Gemini
5 AM	Gemini	Gemini	Gemini; Cancer 6/17
6 AM	Cancer	Cancer	Cancer
7 AM	Cancer	Cancer	Cancer
8 AM	Cancer; Leo 6/8	Leo	Leo
9 AM	Leo	Leo	Leo
10 AM	Leo	Leo; Virgo 6/15	Virgo
11 AM	Virgo	Virgo	Virgo
Noon	Virgo	Virgo	Virgo
1 PM	Virgo; Libra 6/7	Libra	Libra
2 PM	Libra	Libra	Libra
3 PM	Libra	Libra; Scorpio 6/14	Scorpio
4 PM	Scorpio	Scorpio	Scorpio
5 PM	Scorpio	Scorpio	Scorpio
6 PM	Scorpio; Sagittarius 6/7	Sagittarius	Sagittarius
7 PM	Sagittarius	Sagittarius	Sagittarius
8 PM	Sagittarius	Sagittarius; Capricorn 6/12	Sagittarius
9 PM	Capricorn	Capricorn	Capricorn
10 PM	Capricorn	Aquarius	Aquarius
11 PM	Aquarius	Aquarius	Pisces

*See note on facing page.

THE PLACE OF ASTROLOGY IN TODAY'S WORLD

Does astrology have a place in the fast-moving, ultra-scientific world we live in today? Can it be justified in a sophisticated society whose outriders are already preparing to step off the moon into the deep space of the planets themselves? Or is it just a hangover of ancient superstition, a psychological dummy for neurotics and dreamers of every historical age?

These are the kind of questions that any inquiring person can be expected to ask when they approach a subject like astrology which goes beyond, but never excludes, the materialistic side of life.

The simple, single answer is that astrology works. It works for many millions of people in the western world alone. In the United States there are 10 million followers and in Europe, an estimated 25 million. America has more than 4000 practicing astrologers, Europe nearly three times as many. Even down-under Australia has its hundreds of thousands of adherents. In the eastern countries, astrology has enormous followings, again, because it has been proved to work. In India, for example, brides and grooms for centuries have been chosen on the basis of their astrological compatibility.

Astrology today is more vital than ever before, more practicable because all over the world the media devotes much space and time to it, more valid because science itself is confirming the precepts of astrological knowledge with every new exciting step. The ordinary person who daily applies astrology intelligently does not have to wonder whether it is true nor believe in it blindly. He can see it working for himself. And, if he can use it—and this book is designed to help the reader to do just that—he can make living a far richer experience, and become a more developed personality and a better person.

Astrology and Relationships

Astrology is the science of relationships. It is not just a study of planetary influences on man and his environment. It is the study of man himself.

We are at the center of our personal universe, of all our relationships. And our happiness or sadness depends on how we act, how we relate to the people and things that surround us. The emotions that we generate have a distinct effect—for better or worse—on the world around us. Our friends and our enemies will confirm this. Just look in the mirror the next time you are angry. In other words, each of us is a kind of sun or planet or star radiating our feelings on the environment around us. Our influence on our personal universe, whether loving, helpful, or destructive, varies with our changing moods, expressed through our individual character.

Our personal "radiations" are potent in the way they affect our moods and our ability to control them. But we usually are able to throw off our emotion in some sort of action—we have a good cry, walk it off, or tell someone our troubles—before it can build up too far and make us physically ill. Astrology helps us to understand the universal forces working on us, and through this understanding, we can become more properly adjusted to our surroundings so that we find ourselves coping where others may flounder.

The Challenge of Love

The challenge of love lies in recognizing the difference between infatuation, emotion, sex, and, sometimes, the intentional deceit of the other person. Mankind, with its record of broken marriages, despair, and disillusionment, is obviously not very good at making these distinctions.

Can astrology help?

Yes. In the same way that advance knowledge can usually help in any human situation. And there is probably no situation as human, as poignant, as pathetic and universal, as the failure of man's love.

Love, of course, is not just between man and woman. It involves love of children, parents, home, and friends. But the big problems usually involve the choice of partner.

Astrology has established degrees of compatibility that exist between people born under the various signs of the Zodiac. Because people are individuals, there are numerous variations and modifications. So the astrologer, when approached on mate and marriage matters, makes allowances for them. But the fact remains that some groups of people are suited for each other and some are not, and astrology has expressed this in terms of characteristics we all can study and use as a personal guide.

No matter how much enjoyment and pleasure we find in the different aspects of each other's character, if it is not an overall compatibility, the chances of our finding fulfillment or enduring happiness in each other are pretty hopeless. And astrology can help us to find someone compatible.

Astrology and Science

Closely related to our emotions is the "other side" of our personal universe, our physical welfare. Our body, of course, is largely influenced by things around us over which we have very little control. The phone rings, we hear it. The train runs late. We snag our stocking or cut our face shaving. Our body is under a constant bombardment of events that influence our daily lives to varying degrees.

The question that arises from all this is, what makes each of us act so that we have to involve other people and keep the ball of activity and evolution rolling? This is the question that both science and astrology are involved with. The scientists have attacked it from different angles: anthropology, the study of human evolution as body, mind and response to environment; anatomy, the study of bodily structure; psychology, the science of the human mind; and so on. These studies have produced very impressive classifications and valuable information, but because the approach to the problem is fragmented, so is the result. They remain "branches" of science. Science generally studies effects. It keeps turning up wonderful answers but no lasting solutions. Astrology, on the other hand, approaches the question from the broader viewpoint. Astrology began its inquiry with the totality of human experience and saw it as an effect. It then looked to find the cause, or at least the prime movers, and during thousands of years of observation of man and his *universal* environment came up with the extraordinary principle of planetary influence—or astrology, which, from the Greek, means the science of the stars.

Modern science, as we shall see, has confirmed much of astrology's foundations—most of it unintentionally, some of it reluctantly, but still, indisputably.

It is not difficult to imagine that there must be a connection between outer space and Earth. Even today, scientists are not too sure how our Earth was created, but it is generally agreed that it is only a tiny part of the universe. And as a part of the universe, people on Earth see and feel the influence of heavenly bodies in almost every aspect of our existence. There is no doubt that the Sun has the greatest influence on life on this planet. Without it there would be no life, for without it there would be no warmth, no division into day and night, no cycles of time or season at all. This is clear and easy to see. The influence of the Moon, on the other hand, is more subtle, though no less definite.

There are many ways in which the influence of the Moon manifests itself here on Earth, both on human and animal life. It is a well-known fact, for instance, that the large movements of water on our planet—that is the ebb and flow of the tides—are caused by the Moon's gravitational pull. Since this is so, it follows that these water movements do not occur only in the oceans, but that all bodies of water are affected, even down to the tiniest puddle.

The human body, too, which consists of about 70 percent water, falls within the scope of this lunar influence. For example the menstrual cycle of most women corresponds to the 28-day lunar month; the period of pregnancy in humans is 273 days, or equal to nine lunar months. Similarly, many illnesses reach a crisis at the change of the Moon, and statistics in many countries have shown that the crime rate is highest at the time of the Full Moon. Even human sexual desire has been associated with the phases of the Moon. But it is in the movement of the tides that we get the clearest demonstration of planetary influence, which leads to the irresistible correspondence between the so-called metaphysical and the physical.

Tide tables are prepared years in advance by calculating the future positions of the Moon. Science has known for a long time that the Moon is the main cause of tidal action. But only in the last few years has it begun to realize the possible extent of this influence on mankind. To begin with, the ocean tides do not rise and fall as we might imagine from our personal observations of them. The Moon as it orbits around Earth sets up a circular wave of attraction which pulls the oceans of the world after it, broadly in an east to west direction. This influence is like a phantom wave crest, a loop of power stretching from pole to pole which passes over and around the Earth like an invisible shadow. It travels with equal effect across the land masses and, as scientists were recently amazed to observe, caused oysters placed in the dark in the middle of the United States where there is no sea to open their shells to receive the nonexistent tide. If the land-locked oysters react to this invisible signal, what effect does it have on us who not so long ago in evolutionary time came out of the sea and still have its salt in our blood and sweat?

Less well known is the fact that the Moon is also the primary force behind the circulation of blood in human beings and animals, and the movement of sap in trees and plants. Agriculturists have established that the Moon has a distinct influence on crops, which explains why for centuries people have planted according to Moon cycles. The habits of many animals, too, are directed by the movement of the Moon. Migratory birds, for instance, depart only at or near the time of the Full Moon. And certain sea creatures, eels in particular, move only in accordance with certain phases of the Moon.

Know Thyself—Why?

In today's fast-changing world, everyone still longs to know what the future holds. It is the one thing that everyone has in common: rich and poor, famous and infamous, all are deeply concerned about tomorrow.

But the key to the future, as every historian knows, lies in the past. This is as true of individual people as it is of nations. You cannot understand your future without first understanding your past, which is simply another way of saying that you must first of all know yourself.

The motto "know thyself" seems obvious enough nowadays, but it was originally put forward as the foundation of wisdom by the ancient Greek philosophers. It was then adopted by the "mystery religions" of the ancient Middle East, Greece, Rome, and is still used in all genuine schools of mind training or mystical discipline, both in those of the East, based on yoga, and those of the West. So it is universally accepted now, and has been through the ages.

But how do you go about discovering what sort of person you are? The first step is usually classification into some sort of system of types. Astrology did this long before the birth of Christ. Psychology has also done it. So has modern medicine, in its way.

One system classifies people according to the source of the impulses they respond to most readily: the muscles, leading to direct bodily action; the digestive organs, resulting in emotion; or the brain and nerves, giving rise to thinking. Another such system says that character is determined by the endocrine glands, and gives us such labels as "pituitary," "thyroid," and "hyperthyroid" types. These different systems are neither contradictory nor mutually exclusive. In fact, they are very often different ways of saying the same thing.

Very popular, useful classifications were devised by Carl Jung, the eminent disciple of Freud. Jung observed among the different faculties of the mind, four which have a predominant influence on character. These four faculties exist in all of us without exception, but not in perfect balance. So when we say, for instance, that someone is a "thinking type," it means that in any situation he or she tries to be rational. Emotion, which may be the opposite of thinking, will be his or her weakest function. This thinking type can be sensible and reasonable, or calculating and unsympathetic. The emotional type, on the other hand, can often be recognized by exaggerated language—everything is either marvelous or terrible—and in extreme cases they even invent dramas and quarrels out of nothing just to make life more interesting.

The other two faculties are intuition and physical sensation. The sensation type does not only care for food and drink, nice clothes and furniture; he or she is also interested in all forms of physical experience. Many scientists are sensation types as are athletes and nature-lovers. Like sensation, intuition is a form of perception and we all possess it. But it works through that part of the mind which is not under conscious control—consequently it sees meanings and connections which are not obvious to thought or emotion. Inventors and original thinkers are always intuitive, but so, too, are superstitious people who see meanings where none exist.

Thus, sensation tells us what is going on in the world, feeling (that is, emotion) tells us how important it is to ourselves, thinking enables us to interpret it and work out what we should do about it, and intuition tells us what it means to ourselves and others. All four faculties are essential, and all are present in every one of us. But some people are guided chiefly by one, others by another. In addition, Jung also observed a division of the human personality into the extrovert and the introvert, which cuts across these four types.

A disadvantage of all these systems of classification is that one cannot tell very easily where to place oneself. Some people are reluctant to admit that they act to please their emotions. So they deceive themselves for years by trying to belong to whichever type they think is the "best." Of course, there is no best; each has its faults and each has its good points.

The advantage of the signs of the Zodiac is that they simplify classification. Not only that, but your date of birth is personal—it is unarguably yours. What better way to know yourself than by going back as far as possible to the very moment of your birth? And this is precisely what your horoscope is all about, as we shall see in the next section.

WHAT IS A HOROSCOPE?

If you had been able to take a picture of the skies at the moment of your birth, that photograph would be your horoscope. Lacking such a snapshot, it is still possible to recreate the picture—and this is at the basis of the astrologer's art. In other words, your horoscope is a representation of the skies with the planets in the exact positions they occupied at the time you were born.

The year of birth tells an astrologer the positions of the distant, slow-moving planets Jupiter, Saturn, Uranus, Neptune, and Pluto. The month of birth indicates the Sun sign, or birth sign as it is commonly called, as well as indicating the positions of the rapidly moving planets Venus, Mercury, and Mars. The day and time of birth will locate the position of our Moon. And the moment—the exact hour and minute—of birth determines the houses through what is called the Ascendant, or Rising sign.

With this information the astrologer consults various tables to calculate the specific positions of the Sun, Moon, and other planets relative to your birthplace at the moment you were born. Then he or she locates them by means of the Zodiac.

The Zodiac

The Zodiac is a band of stars (constellations) in the skies, centered on the Sun's apparent path around the Earth, and is divided into twelve equal segments, or signs. What we are actually dividing up is the Earth's path around the Sun. But from our point of view here on Earth, it seems as if the Sun is making a great circle around our planet in the sky, so we say it is the Sun's apparent path. This twelvefold division, the Zodiac, is a reference system for the astrologer. At any given moment the planets—and in astrology both the Sun and Moon are considered to be planets—can all be located at a specific point along this path.

Now where in all this are you, the subject of the horoscope? Your character is largely determined by the sign the Sun is in. So that is where the astrologer looks first in your horoscope, at your Sun sign.

The Sun Sign and the Cusp

There are twelve signs in the Zodiac, and the Sun spends approximately one month in each sign. But because of the motion of the Earth around the Sun—the Sun's apparent motion—the dates when the Sun enters and leaves each sign may change from year to year. Some people born near the cusp, or edge, of a sign have difficulty determining which is their Sun sign. But in this book a Table of Cusps is provided for the years 1900 to 2000 (page 5) so you can find out what your true Sun sign is.

Here are the twelve signs of the Zodiac, their ancient zodiacal symbol, and the dates when the Sun enters and leaves each sign for the year 1999. Remember, these dates may change from year to year.

ARIES	Ram	March 20–April 20
TAURUS	Bull	April 20–May 21
GEMINI	Twins	May 21–June 21
CANCER	Crab	June 21–July 23
LEO	Lion	July 23–August 23
VIRGO	Virgin	August 23–September 23
LIBRA	Scales	September 23–October 23
SCORPIO	Scorpion	October 23–November 22
SAGITTARIUS	Archer	November 22–December 22
CAPRICORN	Sea Goat	December 22–January 20
AQUARIUS	Water Bearer	January 20–February 18
PISCES	Fish	February 18–March 20

It is possible to draw significant conclusions and make meaningful predictions based simply on the Sun sign of a person. There are many people who have been amazed at the accuracy of the description of their own character based only on the Sun sign. But an astrologer needs more information than just your Sun sign to interpret the photograph that is your horoscope.

The Rising Sign and the Zodiacal Houses

An astrologer needs the exact time and place of your birth in order to construct and interpret your horoscope. The illustration on the next page shows the flat chart, or natural wheel, an astrologer uses. Note the inner circle of the wheel labeled 1 through 12. These 12 divisions are known as the houses of the Zodiac.

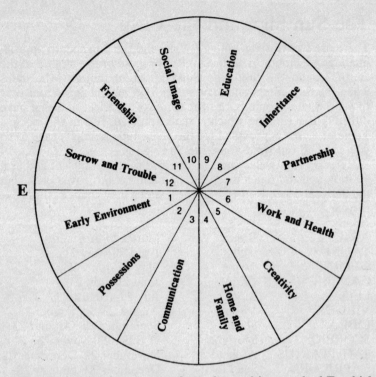

The 1st house always starts from the position marked E, which corresponds to the eastern horizon. The rest of the houses 2 through 12 follow around in a "counterclockwise" direction. The point where each house starts is known as a cusp, or edge.

The cusp, or edge, of the 1st house (point E) is where an astrologer would place your Rising sign, the Ascendant. And, as already noted, the exact time of your birth determines your Rising sign. Let's see how this works.

As the Earth rotates on its axis once every 24 hours, each one of the twelve signs of the Zodiac appears to be "rising" on the horizon, with a new one appearing about every 2 hours. Actually it is the turning of the Earth that exposes each sign to view, but in our astrological work we are discussing apparent motion. This Rising sign marks the Ascendant, and it colors the whole orientation of a horoscope. It indicates the sign governing the 1st house of the chart, and will thus determine which signs will govern all the other houses.

To visualize this idea, imagine two color wheels with twelve divisions superimposed upon each other. For just as the Zodiac is divided into twelve constellations that we identify as the signs, another twelvefold division is used to denote the houses. Now imagine one wheel (the signs) moving slowly while the other wheel (the houses) remains still. This analogy may help you see how the signs keep shifting the "color" of the houses as the Rising sign continues to change every two hours. To simplify things, a Table of Rising Signs has been provided (pages 8–9) for your specific Sun sign.

Once your Rising sign has been placed on the cusp of the 1st house, the signs that govern the rest of the 11 houses can be placed on the chart. In any individual's horoscope the signs do not necessarily correspond with the houses. For example, it could be that a sign covers part of two adjacent houses. It is the interpretation of such variations in an individual's horoscope that marks the professional astrologer.

But to gain a workable understanding of astrology, it is not necessary to go into great detail. In fact, we just need a description of the houses and their meanings, as is shown in the illustration above and in the table below.

THE 12 HOUSES OF THE ZODIAC

1st	Individuality, body appearance, general outlook on life	Personality house
2nd	Finance, possessions, ethical principles, gain or loss	Money house
3rd	Relatives, communication, short journeys, writing, education	Relatives house
4th	Family and home, parental ties, land and property, security	Home house
5th	Pleasure, children, creativity, entertainment, risk	Pleasure house
6th	Health, harvest, hygiene, work and service, employees	Health house
7th	Marriage and divorce, the law, partnerships and alliances	Marriage house
8th	Inheritance, secret deals, sex, death, regeneration	Inheritance house
9th	Travel, sports, study, philosophy and religion	Travel house
10th	Career, social standing, success and honor	Business house
11th	Friendship, social life, hopes and wishes	Friends house
12th	Troubles, illness, secret enemies, hidden agendas	Trouble house

The Planets in the Houses

An astrologer, knowing the exact time and place of your birth, will use tables of planetary motion in order to locate the planets in your horoscope chart. He or she will determine which planet or planets are in which sign and in which house. It is not uncommon, in an individual's horoscope, for there to be two or more planets in the same sign and in the same house.

The characteristics of the planets modify the influence of the Sun according to their natures and strengths.

Sun: Source of life. Basic temperament according to the Sun sign. The conscious will. Human potential.

Moon: Emotions. Moods. Customs. Habits. Changeable. Adaptive. Nurturing.

Mercury: Communication. Intellect. Reasoning power. Curiosity. Short travels.

Venus: Love. Delight. Charm. Harmony. Balance. Art. Beautiful possessions.

Mars: Energy. Initiative. War. Anger. Adventure. Courage. Daring. Impulse.

Jupiter: Luck. Optimism. Generous. Expansive. Opportunities. Protection.

Saturn: Pessimism. Privation. Obstacles. Delay. Hard work. Research. Lasting rewards after long struggle.

Uranus: Fashion. Electricity. Revolution. Independence. Freedom. Sudden changes. Modern science.

Neptune: Sensationalism. Theater. Dreams. Inspiration. Illusion. Deception.

Pluto: Creation and destruction. Total transformation. Lust for power. Strong obsessions.

Superimpose the characteristics of the planets on the functions of the house in which they appear. Express the result through the character of the Sun sign, and you will get the basic idea.

Of course, many other considerations have been taken into account in producing the carefully worked out predictions in this book: the aspects of the planets to each other; their strength according to position and sign; whether they are in a house of exaltation or decline; whether they are natural enemies or not; whether a planet occupies its own sign; the position of a planet in relation to its own house or sign; whether the sign is male or female; whether the sign is a fire, earth, water, or air sign. These are only a few of the colors on the astrologer's pallet which he or she must mix with the inspiration of the artist and the accuracy of the mathematician.

How To Use These Predictions

A person reading the predictions in this book should understand that they are produced from the daily position of the planets for a group of people and are not, of course, individually specialized. To get the full benefit of them our readers should relate the predictions to their own character and circumstances, coordinate them, and draw their own conclusions from them.

If you are a serious observer of your own life, you should find a definite pattern emerging that will be a helpful and reliable guide.

The point is that we always retain our free will. The stars indicate certain directional tendencies but we are not compelled to follow. We can do or not do, and wisdom must make the choice.

We all have our good and bad days. Sometimes they extend into cycles of weeks. It is therefore advisable to study daily predictions in a span ranging from the day before to several days ahead.

Daily predictions should be taken very generally. The word "difficult" does not necessarily indicate a whole day of obstruction or inconvenience. It is a warning to you to be cautious. Your caution will often see you around the difficulty before you are involved. This is the correct use of astrology.

In another section (pages 78–84), detailed information is given about the influence of the Moon as it passes through each of the twelve signs of the Zodiac. There are instructions on how to use the Moon Tables (pages 85–92), which provide Moon Sign Dates throughout the year as well as the Moon's role in health and daily affairs. This information should be used in conjunction with the daily forecasts to give a fuller picture of the astrological trends.

HISTORY OF ASTROLOGY

The origins of astrology have been lost far back in history, but we do know that reference is made to it as far back as the first written records of the human race. It is not hard to see why. Even in primitive times, people must have looked for an explanation for the various happenings in their lives. They must have wanted to know why people were different from one another. And in their search they turned to the regular movements of the Sun, Moon, and stars to see if they could provide an answer.

It is interesting to note that as soon as man learned to use his tools in any type of design, or his mind in any kind of calculation, he turned his attention to the heavens. Ancient cave dwellings reveal dim crescents and circles representative of the Sun and Moon, rulers of day and night. Mesopotamia and the civilization of Chaldea, in itself the foundation of those of Babylonia and Assyria, show a complete picture of astronomical observation and well-developed astrological interpretation.

Humanity has a natural instinct for order. The study of anthropology reveals that primitive people—even as far back as prehistoric times—were striving to achieve a certain order in their lives. They tried to organize the apparent chaos of the universe. They had the desire to attach meaning to things. This demand for order has persisted throughout the history of man. So that observing the regularity of the heavenly bodies made it logical that primitive peoples should turn heavenward in their search for an understanding of the world in which they found themselves so random and alone.

And they did find a significance in the movements of the stars. Shepherds tending their flocks, for instance, observed that when the cluster of stars now known as the constellation Aries was in sight, it was the time of fertility and they associated it with the Ram. And they noticed that the growth of plants and plant life corresponded with different phases of the Moon, so that certain times were favorable for the planting of crops, and other times were not. In this way, there grew up a tradition of seasons and causes connected with the passage of the Sun through the twelve signs of the Zodiac.

Astrology was valued so highly that the king was kept informed of the daily and monthly changes in the heavenly bodies, and the results of astrological studies regarding events of the future. Head astrologers were clearly men of great rank and position, and the office was said to be a hereditary one.

Omens were taken, not only from eclipses and conjunctions of the Moon or Sun with one of the planets, but also from storms and earthquakes. In the eastern civilizations, particularly, the reverence inspired by astrology appears to have remained unbroken since the very earliest days. In ancient China, astrology, astronomy, and religion went hand in hand. The astrologer, who was also an astronomer, was part of the official government service and had his own corner in the Imperial Palace. The duties of the Imperial astrologer, whose office was one of the most important in the land, were clearly defined, as this extract from early records shows:

> This exalted gentleman must concern himself with the stars in the heavens, keeping a record of the changes and movements of the Planets, the Sun and the Moon, in order to examine the movements of the terrestrial world with the object of prognosticating good and bad fortune. He divides the territories of the nine regions of the empire in accordance with their dependence on particular celestial bodies. All the fiefs and principalities are connected with the stars and from this their prosperity or misfortune should be ascertained. He makes prognostications according to the twelve years of the Jupiter cycle of good and evil of the terrestrial world. From the colors of the five kinds of clouds, he determines the coming of floods or droughts, abundance or famine. From the twelve winds, he draws conclusions about the state of harmony of heaven and earth, and takes note of good and bad signs that result from their accord or disaccord. In general, he concerns himself with five kinds of phenomena so as to warn the Emperor to come to the aid of the government and to allow for variations in the ceremonies according to their circumstances.

The Chinese were also keen observers of the fixed stars, giving them such unusual names as Ghost Vehicle, Sun of Imperial Concubine, Imperial Prince, Pivot of Heaven, Twinkling Brilliance, Weaving Girl. But, great astrologers though they may have been, the Chinese lacked one aspect of mathematics that the Greeks applied to astrology—deductive geometry. Deductive geometry was the basis of much classical astrology in and after the time of the Greeks, and this explains the different methods of prognostication used in the East and West.

Down through the ages the astrologer's art has depended, not so much on the uncovering of new facts, though this is important, as on the interpretation of the facts already known. This is the essence of the astrologer's skill.

But why should the signs of the Zodiac have any effect at all on the formation of human character? It is easy to see why people thought they did, and even now we constantly use astrological expressions in our everyday speech. The thoughts of "lucky star," "ill-fated," "star-crossed," "mooning around," are interwoven into the very structure of our language.

Wherever the concept of the Zodiac is understood and used, it could well appear to have an influence on the human character. Does this mean, then, that the human race, in whose civilization the idea of the twelve signs of the Zodiac has long been embedded, is divided into only twelve types? Can we honestly believe that it is really as simple as that? If so, there must be pretty wide ranges of variation within each type. And if, to explain the variation, we call in heredity and environment, experiences in early childhood, the thyroid and other glands, and also the four functions of the mind together with extroversion and introversion, then one begins to wonder if the original classification was worth making at all. No sensible person believes that his favorite system explains everything. But even so, he will not find the system much use at all if it does not even save him the trouble of bothering with the others.

In the same way, if we were to put every person under only one sign of the Zodiac, the system becomes too rigid and unlike life. Besides, it was never intended to be used like that. It may be convenient to have only twelve types, but we know that in practice there is every possible gradation between aggressiveness and timidity, or between conscientiousness and laziness. How, then, do we account for this?

A person born under any given Sun sign can be mainly influenced by one or two of the other signs that appear in their individual horoscope. For instance, famous persons born under the sign of Gemini include Henry VIII, whom nothing and no one could have induced to abdicate, and Edward VIII, who did just that. Obviously, then, the sign Gemini does not fully explain the complete character of either of them.

Again, under the opposite sign, Sagittarius, were both Stalin, who was totally consumed with the notion of power, and Charles V, who freely gave up an empire because he preferred to go into a monastery. And we find under Scorpio many uncompromising characters such as Luther, de Gaulle, Indira Gandhi, and Montgomery, but also Petain, a successful commander whose name later became synonymous with collaboration.

A single sign is therefore obviously inadequate to explain the differences between people; it can only explain resemblances, such as the combativeness of the Scorpio group, or the far-reaching devotion of Charles V and Stalin to their respective ideals—the Christian heaven and the Communist utopia.

But very few people have only one sign in their horoscope chart. In addition to the month of birth, the day and, even more, the hour to the nearest minute if possible, ought to be considered. Without this, it is impossible to have an actual horoscope, for the word horoscope literally means "a consideration of the hour."

The month of birth tells you only which sign of the Zodiac was occupied by the Sun. The day and hour tell you what sign was occupied by the Moon. And the minute tells you which sign was rising on the eastern horizon. This is called the Ascendant, and, as some astrologers believe, it is supposed to be the most important thing in the whole horoscope.

The Sun is said to signify one's heart, that is to say, one's deepest desires and inmost nature. This is quite different from the Moon, which signifies one's superficial way of behaving. When the ancient Romans referred to the Emperor Augustus as a Capricorn, they meant that he had the Moon in Capricorn. Or, to take another example, a modern astrologer would call Disraeli a Scorpion because he had Scorpio Rising, but most people would call him Sagittarius because he had the Sun there. The Romans would have called him Leo because his Moon was in Leo.

So if one does not seem to fit one's birth month, it is always worthwhile reading the other signs, for one may have been born at a time when any of them were rising or occupied by the Moon. It also seems to be the case that the influence of the Sun develops as life goes on, so that the month of birth is easier to guess in people over the age of forty. The young are supposed to be influenced mainly by their Ascendant, the Rising sign, which characterizes the body and physical personality as a whole.

It is nonsense to assume that all people born at a certain time will exhibit the same characteristics, or that they will even behave in the same manner. It is quite obvious that, from the very moment of its birth, a child is subject to the effects of its environment, and that this in turn will influence its character and heritage to a decisive extent. Also to be taken into account are education and economic conditions, which play a very important part in the formation of one's character as well.

People have, in general, certain character traits and qualities which, according to their environment, develop in either a positive or a negative manner. Therefore, selfishness (inherent selfishness, that is) might emerge as unselfishness; kindness and consideration as cruelty and lack of consideration toward others. In the same way, a naturally constructive person may, through frustration, become destructive, and so on. The latent characteristics with which people are born can, therefore, through environment and good or bad training, become something that would appear to be its opposite, and so give the lie to the astrologer's description of their character. But this is not the case. The true character is still there, but it is buried deep beneath these external superficialities.

Careful study of the character traits of various signs of the Zodiac are of immeasurable help, and can render beneficial service to the intelligent person. Undoubtedly, the reader will already have discovered that, while he is able to get on very well with some people, he just "cannot stand" others. The causes sometimes seem inexplicable. At times there is intense dislike, at other times immediate sympathy. And there is, too, the phenomenon of love at first sight, which is also apparently inexplicable. People appear to be either sympathetic or unsympathetic toward each other for no apparent reason.

Now if we look at this in the light of the Zodiac, we find that people born under different signs are either compatible or incompatible with each other. In other words, there are good and bad interrelating factors among the various signs. This does not, of course, mean that humanity can be divided into groups of hostile camps. It would be quite wrong to be hostile or indifferent toward people who happen to be born under an incompatible sign. There is no reason why everybody should not, or cannot, learn to control and adjust their feelings and actions, especially after they are aware of the positive qualities of other people by studying their character analyses, among other things.

Every person born under a certain sign has both positive and negative qualities, which are developed more or less according to our free will. Nobody is entirely good or entirely bad, and it is up to each of us to learn to control ourselves on the one hand and at the same time to endeavor to learn about ourselves and others.

It cannot be emphasized often enough that it is free will that determines whether we will make really good use of our talents and abilities. Using our free will, we can either overcome our failings or allow them to rule us. Our free will enables us to exert sufficient willpower to control our failings so that they do not harm ourselves or others.

Astrology can reveal our inclinations and tendencies. Astrology can tell us about ourselves so that we are able to use our free will to overcome our shortcomings. In this way astrology helps us do our best to become needed and valuable members of society as well as helpmates to our family and our friends. Astrology also can save us a great deal of unhappiness and remorse.

Yet it may seem absurd that an ancient philosophy could be a prop to modern men and women. But below the materialistic surface of modern life, there are hidden streams of feeling and thought. Symbology is reappearing as a study worthy of the scholar; the psychosomatic factor in illness has passed from the writings of the crank to those of the specialist; spiritual healing in all its forms is no longer a pious hope but an accepted phenomenon. And it is into this context that we consider astrology, in the sense that it is an analysis of human types.

Astrology and medicine had a long journey together, and only parted company a couple of centuries ago. There still remain in medical language such astrological terms as "saturnine," "choleric," and "mercurial," used in the diagnosis of physical tendencies. The herbalist, for long the handyman of the medical profession, has been dominated by astrology since the days of the Greeks. Certain herbs traditionally respond to certain planetary influences, and diseases must therefore be treated to ensure harmony between the medicine and the disease.

But the stars are expected to foretell and not only to diagnose. Astrological forecasting has been remarkably accurate, but often it is wide of the mark. The brave person who cares to predict world events takes dangerous chances. Individual forecasting is less clear cut; it can be a help or a disillusionment. Then we come to the nagging question: if it is possible to foreknow, is it right to foretell? This is a point of ethics on which it is hard to pronounce judgment. The doctor faces the same dilemma if he finds that symptoms of a mortal disease are present in his patient and that he can only prognosticate a steady decline. How much to tell an individual in a crisis is a problem that has perplexed many distinguished scholars. Honest and conscientious astrologers in this modern world, where so many people are seeking guidance, face the same problem.

Five hundred years ago it was customary to call in a learned man who was an astrologer who was probably also a doctor and a philosopher. By his knowledge of astrology, his study of planetary influences, he felt himself qualified to guide those in distress. The world has moved forward at a fantastic rate since then, and yet people are still uncertain of themselves. At first sight it seems fantastic in the light of modern thinking that they turn to the most ancient of all studies, and get someone to calculate a horoscope for them. But is it *really* so fantastic if you take a second look? For astrology is concerned with tomorrow, with survival. And in a world such as ours, tomorrow and survival are the keywords for the twenty-first century.

ASTROLOGICAL BRIDGE TO THE 21st CENTURY

As the last decade of the twentieth century comes to a close, planetary aspects for its final years connect you with the future. Major changes completed in 1995 and 1996 give rise to new planetary cycles that form the bridge to the twenty-first century and new horizons. The years 1996 through 1999 and into the year 2000 reveal hidden paths and personal hints for achieving your potential, for making the most of your message from the planets.

All the major planets begin new cycles in the late 1990s. Jupiter, planet of good fortune, transits four zodiacal signs from 1996 through 1999 and goes through a complete cycle in each of the elements earth, air, fire, and water. Jupiter is in Capricorn, then in Aquarius, next in Pisces, and finally in Aries as the century turns. With the dawning of the twenty-first century, each new yearly Jupiter cycle follows the natural progression of the Zodiac, from Aries in 2000, then Taurus in 2001, next Gemini in 2002, and so on through Pisces in 2011. The beneficent planet Jupiter promotes your professional and educational goals while urging informed choice and deliberation. Jupiter sharpens your focus and hones your skills. And while safeguarding good luck, Jupiter can turn unusual risks into achievable aims.

Saturn, planet of reason and responsibility, has begun a new cycle in the spring of 1996 when it entered fiery Aries. Saturn in Aries through March 1999 heightens a longing for independence. Your movements are freed from everyday restrictions, allowing you to travel, to explore, to act on a variety of choices. With Saturn in Aries you get set to blaze a new trail. Saturn enters earthy Taurus in March 1999 for a three-year stay over the turn of the century into the year 2002. Saturn in Taurus inspires industry and affection. Practicality, perseverance, and planning can reverse setbacks and minimize risk. Saturn in Taurus lends beauty, order, and structure to your life. In order to take advantage of opportunity through responsibility, to persevere against adversity, look to beautiful planet Saturn.

Uranus, planet of innovation and surprise, started an important new cycle in January of 1996. At that time Uranus entered its natural home in airy Aquarius. Uranus in Aquarius into the year 2003 has a profound effect on your personality and the lens through which you see the world. A basic change in the way you project yourself is just one impact of Uranus in Aquarius. More significantly, a whole new consciousness is evolving. Winds of change blowing your way emphasize movement and freedom. Uranus in Aquarius poses involvement in the larger community beyond self, family, friends, lovers, associates. Radical ideas and progressive thought signal a journey of liberation. As the century turns, follow Uranus on the path of humanitarianism. While you carve a prestigious niche in public life, while you preach social reform and justice, you will be striving to make the world a better place for all people.

Neptune, planet of vision and mystery, is in earthy Capricorn until late 1998. Neptune in Capricorn excites creativity while restraining fanciful thinking. Wise use of resources helps you build persona and prestige. Then Neptune enters airy Aquarius during November 1998 and is there into the year 2011. Neptune in Aquarius, the sign of the Water Bearer, represents two sides of the coin of wisdom: inspiration and reason. Here Neptune stirs powerful currents bearing a rich and varied harvest, the fertile breeding ground for idealistic aims and practical considerations. Neptune's fine intuition tunes in to your dreams, your imagination, your spirituality. You can never turn your back on the mysteries of life. Uranus and Neptune, the planets of enlightenment and renewed idealism both in the sign of Aquarius, give you glimpses into the future, letting you peek through secret doorways into the twenty-first century.

Pluto, planet of beginnings and endings, has completed one cycle of growth November 1995 in the sign of Scorpio. Pluto in Scorpio marked a long period of experimentation and rejuvenation. Then Pluto entered the fiery sign of Sagittarius on November 10, 1995 and is there into the year 2007. Pluto in Sagittarius during its long stay of twelve years can create significant change. The great power of Pluto in Sagittarius may already be starting its transformation of your character and lifestyle. Pluto in Sagittarius takes you on a new journey of exploration and learning. The awakening you experience on intellectual and artistic levels heralds a new cycle of growth. Uncompromising Pluto, seeker of truth, challenges your identity, persona, and self-expression. Uncovering the real you, Pluto holds the key to understanding and meaningful communication. Pluto in Sagittarius can be the guiding light illuminating the first decade of the twenty-first century. Good luck is riding on the waves of change.

THE SIGNS OF THE ZODIAC

Dominant Characteristics

Aries: March 21–April 20

The Positive Side of Aries

The Aries has many positive points to his character. People born under this first sign of the Zodiac are often quite strong and enthusiastic. On the whole, they are forward-looking people who are not easily discouraged by temporary setbacks. They know what they want out of life and they go out after it. Their personalities are strong. Others are usually quite impressed by the Ram's way of doing things. Quite often they are sources of inspiration for others traveling the same route. Aries men and women have a special zest for life that can be contagious; for others, they are a fine example of how life should be lived.

The Aries person usually has a quick and active mind. He is imaginative and inventive. He enjoys keeping busy and active. He generally gets along well with all kinds of people. He is interested in mankind, as a whole. He likes to be challenged. Some would say he thrives on opposition, for it is when he is set against that he often does his best. Getting over or around obstacles is a challenge he generally enjoys. All in all, Aries is quite positive and young-thinking. He likes to keep abreast of new things that are happening in the world. Aries are often fond of speed. They like things to be done quickly, and this sometimes aggravates their slower colleagues and associates.

The Aries man or woman always seems to remain young. Their whole approach to life is youthful and optimistic. They never say die, no matter what the odds. They may have an occasional setback, but it is not long before they are back on their feet again.

The Negative Side of Aries

Everybody has his less positive qualities—and Aries is no exception. Sometimes the Aries man or woman is not very tactful in communicating with others; in his hurry to get things done he is apt to be a little callous or inconsiderate. Sensitive people are likely to find him somewhat sharp-tongued in some situations. Often in his eagerness to get the show on the road, he misses the mark altogether and cannot achieve his aims.

At times Aries can be too impulsive. He can occasionally be stubborn and refuse to listen to reason. If things do not move quickly enough to suit the Aries man or woman, he or she is apt to become rather nervous or irritable. The uncultivated Aries is not unfamiliar with moments of doubt and fear. He is capable of being destructive if he does not get his way. He can overcome some of his emotional problems by steadily trying to express himself as he really is, but this requires effort.

Taurus: April 21–May 20

The Positive Side of Taurus

The Taurus person is known for his ability to concentrate and for his tenacity. These are perhaps his strongest qualities. The Taurus man or woman generally has very little trouble in getting along with others; it's his nature to be helpful toward people in need. He can always be depended on by his friends, especially those in trouble.

Taurus generally achieves what he wants through his ability to persevere. He never leaves anything unfinished but works on something until it has been completed. People can usually take him at his word; he is honest and forthright in most of his dealings. The Taurus person has a good chance to make a success of his life because of his many positive qualities. The Taurus who aims high seldom falls short of his mark. He learns well by experience. He is thorough and does not believe in shortcuts of any kind. The Bull's thoroughness pays off in the end, for through his deliberateness he learns how to rely on himself and what he has learned. The Taurus person tries to get along with others, as a rule. He is not overly critical and likes people to be themselves. He is a tolerant person and enjoys peace and harmony—especially in his home life.

Taurus is usually cautious in all that he does. He is not a person who believes in taking unnecessary risks. Before adopting any one line of action, he will weigh all of the pros and cons. The Taurus person is steadfast. Once his mind is made up it seldom changes. The person born under this sign usually is a good family person— reliable and loving.

The Negative Side of Taurus

Sometimes the Taurus man or woman is a bit too stubborn. He won't listen to other points of view if his mind is set on something. To others, this can be quite annoying. Taurus also does not like to be told what to do. He becomes rather angry if others think him not too bright. He does not like to be told he is wrong, even when he is. He dislikes being contradicted.

Some people who are born under this sign are very suspicious of others—even of those persons close to them. They find it difficult to trust people fully. They are often afraid of being deceived or taken advantage of. The Bull often finds it difficult to forget or forgive. His love of material things sometimes makes him rather avaricious and petty.

Gemini: May 21–June 20

The Positive Side of Gemini

The person born under this sign of the Heavenly Twins is usually quite bright and quick-witted. Some of them are capable of doing many different things. The Gemini person very often has many different interests. He keeps an open mind and is always anxious to learn new things.

Gemini is often an analytical person. He is a person who enjoys making use of his intellect. He is governed more by his mind than by his emotions. He is a person who is not confined to one view; he can often understand both sides to a problem or question. He knows how to reason, how to make rapid decisions if need be.

He is an adaptable person and can make himself at home almost anywhere. There are all kinds of situations he can adapt to. He is a person who seldom doubts himself; he is sure of his talents and his ability to think and reason. Gemini is generally most satisfied

when he is in a situation where he can make use of his intellect. Never short of imagination, he often has strong talents for invention. He is rather a modern person when it comes to life; Gemini almost always moves along with the times—perhaps that is why he remains so youthful throughout most of his life.

Literature and art appeal to the person born under this sign. Creativity in almost any form will interest and intrigue the Gemini man or woman.

The Gemini is often quite charming. A good talker, he often is the center of attraction at any gathering. People find it easy to like a person born under this sign because he can appear easygoing and usually has a good sense of humor.

The Negative Side of Gemini

Sometimes the Gemini person tries to do too many things at one time—and as a result, winds up finishing nothing. Some Twins are easily distracted and find it rather difficult to concentrate on one thing for too long a time. Sometimes they give in to trifling fancies and find it rather boring to become too serious about any one thing. Some of them are never dependable, no matter what they promise.

Although the Gemini man or woman often appears to be well-versed on many subjects, this is sometimes just a veneer. His knowledge may be only superficial, but because he speaks so well he gives people the impression of erudition. Some Geminis are sharp-tongued and inconsiderate; they think only of themselves and their own pleasure.

Cancer: June 21–July 20

The Positive Side of Cancer

The Moon Child's most positive point is his understanding nature. On the whole, he is a loving and sympathetic person. He would never go out of his way to hurt anyone. The Cancer man or woman is often very kind and tender; they give what they can to others. They hate to see others suffering and will do what they can to help someone in less fortunate circumstances than themselves. They are often very concerned about the world. Their interest in people generally goes beyond that of just their own families and close friends; they have a deep sense of community and respect humanitarian values. The Moon Child means what he says, as a rule; he is honest about his feelings.

The Cancer man or woman is a person who knows the art of patience. When something seems difficult, he is willing to wait until the situation becomes manageable again. He is a person who knows how to bide his time. Cancer knows how to concentrate on one thing at a time. When he has made his mind up he generally sticks with what he does, seeing it through to the end.

Cancer is a person who loves his home. He enjoys being surrounded by familiar things and the people he loves. Of all the signs, Cancer is the most maternal. Even the men born under this sign often have a motherly or protective quality about them. They like to take care of people in their family—to see that they are well loved and well provided for. They are usually loyal and faithful. Family ties mean a lot to the Cancer man or woman. Parents and in-laws are respected and loved. Young Cancer responds very well to adults who show faith in him. The Moon Child has a strong sense of tradition. He is very sensitive to the moods of others.

The Negative Side of Cancer

Sometimes Cancer finds it rather hard to face life. It becomes too much for him. He can be a little timid and retiring, when things don't go too well. When unfortunate things happen, he is apt to just shrug and say, "Whatever will be will be." He can be fatalistic to a fault. The uncultivated Cancer is a bit lazy. He doesn't have very much ambition. Anything that seems a bit difficult he'll gladly leave to others. He may be lacking in initiative. Too sensitive, when he feels he's been injured, he'll crawl back into his shell and nurse his imaginary wounds. The immature Moon Child often is given to crying when the smallest thing goes wrong.

Some Cancers find it difficult to enjoy themselves in environments outside their homes. They make heavy demands on others, and need to be constantly reassured that they are loved. Lacking such reassurance, they may resort to sulking in silence.

Leo: July 21–August 21

The Positive Side of Leo

Often Leos make good leaders. They seem to be good organizers and administrators. Usually they are quite popular with others. Whatever group it is that they belong to, the Leo man or woman is almost sure to be or become the leader. Loyalty, one of the Lion's noblest traits, enables him or her to maintain this leadership position.

Leo is generous most of the time. It is his best characteristic. He or she likes to give gifts and presents. In making others happy, the Leo person becomes happy himself. He likes to splurge when spending money on others. In some instances it may seem that the Lion's generosity knows no boundaries. A hospitable person, the Leo man or woman is very fond of welcoming people to his house and entertaining them. He is never short of company.

Leo has plenty of energy and drive. He enjoys working toward some specific goal. When he applies himself correctly, he gets what he wants most often. The Leo person is almost never unsure of himself. He has plenty of confidence and aplomb. He is a person who is direct in almost everything he does. He has a quick mind and can make a decision in a very short time.

He usually sets a good example for others because of his ambitious manner and positive ways. He knows how to stick to something once he's started. Although Leo may be good at making a joke, he is not superficial or glib. He is a loving person, kind and thoughtful.

There is generally nothing small or petty about the Leo man or woman. He does what he can for those who are deserving. He is a person others can rely upon at all times. He means what he says. An honest person, generally speaking, he is a friend who is valued and sought out.

The Negative Side of Leo

Leo, however, does have his faults. At times, he can be just a bit too arrogant. He thinks that no one deserves a leadership position except him. Only he is capable of doing things well. His opinion of himself is often much too high. Because of his conceit, he is

sometimes rather unpopular with a good many people. Some Leos are too materialistic; they can only think in terms of money and profit.

Some Leos enjoy lording it over others—at home or at their place of business. What is more, they feel they have the right to. Egocentric to an impossible degree, this sort of Leo cares little about how others think or feel. He can be rude and cutting.

Virgo: August 22–September 22

The Positive Side of Virgo

The person born under the sign of Virgo is generally a busy person. He knows how to arrange and organize things. He is a good planner. Above all, he is practical and is not afraid of hard work.

Often called the sign of the Harvester, Virgo knows how to attain what he desires. He sticks with something until it is finished. He never shirks his duties, and can always be depended upon. The Virgo person can be thoroughly trusted at all times.

The man or woman born under this sign tries to do everything to perfection. He doesn't believe in doing anything halfway. He always aims for the top. He is the sort of a person who is always learning and constantly striving to better himself—not because he wants more money or glory, but because it gives him a feeling of accomplishment.

The Virgo man or woman is a very observant person. He is sensitive to how others feel, and can see things below the surface of a situation. He usually puts this talent to constructive use.

It is not difficult for the Virgo to be open and earnest. He believes in putting his cards on the table. He is never secretive or underhanded. He's as good as his word. The Virgo person is generally plainspoken and down to earth. He has no trouble in expressing himself.

The Virgo person likes to keep up to date on new developments in his particular field. Well-informed, generally, he sometimes has a keen interest in the arts or literature. What he knows, he knows well. His ability to use his critical faculties is well-developed and sometimes startles others because of its accuracy.

Virgos adhere to a moderate way of life; they avoid excesses. Virgo is a responsible person and enjoys being of service.

The Negative Side of Virgo

Sometimes a Virgo person is too critical. He thinks that only he can do something the way it should be done. Whatever anyone else does is inferior. He can be rather annoying in the way he quibbles over insignificant details. In telling others how things should be done, he can be rather tactless and mean.

Some Virgos seem rather emotionless and cool. They feel emotional involvement is beneath them. They are sometimes too tidy, too neat. With money they can be rather miserly. Some Virgos try to force their opinions and ideas on others.

Libra: September 23–October 22

The Positive Side of Libra

Libras love harmony. It is one of their most outstanding character traits. They are interested in achieving balance; they admire beauty and grace in things as well as in people. Generally speaking, they are kind and considerate people. Libras are usually very sympathetic. They go out of their way not to hurt another person's feelings. They are outgoing and do what they can to help those in need.

People born under the sign of Libra almost always make good friends. They are loyal and amiable. They enjoy the company of others. Many of them are rather moderate in their views; they believe in keeping an open mind, however, and weighing both sides of an issue fairly before making a decision.

Alert and intelligent, Libra, often known as the Lawgiver, is always fair-minded and tries to put himself in the position of the other person. They are against injustice; quite often they take up for the underdog. In most of their social dealings, they try to be tactful and kind. They dislike discord and bickering, and most Libras strive for peace and harmony in all their relationships.

The Libra man or woman has a keen sense of beauty. They appreciate handsome furnishings and clothes. Many of them are artistically inclined. Their taste is usually impeccable. They know how to use color. Their homes are almost always attractively arranged and inviting. They enjoy entertaining people and see to it that their guests always feel at home and welcome.

Libra gets along with almost everyone. He is well-liked and socially much in demand.

The Negative Side of Libra

Some people born under this sign tend to be rather insincere. So eager are they to achieve harmony in all relationships that they will even go so far as to lie. Many of them are escapists. They find facing the truth an ordeal and prefer living in a world of make-believe.

In a serious argument, some Libras give in rather easily even when they know they are right. Arguing, even about something they believe in, is too unsettling for some of them.

Libras sometimes care too much for material things. They enjoy possessions and luxuries. Some are vain and tend to be jealous.

Scorpio: October 23–November 22

The Positive Side of Scorpio

The Scorpio man or woman generally knows what he or she wants out of life. He is a determined person. He sees something through to the end. Scorpio is quite sincere, and seldom says anything he doesn't mean. When he sets a goal for himself he tries to go about achieving it in a very direct way.

The Scorpion is brave and courageous. They are not afraid of hard work. Obstacles do not frighten them. They forge ahead until they achieve what they set out for. The Scorpio man or woman has a strong will.

Although Scorpio may seem rather fixed and determined, inside he is often quite tender and loving. He can care very much for others. He believes in sincerity in all relationships. His feelings about someone tend to last; they are profound and not superficial.

The Scorpio person is someone who adheres to his principles no matter what happens. He will not be deterred from a path he believes to be right.

Because of his many positive strengths, the Scorpion can often achieve happiness for himself and for those that he loves.

He is a constructive person by nature. He often has a deep understanding of people and of life, in general. He is perceptive and unafraid. Obstacles often seem to spur him on. He is a positive person who enjoys winning. He has many strengths and resources; challenge of any sort often brings out the best in him.

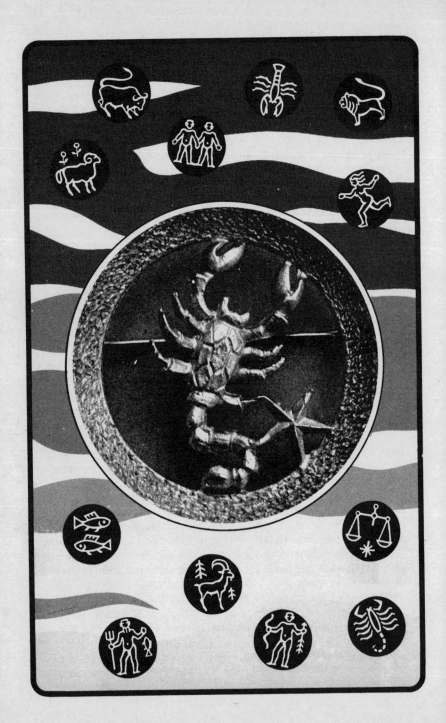

The Negative Side of Scorpio

The Scorpio person is sometimes hypersensitive. Often he imagines injury when there is none. He feels that others do not bother to recognize him for his true worth. Sometimes he is given to excessive boasting in order to compensate for what he feels is neglect.

Scorpio can be proud, arrogant, and competitive. They can be sly when they put their minds to it and they enjoy outwitting persons or institutions noted for their cleverness.

Their tactics for getting what they want are sometimes devious and ruthless. They don't care too much about what others may think. If they feel others have done them an injustice, they will do their best to seek revenge. The Scorpion often has a sudden, violent temper; and this person's interest in sex is sometimes quite unbalanced or excessive.

Sagittarius: November 23–December 20

The Positive Side of Sagittarius

People born under this sign are honest and forthright. Their approach to life is earnest and open. Sagittarius is often quite adult in his way of seeing things. They are broad-minded and tolerant people. When dealing with others the person born under the sign of the Archer is almost always open and forthright. He doesn't believe in deceit or pretension. His standards are high. People who associate with Sagittarius generally admire and respect his tolerant viewpoint.

The Archer trusts others easily and expects them to trust him. He is never suspicious or envious and almost always thinks well of others. People always enjoy his company because he is so friendly and easygoing. The Sagittarius man or woman is often good-humored. He can always be depended upon by his friends, family, and co-workers.

The person born under this sign of the Zodiac likes a good joke every now and then. Sagittarius is eager for fun and laughs, which makes him very popular with others.

A lively person, he enjoys sports and outdoor life. The Archer is fond of animals. Intelligent and interesting, he can begin an

animated conversation with ease. He likes exchanging ideas and discussing various views.

He is not selfish or proud. If someone proposes an idea or plan that is better than his, he will immediately adopt it. Imaginative yet practical, he knows how to put ideas into practice.

The Archer enjoys sport and games, and it doesn't matter if he wins or loses. He is a forgiving person, and never sulks over something that has not worked out in his favor.

He is seldom critical, and is almost always generous.

The Negative Side of Sagittarius

Some Sagittarius are restless. They take foolish risks and seldom learn from the mistakes they make. They don't have heads for money and are often mismanaging their finances. Some of them devote much of their time to gambling.

Some are too outspoken and tactless, always putting their feet in their mouths. They hurt others carelessly by being honest at the wrong time. Sometimes they make promises which they don't keep. They don't stick close enough to their plans and go from one failure to another. They are undisciplined and waste a lot of energy.

Capricorn: December 21–January 19

The Positive Side of Capricorn

The person born under the sign of Capricorn, known variously as the Mountain Goat or Sea Goat, is usually very stable and patient. He sticks to whatever tasks he has and sees them through. He can always be relied upon and he is not averse to work.

An honest person, Capricorn is generally serious about whatever he does. He does not take his duties lightly. He is a practical person and believes in keeping his feet on the ground.

Quite often the person born under this sign is ambitious and knows how to get what he wants out of life. The Goat forges ahead and never gives up his goal. When he is determined about something, he almost always wins. He is a good worker—a hard worker. Although things may not come easy to him, he will not complain, but continue working until his chores are finished.

He is usually good at business matters and knows the value of money. He is not a spendthrift and knows how to put something away for a rainy day; he dislikes waste and unnecessary loss.

Capricorn knows how to make use of his self-control. He can apply himself to almost anything once he puts his mind to it. His ability to concentrate sometimes astounds others. He is diligent and does well when involved in detail work.

The Capricorn man or woman is charitable, generally speaking, and will do what is possible to help others less fortunate. As a friend, he is loyal and trustworthy. He never shirks his duties or responsibilities. He is self-reliant and never expects too much of the other fellow. He does what he can on his own. If someone does him a good turn, then he will do his best to return the favor.

The Negative Side of Capricorn

Like everyone, Capricorn, too, has faults. At times, the Goat can be overcritical of others. He expects others to live up to his own high standards. He thinks highly of himself and tends to look down on others.

His interest in material things may be exaggerated. The Capricorn man or woman thinks too much about getting on in the world and having something to show for it. He may even be a little greedy.

He sometimes thinks he knows what's best for everyone. He is too bossy. He is always trying to organize and correct others. He may be a little narrow in his thinking.

Aquarius: January 20–February 18

The Positive Side of Aquarius

The Aquarius man or woman is usually very honest and forthright. These are his two greatest qualities. His standards for himself are generally very high. He can always be relied upon by others. His word is his bond.

Aquarius is perhaps the most tolerant of all the Zodiac personalities. He respects other people's beliefs and feels that everyone is entitled to his own approach to life.

He would never do anything to injure another's feelings. He is never unkind or cruel. Always considerate of others, the Water

Bearer is always willing to help a person in need. He feels a very strong tie between himself and all the other members of mankind.

The person born under this sign, called the Water Bearer, is almost always an individualist. He does not believe in teaming up with the masses, but prefers going his own way. His ideas about life and mankind are often quite advanced. There is a saying to the effect that the average Aquarius is fifty years ahead of his time.

Aquarius is community-minded. The problems of the world concern him greatly. He is interested in helping others no matter what part of the globe they live in. He is truly a humanitarian sort. He likes to be of service to others.

Giving, considerate, and without prejudice, Aquarius have no trouble getting along with others.

The Negative Side of Aquarius

Aquarius may be too much of a dreamer. He makes plans but seldom carries them out. He is rather unrealistic. His imagination has a tendency to run away with him. Because many of his plans are impractical, he is always in some sort of a dither.

Others may not approve of him at all times because of his unconventional behavior. He may be a bit eccentric. Sometimes he is so busy with his own thoughts that he loses touch with the realities of existence.

Some Aquarius feel they are more clever and intelligent than others. They seldom admit to their own faults, even when they are quite apparent. Some become rather fanatic in their views. Their criticism of others is sometimes destructive and negative.

Pisces: February 19–March 20

The Positive Side of Pisces

Known as the sign of the Fishes, Pisces has a sympathetic nature. Kindly, he is often dedicated in the way he goes about helping others. The sick and the troubled often turn to him for advice and assistance. Possessing keen intuition, Pisces can easily understand people's deepest problems.

He is very broad-minded and does not criticize others for their faults. He knows how to accept people for what they are. On the whole, he is a trustworthy and earnest person. He is loyal to his friends and will do what he can to help them in time of need. Generous and good-natured, he is a lover of peace; he is often willing to help others solve their differences. People who have taken a wrong turn in life often interest him and he will do what he can to persuade them to rehabilitate themselves.

He has a strong intuitive sense and most of the time he knows how to make it work for him. Pisces is unusually perceptive and often knows what is bothering someone before that person, himself, is aware of it. The Pisces man or woman is an idealistic person, basically, and is interested in making the world a better place in which to live. Pisces believes that everyone should help each other. He is willing to do more than his share in order to achieve cooperation with others.

The person born under this sign often is talented in music or art. He is a receptive person; he is able to take the ups and downs of life with philosophic calm.

The Negative Side of Pisces

Some Pisces are often depressed; their outlook on life is rather glum. They may feel that they have been given a bad deal in life and that others are always taking unfair advantage of them. Pisces sometimes feel that the world is a cold and cruel place. The Fishes can be easily discouraged. The Pisces man or woman may even withdraw from the harshness of reality into a secret shell of his own where he dreams and idles away a good deal of his time.

Pisces can be lazy. He lets things happen without giving the least bit of resistance. He drifts along, whether on the high road or on the low. He can be lacking in willpower.

Some Pisces people seek escape through drugs or alcohol. When temptation comes along they find it hard to resist. In matters of sex, they can be rather permissive.

Sun Sign Personalities

ARIES: Hans Christian Andersen, Pearl Bailey, Marlon Brando, Wernher Von Braun, Charlie Chaplin, Joan Crawford, Da Vinci, Bette Davis, Doris Day, W. C. Fields, Alec Guinness, Adolf Hitler, William Holden, Thomas Jefferson, Nikita Khrushchev, Elton John, Arturo Toscanini, J. P. Morgan, Paul Robeson, Gloria Steinem, Sarah Vaughn, Vincent van Gogh, Tennessee Williams

TAURUS: Fred Astaire, Charlotte Brontë, Carol Burnett, Irving Berlin, Bing Crosby, Salvador Dali, Tchaikovsky, Queen Elizabeth II, Duke Ellington, Ella Fitzgerald, Henry Fonda, Sigmund Freud, Orson Welles, Joe Louis, Lenin, Karl Marx, Golda Meir, Eva Peron, Bertrand Russell, Shakespeare, Kate Smith, Benjamin Spock, Barbra Streisand, Shirley Temple, Harry Truman

GEMINI: Ruth Benedict, Josephine Baker, Rachel Carson, Carlos Chavez, Walt Whitman, Bob Dylan, Ralph Waldo Emerson, Judy Garland, Paul Gauguin, Allen Ginsberg, Benny Goodman, Bob Hope, Burl Ives, John F. Kennedy, Peggy Lee, Marilyn Monroe, Joe Namath, Cole Porter, Laurence Olivier, Harriet Beecher Stowe, Queen Victoria, John Wayne, Frank Lloyd Wright

CANCER: "Dear Abby," Lizzie Borden, David Brinkley, Yul Brynner, Pearl Buck, Marc Chagall, Princess Diana, Babe Didrikson, Mary Baker Eddy, Henry VIII, John Glenn, Ernest Hemingway, Lena Horne, Oscar Hammerstein, Helen Keller, Ann Landers, George Orwell, Nancy Reagan, Rembrandt, Richard Rodgers, Ginger Rogers, Rubens, Jean-Paul Sartre, O. J. Simpson

LEO: Neil Armstrong, James Baldwin, Lucille Ball, Emily Brontë, Wilt Chamberlain, Julia Child, William J. Clinton, Cecil B. De Mille, Ogden Nash, Amelia Earhart, Edna Ferber, Arthur Goldberg, Alfred Hitchcock, Mick Jagger, George Meany, Annie Oakley, George Bernard Shaw, Napoleon, Jacqueline Onassis, Henry Ford, Francis Scott Key, Andy Warhol, Mae West, Orville Wright

VIRGO: Ingrid Bergman, Warren Burger, Maurice Chevalier, Agatha Christie, Sean Connery, Lafayette, Peter Falk, Greta Garbo, Althea Gibson, Arthur Godfrey, Goethe, Buddy Hackett, Michael Jackson, Lyndon Johnson, D. H. Lawrence, Sophia Loren, Grandma Moses, Arnold Palmer, Queen Elizabeth I, Walter Reuther, Peter Sellers, Lily Tomlin, George Wallace

LIBRA: Brigitte Bardot, Art Buchwald, Truman Capote, Dwight D. Eisenhower, William Faulkner, F. Scott Fitzgerald, Gandhi, George Gershwin, Micky Mantle, Helen Hayes, Vladimir Horowitz, Doris Lessing, Martina Navratalova, Eugene O'Neill, Luciano Pavarotti, Emily Post, Eleanor Roosevelt, Bruce Springsteen, Margaret Thatcher, Gore Vidal, Barbara Walters, Oscar Wilde

SCORPIO: Vivien Leigh, Richard Burton, Art Carney, Johnny Carson, Billy Graham, Grace Kelly, Walter Cronkite, Marie Curie, Charles de Gaulle, Linda Evans, Indira Gandhi, Theodore Roosevelt, Rock Hudson, Katherine Hepburn, Robert F. Kennedy, Billie Jean King, Martin Luther, Georgia O'Keeffe, Pablo Picasso, Jonas Salk, Alan Shepard, Robert Louis Stevenson

SAGITTARIUS: Jane Austen, Louisa May Alcott, Woody Allen, Beethoven, Willy Brandt, Mary Martin, William F. Buckley, Maria Callas, Winston Churchill, Noel Coward, Emily Dickinson, Walt Disney, Benjamin Disraeli, James Doolittle, Kirk Douglas, Chet Huntley, Jane Fonda, Chris Evert Lloyd, Margaret Mead, Charles Schulz, John Milton, Frank Sinatra, Steven Spielberg

CAPRICORN: Muhammad Ali, Isaac Asimov, Pablo Casals, Dizzy Dean, Marlene Dietrich, James Farmer, Ava Gardner, Barry Goldwater, Cary Grant, J. Edgar Hoover, Howard Hughes, Joan of Arc, Gypsy Rose Lee, Martin Luther King, Jr., Rudyard Kipling, Mao Tse-tung, Richard Nixon, Gamal Nasser, Louis Pasteur, Albert Schweitzer, Stalin, Benjamin Franklin, Elvis Presley

AQUARIUS: Marian Anderson, Susan B. Anthony, Jack Benny, John Barrymore, Mikhail Baryshnikov, Charles Darwin, Charles Dickens, Thomas Edison, Clark Gable, Jascha Heifetz, Abraham Lincoln, Yehudi Menuhin, Mozart, Jack Nicklaus, Ronald Reagan, Jackie Robinson, Norman Rockwell, Franklin D. Roosevelt, Gertrude Stein, Charles Lindbergh, Margaret Truman

PISCES: Edward Albee, Harry Belafonte, Alexander Graham Bell, Chopin, Adelle Davis, Albert Einstein, Golda Meir, Jackie Gleason, Winslow Homer, Edward M. Kennedy, Victor Hugo, Mike Mansfield, Michelangelo, Edna St. Vincent Millay, Liza Minelli, John Steinbeck, Linus Pauling, Ravel, Renoir, Diana Ross, William Shirer, Elizabeth Taylor, George Washington

The Signs and Their Key Words

		POSITIVE	NEGATIVE
ARIES	self	courage, initiative, pioneer instinct	brash rudeness, selfish impetuosity
TAURUS	money	endurance, loyalty, wealth	obstinacy, gluttony
GEMINI	mind	versatility	capriciousness, unreliability
CANCER	family	sympathy, homing instinct	clannishness, childishness
LEO	children	love, authority, integrity	egotism, force
VIRGO	work	purity, industry, analysis	faultfinding, cynicism
LIBRA	marriage	harmony, justice	vacillation, superficiality
SCORPIO	sex	survival, regeneration	vengeance, discord
SAGITTARIUS	travel	optimism, higher learning	lawlessness
CAPRICORN	career	depth	narrowness, gloom
AQUARIUS	friends	human fellowship, genius	perverse unpredictability
PISCES	confinement	spiritual love, universality	diffusion, escapism

The Elements and Qualities of The Signs

Every sign has both an *element* and a *quality* associated with it. The element indicates the basic makeup of the sign, and the quality describes the kind of activity associated with each.

Element	Sign	Quality	Sign
FIRE	ARIES LEO SAGITTARIUS	CARDINAL....	ARIES LIBRA CANCER CAPRICORN
EARTH	TAURUS VIRGO CAPRICORN	FIXED	TAURUS LEO SCORPIO AQUARIUS
AIR.........	GEMINI LIBRA AQUARIUS	MUTABLE	GEMINI VIRGO SAGITTARIUS PISCES
WATER....	CANCER SCORPIO PISCES		

Signs can be grouped together according to their element and quality. Signs of the same element share many basic traits in common. They tend to form stable configurations and ultimately harmonious relationships. Signs of the same quality are often less harmonious, but they share many dynamic potentials for growth as well as profound fulfillment.

Further discussion of each of these sign groupings is provided on the following pages.

The Fire Signs

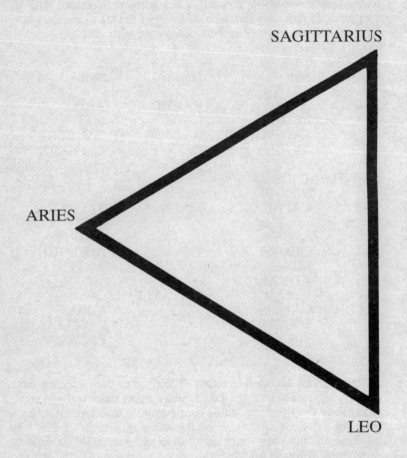

This is the fire group. On the whole these are emotional, volatile types, quick to anger, quick to forgive. They are adventurous, powerful people and act as a source of inspiration for everyone. They spark into action with immediate exuberant impulses. They are intelligent, self-involved, creative, and idealistic. They all share a certain vibrancy and glow that outwardly reflects an inner flame and passion for living.

The Earth Signs

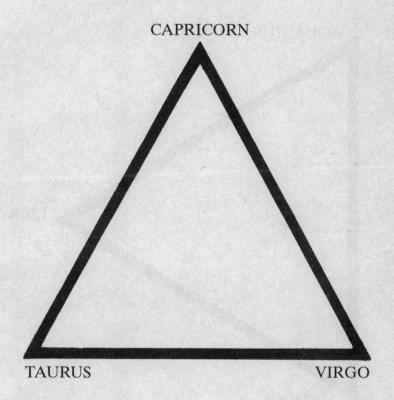

CAPRICORN

TAURUS

VIRGO

This is the earth group. They are in constant touch with the material world and tend to be conservative. Although they are all capable of spartan self-discipline, they are earthy, sensual people who are stimulated by the tangible, elegant, and luxurious. The thread of their lives is always practical, but they do fantasize and are often attracted to dark, mysterious, emotional people. They are like great cliffs overhanging the sea, forever married to the ocean but always resisting erosion from the dark, emotional forces that thunder at their feet.

The Air Signs

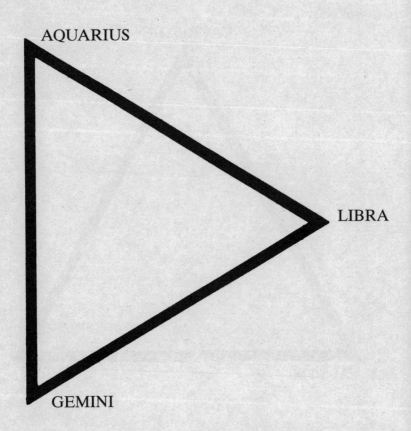

This is the air group. They are light, mental creatures desirous of contact, communication, and relationship. They are involved with people and the forming of ties on many levels. Original thinkers, they are the bearers of human news. Their language is their sense of word, color, style, and beauty. They provide an atmosphere suitable and pleasant for living. They add change and versatility to the scene, and it is through them that we can explore new territory of human intelligence and experience.

The Water Signs

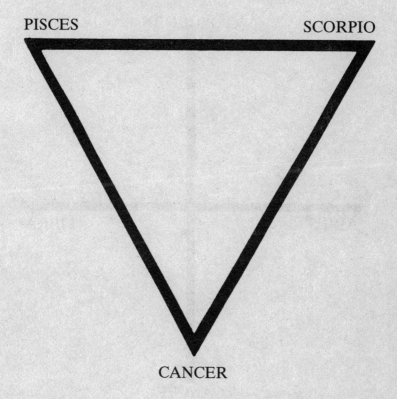

PISCES

SCORPIO

CANCER

This is the water group. Through the water people, we are all joined together on emotional, nonverbal levels. They are silent, mysterious types whose magic hypnotizes even the most determined realist. They have uncanny perceptions about people and are as rich as the oceans when it comes to feeling, emotion, or imagination. They are sensitive, mystical creatures with memories that go back beyond time. Through water, life is sustained. These people have the potential for the depths of darkness or the heights of mysticism and art.

The Cardinal Signs

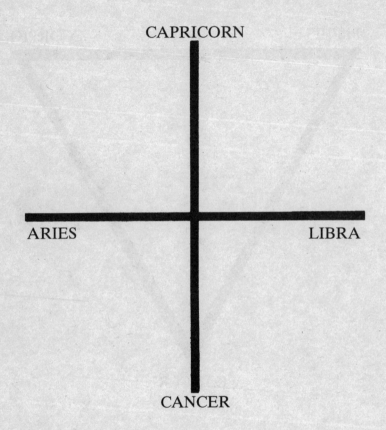

Put together, this is a clear-cut picture of dynamism, activity, tremendous stress, and remarkable achievement. These people know the meaning of great change since their lives are often characterized by significant crises and major successes. This combination is like a simultaneous storm of summer, fall, winter, and spring. The danger is chaotic diffusion of energy; the potential is irrepressible growth and victory.

The Fixed Signs

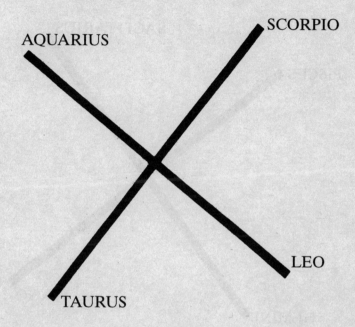

AQUARIUS

SCORPIO

TAURUS

LEO

Fixed signs are always establishing themselves in a given place or area of experience. Like explorers who arrive and plant a flag, these people claim a position from which they do not enjoy being deposed. They are staunch, stalwart, upright, trusty, honorable people, although their obstinacy is well-known. Their contribution is fixity, and they are the angels who support our visible world.

The Mutable Signs

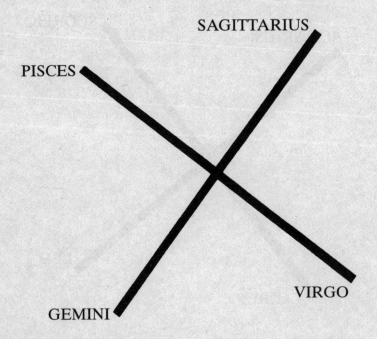

Mutable people are versatile, sensitive, intelligent, nervous, and deeply curious about life. They are the translators of all energy. They often carry out or complete tasks initiated by others. Combinations of these signs have highly developed minds; they are imaginative and jumpy and think and talk a lot. At worst their lives are a Tower of Babel. At best they are adaptable and ready creatures who can assimilate one kind of experience and enjoy it while anticipating coming changes.

THE PLANETS
OF THE SOLAR SYSTEM

This section describes the planets of the solar system. In astrology, both the Sun and the Moon are considered to be planets. Because of the Moon's influence in our day-to-day lives, the Moon is described in a separate section following this one.

The Planets and the Signs They Rule

The signs of the Zodiac are linked to the planets in the following way. Each sign is governed or ruled by one or more planets. No matter where the planets are located in the sky at any given moment, they still rule their respective signs, and when they travel through the signs they rule, they have special dignity and their effects are stronger.

Following is a list of the planets and the signs they rule. After looking at the list, read the definitions of the planets and see if you can determine how the planet ruling *your* Sun sign has affected your life.

SIGNS	RULING PLANETS
Aries	Mars, Pluto
Taurus	Venus
Gemini	Mercury
Cancer	Moon
Leo	Sun
Virgo	Mercury
Libra	Venus
Scorpio	Mars, Pluto
Sagittarius	Jupiter
Capricorn	Saturn
Aquarius	Saturn, Uranus
Pisces	Jupiter, Neptune

Characteristics of the Planets

The following pages give the meaning and characteristics of the planets of the solar system. They all travel around the Sun at different speeds and different distances. Taken with the Sun, they all distribute individual intelligence and ability throughout the entire chart.

The planets modify the influence of the Sun in a chart according to their own particular natures, strengths, and positions. Their positions must be calculated for each year and day, and their function and expression in a horoscope will change as they move from one area of the Zodiac to another.

We start with a description of the sun.

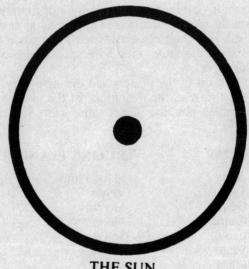

THE SUN

SUN

This is the center of existence. Around this flaming sphere all the planets revolve in endless orbits. Our star is constantly sending out its beams of light and energy without which no life on Earth would be possible. In astrology it symbolizes everything we are trying to become, the center around which all of our activity in life will always revolve. It is the symbol of our basic nature and describes the natural and constant thread that runs through everything that we do from birth to death on this planet.

To early astrologers, the Sun seemed to be another planet because it crossed the heavens every day, just like the rest of the bodies in the sky.

It is the only star near enough to be seen well—it is, in fact, a dwarf star. Approximately 860,000 miles in diameter, it is about ten times as wide as the giant planet Jupiter. The next nearest star is nearly 300,000 times as far away, and if the Sun were located as far away as most of the bright stars, it would be too faint to be seen without a telescope.

Everything in the horoscope ultimately revolves around this singular body. Although other forces may be prominent in the charts of some individuals, still the Sun is the total nucleus of being and symbolizes the complete potential of every human being alive. It is vitality and the life force. Your whole essence comes from the position of the Sun.

You are always trying to express the Sun according to its position by house and sign. Possibility for all development is found in the Sun, and it marks the fundamental character of your personal radiations all around you.

It is the symbol of strength, vigor, wisdom, dignity, ardor, and generosity, and the ability for a person to function as a mature individual. It is also a creative force in society. It is consciousness of the gift of life.

The underdeveloped solar nature is arrogant, pushy, undependable, and proud, and is constantly using force.

MERCURY

Mercury is the planet closest to the Sun. It races around our star, gathering information and translating it to the rest of the system. Mercury represents your capacity to understand the desires of your own will and to translate those desires into action.

In other words it is the planet of mind and the power of communication. Through Mercury we develop an ability to think, write, speak, and observe—to become aware of the world around us. It colors our attitudes and vision of the world, as well as our capacity to communicate our inner responses to the outside world. Some people who have serious disabilities in their power of verbal communication have often wrongly been described as people lacking intelligence.

Although this planet (and its position in the horoscope) indicates your power to communicate your thoughts and perceptions to the world, intelligence is something deeper. Intelligence is distributed throughout all the planets. It is the relationship of the planets to each other that truly describes what we call intelligence. Mercury rules speaking, language, mathematics, draft and design, students, messengers, young people, offices, teachers, and any pursuits where the mind of man has wings.

VENUS

Venus is beauty. It symbolizes the harmony and radiance of a rare and elusive quality: beauty itself. It is refinement and delicacy, softness and charm. In astrology it indicates grace, balance, and the aesthetic sense. Where Venus is we see beauty, a gentle drawing in of energy and the need for satisfaction and completion. It is a special touch that finishes off rough edges. It is sensitivity, and affection, and it is always the place for that other elusive phenomenon: love. Venus describes our sense of what is beautiful and loving. Poorly developed, it is vulgar, tasteless, and self-indulgent. But its ideal is the flame of spiritual love—Aphrodite, goddess of love, and the sweetness and power of personal beauty.

MARS

Mars is raw, crude energy. The planet next to Earth but outward from the Sun is a fiery red sphere that charges through the horoscope with force and fury. It represents the way you reach out for new adventure and new experience. It is energy and drive, initiative, courage, and daring. It is the power to start something and see it through. It can be thoughtless, cruel and wild, angry and hostile, causing cuts, burns, scalds, and wounds. It can stab its way through a chart, or it can be the symbol of healthy spirited adventure, well-channeled constructive power to begin and keep up the drive. If you have trouble starting things, if you lack the get-up-and-go to start the ball rolling, if you lack aggressiveness and self-confidence, chances are there's another planet influencing your Mars. Mars rules soldiers, butchers, surgeons, salesmen—any field that requires daring, bold skill, operational technique, or self-promotion.

JUPITER

This is the largest planet of the solar system. Scientists have recently learned that Jupiter reflects more light than it receives from the Sun. In a sense it is like a star itself. In astrology it rules good luck and good cheer, health, wealth, optimism, happiness, success, and joy. It is the symbol of opportunity and always opens the way for new possibilities in your life. It rules exuberance, enthusiasm, wisdom, knowledge, generosity, and all forms of expansion in general. It rules actors, statesmen, clerics, professional people, religion, publishing, and the distribution of many people over large areas.

Sometimes Jupiter makes you think you deserve everything, and you become sloppy, wasteful, careless and rude, prodigal and lawless, in the illusion that nothing can ever go wrong. Then there is the danger of overconfidence, exaggeration, undependability, and overindulgence.

Jupiter is the minimization of limitation and the emphasis on spirituality and potential. It is the thirst for knowledge and higher learning.

SATURN

Saturn circles our system in dark splendor with its mysterious rings, forcing us to be awakened to whatever we have neglected in the past. It will present real puzzles and problems to be solved, causing delays, obstacles, and hindrances. By doing so, Saturn stirs our own sensitivity to those areas where we are laziest.

Here we must patiently develop *method*, and only through painstaking effort can our ends be achieved. It brings order to a horoscope and imposes reason just where we are feeling least reasonable. By creating limitations and boundary, Saturn shows the consequences of being human and demands that we accept the changing cycles inevitable in human life. Saturn rules time, old age, and sobriety. It can bring depression, gloom, jealousy, and greed, or serious acceptance of responsibilities out of which success will develop. With Saturn there is nothing to do but face facts. It rules laborers, stones, granite, rocks, and crystals of all kinds.

THE OUTER PLANETS:
URANUS, NEPTUNE, PLUTO

Uranus, Neptune, Pluto are the outer planets. They liberate human beings from cultural conditioning, and in that sense are the lawbreakers. In early times it was thought that Saturn was the last planet of the system—the outer limit beyond which we could never go. The discovery of the next three planets ushered in new phases of human history, revolution, and technology.

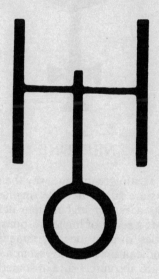

URANUS

Uranus rules unexpected change, upheaval, revolution. It is the symbol of total independence and asserts the freedom of an individual from all restriction and restraint. It is a breakthrough planet and indicates talent, originality, and genius in a horoscope. It usually causes last-minute reversals and changes of plan, unwanted separations, accidents, catastrophes, and eccentric behavior. It can add irrational rebelliousness and perverse bohemianism to a personality or a streak of unaffected brilliance in science and art. It rules technology, aviation, and all forms of electrical and electronic advancement. It governs great leaps forward and topsy-turvy situations, and *always* turns things around at the last minute. Its effects are difficult to predict, since it rules sudden last-minute decisions and events that come like lightning out of the blue.

NEPTUNE

Neptune dissolves existing reality the way the sea erodes the cliffs beside it. Its effects are subtle like the ringing of a buoy's bell in the fog. It suggests a reality higher than definition can usually describe. It awakens a sense of higher responsibility often causing guilt, worry, anxieties, or delusions. Neptune is associated with all forms of escape and can make things seem a certain way so convincingly that you are absolutely sure of something that eventually turns out to be quite different.

It is the planet of illusion and therefore governs the invisible realms that lie beyond our ordinary minds, beyond our simple factual ability to prove what is "real." Treachery, deceit, disillusionment, and disappointment are linked to Neptune. It describes a vague reality that promises eternity and the divine, yet in a manner so complex that we cannot really fathom it at all. At its worst Neptune is a cheap intoxicant; at its best it is the poetry, music, and inspiration of the higher planes of spiritual love. It has dominion over movies, photographs, and much of the arts.

PLUTO

Pluto lies at the outpost of our system and therefore rules finality in a horoscope—the final closing of chapters in your life, the passing of major milestones and points of development from which there is no return. It is a final wipeout, a closeout, an evacuation. It is a distant, subtle but powerful catalyst in all transformations that occur. It creates, destroys, then recreates. Sometimes Pluto starts its influence with a minor event or insignificant incident that might even go unnoticed. Slowly but surely, little by little, everything changes, until at last there has been a total transformation in the area of your life where Pluto has been operating. It rules mass thinking and the trends that society first rejects, then adopts, and finally outgrows.

Pluto rules the dead and the underworld—all the powerful forces of creation and destruction that go on all the time beneath, around, and above us. It can bring a lust for power with strong obsessions.

It is the planet that rules the metamorphosis of the caterpillar into a butterfly, for it symbolizes the capacity to change totally and forever a person's lifestyle, way of thought, and behavior.

THE MOON IN EACH SIGN

The Moon is the nearest planet to the Earth. It exerts more observable influence on us from day to day than any other planet. The effect is very personal, very intimate, and if we are not aware of how it works it can make us quite unstable in our ideas. And the annoying thing is that at these times we often see our own instability but can do nothing about it. A knowledge of what can be expected may help considerably. We can then be prepared to stand strong against the Moon's negative influences and use its positive ones to help us to get ahead. Who has not heard of going with the tide?

The Moon reflects, has no light of its own. It reflects the Sun—the life giver—in the form of vital movement. The Moon controls the tides, the blood rhythm, the movement of sap in trees and plants. Its nature is inconstancy and change so it signifies our moods, our superficial behavior—walking, talking, and especially thinking. Being a true reflector of other forces, the Moon is cold, watery like the surface of a still lake, brilliant and scintillating at times, but easily ruffled and disturbed by the winds of change.

The Moon takes about 27⅓ days to make a complete transit of the Zodiac. It spends just over 2¼ days in each sign. During that time it reflects the qualities, energies, and characteristics of the sign and, to a degree, the planet which rules the sign. When the Moon in its transit occupies a sign incompatible with our own birth sign, we can expect to feel a vague uneasiness, perhaps a touch of irritableness. We should not be discouraged nor let the feeling get us down, or, worse still, allow ourselves to take the discomfort out on others. Try to remember that the Moon has to change signs within 55 hours and, provided you are not physically ill, your mood will probably change with it. It is amazing how frequently depression lifts with the shift in the Moon's position. And, of course, when the Moon is transiting a sign compatible or sympathetic to yours, you will probably feel some sort of stimulation or just be plain happy to be alive.

In the horoscope, the Moon is such a powerful indicator that competent astrologers often use the sign it occupied at birth as the birth sign of the person. This is done particularly when the Sun is on the cusp, or edge, of two signs. Most experienced astrologers, however, coordinate both Sun and Moon signs by reading and confirming from one to the other and secure a far more accurate and personalized analysis.

For these reasons, the Moon tables which follow this section (see pages 86–92) are of great importance to the individual. They show the days and the exact times the Moon will enter each sign of the Zodiac for the year. Remember, you have to adjust the indicated times to local time. The corrections, already calculated for most of the main cities, are at the beginning of the tables. What follows now is a guide to the influences that will be reflected to the Earth by the Moon while it transits each of the twelve signs. The influence is at its peak about 26 hours after the Moon enters a sign. As you read the daily forecast, check the Moon sign for any given day and glance back at this guide.

MOON IN ARIES

This is a time for action, for reaching out beyond the usual self-imposed limitations and faint-hearted cautions. If you have plans in your head or on your desk, put them into practice. New ventures, applications, new jobs, new starts of any kind—all have a good chance of success. This is the period when original and dynamic impulses are being reflected onto Earth. Such energies are extremely vital and favor the pursuit of pleasure and adventure in practically every form. Sick people should feel an improvement. Those who are well will probably find themselves exuding confidence and optimism. People fond of physical exercise should find their bodies growing with tone and well-being. Boldness, strength, determination should characterize most of your activities with a readiness to face up to old challenges. Yesterday's problems may seem petty and exaggerated—so deal with them. Strike out alone. Self-reliance will attract others to you. This is a good time for making friends. Business and marriage partners are more likely to be impressed with the man and woman of action. Opposition will be overcome or thrown aside with much less effort than usual. CAUTION: Be dominant but not domineering.

MOON IN TAURUS

The spontaneous, action-packed person of yesterday gives way to the cautious, diligent, hardworking "thinker." In this period ideas will probably be concentrated on ways of improving finances. A great deal of time may be spent figuring out and going over schemes and plans. It is the right time to be careful with detail.

People will find themselves working longer than usual at their desks. Or devoting more time to serious thought about the future. A strong desire to put order into business and financial arrangements may cause extra work. Loved ones may complain of being neglected and may fail to appreciate that your efforts are for their ultimate benefit. Your desire for system may extend to criticism of arrangements in the home and lead to minor upsets. Health may be affected through overwork. Try to secure a reasonable amount of rest and relaxation, although the tendency will be to "keep going" despite good advice. Work done conscientiously in this period should result in a solid contribution to your future security. CAUTION: Try not to be as serious with people as the work you are engaged in.

MOON IN GEMINI
The humdrum of routine and too much work should suddenly end. You are likely to find yourself in an expansive, quicksilver world of change and self-expression. Urges to write, to paint, to experience the freedom of some sort of artistic outpouring, may be very strong. Take full advantage of them. You may find yourself finishing something you began and put aside long ago. Or embarking on something new which could easily be prompted by a chance meeting, a new acquaintance, or even an advertisement. There may be a yearning for a change of scenery, the feeling to visit another country (not too far away), or at least to get away for a few days. This may result in short, quick journeys. Or, if you are planning a single visit, there may be some unexpected changes or detours on the way. Familiar activities will seem to give little satisfaction unless they contain a fresh element of excitement or expectation. The inclination will be toward untried pursuits, particularly those that allow you to express your inner nature. The accent is on new faces, new places. CAUTION: Do not be too quick to commit yourself emotionally.

MOON IN CANCER
Feelings of uncertainty and vague insecurity are likely to cause problems while the Moon is in Cancer. Thoughts may turn frequently to the warmth of the home and the comfort of loved ones. Nostalgic impulses could cause you to bring out old photographs and letters and reflect on the days when your life seemed to be much more rewarding and less demanding. The love and understanding of parents and family may be important, and, if it is not forthcoming, you may have to fight against bouts of self-pity. The cordiality of friends and the thought of good times with them that are sure to be repeated will help to restore you to a happier frame

of mind. The desire to be alone may follow minor setbacks or rebuffs at this time, but solitude is unlikely to help. Better to get on the telephone or visit someone. This period often causes peculiar dreams and upsurges of imaginative thinking which can be helpful to authors of occult and mystical works. Preoccupation with the personal world of simple human needs can overshadow any material strivings. CAUTION: Do not spend too much time thinking—seek the company of loved ones or close friends.

MOON IN LEO
New horizons of exciting and rather extravagant activity open up. This is the time for exhilarating entertainment, glamorous and lavish parties, and expensive shopping sprees. Any merrymaking that relies upon your generosity as a host has every chance of being a spectacular success. You should find yourself right in the center of the fun, either as the life of the party or simply as a person whom happy people like to be with. Romance thrives in this heady atmosphere and friendships are likely to explode unexpectedly into serious attachments. Children and younger people should be attracted to you and you may find yourself organizing a picnic or a visit to a fun-fair, the movies, or the beach. The sunny company and vitality of youthful companions should help you to find some unsuspected energy. In career, you could find an opening for promotion or advancement. This should be the time to make a direct approach. The period favors those engaged in original research. CAUTION: Bask in popularity, not in flattery.

MOON IN VIRGO
Off comes the party cap and out steps the busy, practical worker. He wants to get his personal affairs straight, to rearrange them, if necessary, for more efficiency, so he will have more time for more work. He clears up his correspondence, pays outstanding bills, makes numerous phone calls. He is likely to make inquiries, or sign up for some new insurance and put money into gilt-edged investment. Thoughts probably revolve around the need for future security—to tie up loose ends and clear the decks. There may be a tendency to be "finicky," to interfere in the routine of others, particularly friends and family members. The motive may be a genuine desire to help with suggestions for updating or streamlining their affairs, but these will probably not be welcomed. Sympathy may be felt for less fortunate sections of the community and a flurry of some sort of voluntary service is likely. This may be accompanied by strong feelings of responsibility on several fronts and health may suffer from extra efforts made. CAUTION: Everyone may not want your help or advice.

MOON IN LIBRA

These are days of harmony and agreement and you should find yourself at peace with most others. Relationships tend to be smooth and sweet-flowing. Friends may become closer and bonds deepen in mutual understanding. Hopes will be shared. Progress by cooperation could be the secret of success in every sphere. In business, established partnerships may flourish and new ones get off to a good start. Acquaintances could discover similar interests that lead to congenial discussions and rewarding exchanges of some sort. Love, as a unifying force, reaches its optimum. Marriage partners should find accord. Those who wed at this time face the prospect of a happy union. Cooperation and tolerance are felt to be stronger than dissension and impatience. The argumentative are not quite so loud in their bellowings, nor as inflexible in their attitudes. In the home, there should be a greater recognition of the other point of view and a readiness to put the wishes of the group before selfish insistence. This is a favorable time to join an art group. CAUTION: Do not be too independent—let others help you if they want to.

MOON IN SCORPIO

Driving impulses to make money and to economize are likely to cause upsets all around. No area of expenditure is likely to be spared the ax, including the household budget. This is a time when the desire to cut down on extravagance can become near fanatical. Care must be exercised to try to keep the aim in reasonable perspective. Others may not feel the same urgent need to save and may retaliate. There is a danger that possessions of sentimental value will be sold to realize cash for investment. Buying and selling of stock for quick profit is also likely. The attention turns to organizing, reorganizing, tidying up at home and at work. Neglected jobs could suddenly be done with great bursts of energy. The desire for solitude may intervene. Self-searching thoughts could disturb. The sense of invisible and mysterious energies in play could cause some excitability. The reassurance of loves ones may help. CAUTION: Be kind to the people you love.

MOON IN SAGITTARIUS

These are days when you are likely to be stirred and elevated by discussions and reflections of a religious and philosophical nature. Ideas of faraway places may cause unusual response and excitement. A decision may be made to visit someone overseas, perhaps a person whose influence was important to your earlier character development. There could be a strong resolution to get away from present intellectual patterns, to learn new subjects, and to meet more interesting people. The superficial may be rejected in all its forms. An impatience with old ideas and unimaginative contacts could lead to a change of companions and interests. There may be an upsurge of religious feeling and metaphysical inquiry. Even a new insight into the significance of astrology and other occult studies is likely under the curious stimulus of the Moon in Sagittarius. Physically, you may express this need for fundamental change by spending more time outdoors: sports, gardening, long walks appeal. CAUTION: Try to channel any restlessness into worthwhile study.

MOON IN CAPRICORN

Life in these hours may seem to pivot around the importance of gaining prestige and honor in the career, as well as maintaining a spotless reputation. Ambitious urges may be excessive and could be accompanied by quite acquisitive drives for money. Effort should be directed along strictly ethical lines where there is no possibility of reproach or scandal. All endeavors are likely to be characterized by great earnestness, and an air of authority and purpose which should impress those who are looking for leadership or reliability. The desire to conform to accepted standards may extend to sharp criticism of family members. Frivolity and unconventional actions are unlikely to amuse while the Moon is in Capricorn. Moderation and seriousness are the orders of the day. Achievement and recognition in this period could come through community work or organizing for the benefit of some amateur group. CAUTION: Dignity and esteem are not always self-awarded.

MOON IN AQUARIUS

Moon in Aquarius is in the second last sign of the Zodiac where ideas can become disturbingly fine and subtle. The result is often a mental "no-man's land" where imagination cannot be trusted with the same certitude as other times. The dangers for the individual are the extremes of optimism and pessimism. Unless the imagination is held in check, situations are likely to be misread, and rosy conclusions drawn where they do not exist. Consequences for the unwary can be costly in career and business. Best to think twice and not speak or act until you think again. Pessimism can be a cruel self-inflicted penalty for delusion at this time. Between the two extremes are strange areas of self-deception which, for example, can make the selfish person think he is actually being generous. Eerie dreams which resemble the reality and even seem to continue into the waking state are also possible. CAUTION: Look for the fact and not just for the image in your mind.

MOON IN PISCES

Everything seems to come to the surface now. Memory may be crystal clear, throwing up long-forgotten information which could be valuable in the career or business. Flashes of clairvoyance and intuition are possible along with sudden realizations of one's own nature, which may be used for self-improvement. A talent, never before suspected, may be discovered. Qualities not evident before in friends and marriage partners are likely to be noticed. As this is a period in which the truth seems to emerge, the discovery of false characteristics is likely to lead to disenchantment or a shift in attachments. However, when qualities are accepted, it should lead to happiness and deeper feeling. Surprise solutions could bob up for old problems. There may be a public announcement of the solving of a crime or mystery. People with secrets may find someone has "guessed" correctly. The secrets of the soul or the inner self also tend to reveal themselves. Religious and philosophical groups may make some interesting discoveries. CAUTION: Not a time for activities that depend on secrecy.

NOTE: When you read your daily forecasts, use the Moon Sign Dates that are provided in the following section of Moon Tables. Then you may want to glance back here for the Moon's influence in a given sign.

MOON TABLES

Atlanta, Boston, Detroit, Miami, Washington, Montreal, Ottawa, Quebec, Bogota, Havana, Lima, Santiago .. Same time

Chicago, New Orleans, Houston, Winnipeg, Churchill, Mexico City .... Deduct 1 hour

Albuquerque, Denver, Phoenix, El Paso, Edmonton, Helena .... Deduct 2 hours

Los Angeles, San Francisco, Reno, Portland, Seattle, Vancouver .... Deduct 3 hours

Honolulu, Anchorage, Fairbanks, Kodiak .... Deduct 5 hours

Nome, Samoa, Tonga, Midway.................... Deduct 6 hours

Halifax, Bermuda, San Juan, Caracas, La Paz, Barbados ....Add 1 hour

St. John's, Brasilia, Rio de Janeiro, Sao Paulo, Buenos Aires, Montevideo.........................Add 2 hours

Azores, Cape Verde Islands...........................Add 3 hours

Canary Islands, Madeira, Reykjavik ....Add 4 hours

London, Paris, Amsterdam, Madrid, Lisbon, Gibraltar, Belfast, Rabat ....Add 5 hours

Frankfurt, Rome, Oslo, Stockholm, Prague, Belgrade..Add 6 hours

Bucharest, Beirut, Tel Aviv, Athens, Istanbul, Cairo, Alexandria, Cape Town, Johannesburg ....Add 7 hours

Moscow, Leningrad, Baghdad, Dhahran, Addis Ababa, Nairobi, Teheran, Zanzibar.........Add 8 hours

Bombay, Calcutta, Sri Lanka..................... Add 10 ½ hours

Hong Kong, Shanghai, Manila, Peking, Perth...... Add 13 hours

Tokyo, Okinawa, Darwin, Pusan.................... Add 14 hours

Sydney, Melbourne, Port Moresby, Guam.......... Add 15 hours

Auckland, Wellington, Suva, Wake................. Add 17 hours

1999 MOON SIGN DATES—
NEW YORK TIME

JANUARY		FEBRUARY		MARCH	
Day Moon Enters		**Day Moon Enters**		**Day Moon Enters**	
1. Cancer	3:16 am	1. Virgo	8:38 pm	1. Virgo	5:06 am
2. Cancer		2. Virgo		2. Virgo	
3. Leo	5:32 am	3. Virgo		3. Libra	1:35 pm
4. Leo		4. Libra	4:57 am	4. Libra	
5. Virgo	10:50 am	5. Libra		5. Libra	
6. Virgo		6. Scorp.	4:07 pm	6. Scorp.	0:23 am
7. Libra	7:54 pm	7. Scorp.		7. Scorp.	
8. Libra		8. Scorp.		8. Sagitt.	0:47 pm
9. Libra		9. Sagitt.	4:39 am	9. Sagitt.	
10. Scorp.	7:50 am	10. Sagitt.		10. Sagitt.	
11. Scorp.		11. Capric.	4:11 pm	11. Capric.	0:55 am
12. Sagitt.	8:24 pm	12. Capric.		12. Capric.	
13. Sagitt.		13. Capric.		13. Aquar.	10:33 am
14. Sagitt.		14. Aquar.	0:58 am	14. Aquar.	
15. Capric.	7:30 am	15. Aquar.		15. Pisces	4:31 pm
16. Capric.		16. Pisces	6:41 am	16. Pisces	
17. Aquar.	4:12 pm	17. Pisces		17. Aries	7:14 pm
18. Aquar.		18. Aries	10:07 am	18. Aries	
19. Pisces	10:41 pm	19. Aries		19. Taurus	8:10 pm
20. Pisces		20. Taurus	0:30 pm	20. Taurus	
21. Pisces		21. Taurus		21. Gemini	9:06 pm
22. Aries	3:26 am	22. Gemini	2:55 pm	22. Gemini	
23. Aries		23. Gemini		23. Cancer	11:34 pm
24. Taurus	6:53 am	24. Cancer	6:10 pm	24. Cancer	
25. Taurus		25. Cancer		25. Cancer	
26. Gemini	9:30 am	26. Leo	10:45 pm	26. Leo	4:23 am
27. Gemini		27. Leo		27. Leo	
28. Cancer	11:58 am	28. Leo		28. Virgo	11:35 am
29. Cancer				29. Virgo	
30. Leo	3:17 pm			30. Libra	8:50 pm
31. Leo				31. Libra	

Summer time to be considered where applicable.

1999 MOON SIGN DATES—
NEW YORK TIME

APRIL		MAY		JUNE	
Day Moon Enters		**Day Moon Enters**		**Day Moon Enters**	
1. Libra		1. Scorp.		1. Capric.	
2. Scorp.	7:50 am	2. Sagitt.	2:37 am	2. Capric.	
3. Scorp.		3. Sagitt.		3. Aquar.	8:38 am
4. Sagitt.	8:08 pm	4. Capric.	3:13 pm	4. Aquar.	
5. Sagitt.		5. Capric.		5. Pisces	6:02 pm
6. Sagitt.		6. Capric.		6. Pisces	
7. Capric.	8:40 am	7. Aquar.	2:41 am	7. Pisces	
8. Capric.		8. Aquar.		8. Aries	0:09 am
9. Aquar.	7:25 pm	9. Pisces	11:17 am	9. Aries	
10. Aquar.		10. Pisces		10. Taurus	2:44 am
11. Aquar.		11. Aries	3:54 pm	11. Taurus	
12. Pisces	2:36 am	12. Aries		12. Gemini	2:49 am
13. Pisces		13. Taurus	4:57 pm	13. Gemini	
14. Aries	5:47 am	14. Taurus		14. Cancer	2:15 am
15. Aries		15. Gemini	4:08 pm	15. Cancer	
16. Taurus	6:08 am	16. Gemini		16. Leo	3:08 am
17. Taurus		17. Cancer	3:40 pm	17. Leo	
18. Gemini	5:40 am	18. Cancer		18. Virgo	7:13 am
19. Gemini		19. Leo	5:38 pm	19. Virgo	
20. Cancer	6:28 am	20. Leo		20. Libra	3:11 pm
21. Cancer		21. Virgo	11:16 pm	21. Libra	
22. Leo	10:07 am	22. Virgo		22. Libra	
23. Leo		23. Virgo		23. Scorp.	2:19 am
24. Virgo	5:05 pm	24. Libra	8:30 am	24. Scorp.	
25. Virgo		25. Libra		25. Sagitt.	2:52 pm
26. Virgo		26. Scorp.	8:06 pm	26. Sagitt.	
27. Libra	2:47 am	27. Scorp.		27. Sagitt.	
28. Libra		28. Scorp.		28. Capric.	3:13 am
29. Scorp.	2:14 pm	29. Sagitt.	8:38 am	29. Capric.	
30. Scorp.		30. Sagitt.		30. Aquar.	2:20 pm
		31. Capric.	9:07 pm		

Summer time to be considered where applicable.

1999 MOON SIGN DATES—
NEW YORK TIME

JULY		AUGUST		SEPTEMBER	
Day Moon Enters		Day Moon Enters		Day Moon Enters	
1. Aquar.		1. Aries	11:48 am	1. Taurus	
2. Pisces	11:35 pm	2. Aries		2. Gemini	0:26 am
3. Pisces		3. Taurus	4:10 pm	3. Gemini	
4. Pisces		4. Taurus		4. Cancer	3:11 am
5. Aries	6:22 am	5. Gemini	6:58 pm	5. Cancer	
6. Aries		6. Gemini		6. Leo	6:30 am
7. Taurus	10:23 am	7. Cancer	8:54 pm	7. Leo	
8. Taurus		8. Cancer		8. Virgo	10:58 am
9. Gemini	0:01 pm	9. Leo	10:57 pm	9. Virgo	
10. Gemini		10. Leo		10. Libra	5:17 pm
11. Cancer	0:28 pm	11. Leo		11. Libra	
12. Cancer		12. Virgo	2:23 am	12. Libra	
13. Leo	1:27 pm	13. Virgo		13. Scorp.	2:09 am
14. Leo		14. Libra	8:25 am	14. Scorp.	
15. Virgo	4:40 pm	15. Libra		15. Sagitt.	1:36 pm
16. Virgo		16. Scorp.	5:41 pm	16. Sagitt.	
17. Libra	11:20 pm	17. Scorp.		17. Sagitt.	
18. Libra		18. Scorp.		18. Capric.	2:14 am
19. Libra		19. Sagitt.	5:33 am	19. Capric.	
20. Scorp.	9:31 am	20. Sagitt.		20. Aquar.	1:39 pm
21. Scorp.		21. Capric.	6:00 pm	21. Aquar.	
22. Sagitt.	9:49 pm	22. Capric.		22. Pisces	9:52 pm
23. Sagitt.		23. Capric.		23. Pisces	
24. Sagitt.		24. Aquar.	4:50 am	24. Pisces	
25. Capric.	10:09 am	25. Aquar.		25. Aries	2:35 am
26. Capric.		26. Pisces	0:51 pm	26. Aries	
27. Aquar.	8:55 pm	27. Pisces		27. Taurus	4:52 am
28. Aquar.		28. Aries	6:10 pm	28. Taurus	
29. Aquar.		29. Aries		29. Gemini	6:22 am
30. Pisces	5:28 am	30. Taurus	9:42 pm	30. Gemini	
31. Pisces		31. Taurus			

Summer time to be considered where applicable.

1999 MOON SIGN DATES— NEW YORK TIME

OCTOBER		NOVEMBER		DECEMBER	
Day Moon Enters		**Day Moon Enters**		**Day Moon Enters**	
1. Cancer	8:32 am	1. Virgo	11:08 pm	1. Libra	0:30 pm
2. Cancer		2. Virgo		2. Libra	
3. Leo	0:14 pm	3. Virgo		3. Scorp.	10:36 pm
4. Leo		4. Libra	6:58 am	4. Scorp.	
5. Virgo	5:41 pm	5. Libra		5. Scorp.	
6. Virgo		6. Scorp.	4:47 pm	6. Sagitt.	10:28 am
7. Virgo		7. Scorp.		7. Sagitt.	
8. Libra	0:53 am	8. Scorp.		8. Capric.	11:15 pm
9. Libra		9. Sagitt.	4:16 am	9. Capric.	
10. Scorp.	10:02 am	10. Sagitt.		10. Capric.	
11. Scorp.		11. Capric.	5:01 pm	11. Aquar.	12:00 pm
12. Sagitt.	9:20 pm	12. Capric.		12. Aquar.	
13. Sagitt.		13. Capric.		13. Pisces	11:19 pm
14. Sagitt.		14. Aquar.	5:47 am	14. Pisces	
15. Capric.	10:05 am	15. Aquar.		15. Pisces	
16. Capric.		16. Pisces	4:22 pm	16. Aries	7:31 am
17. Aquar.	10:18 pm	17. Pisces		17. Aries	
18. Aquar.		18. Aries	10:58 pm	18. Taurus	11:46 am
19. Aquar.		19. Aries		19. Taurus	
20. Pisces	7:34 am	20. Aries		20. Gemini	0:40 pm
21. Pisces		21. Taurus	1:27 am	21. Gemini	
22. Aries	0:42 pm	22. Taurus		22. Cancer	11:53 am
23. Aries		23. Gemini	1:15 am	23. Cancer	
24. Taurus	2:26 pm	24. Gemini		24. Leo	11:33 am
25. Taurus		25. Cancer	0:30 am	25. Leo	
26. Gemini	2:34 pm	26. Cancer		26. Virgo	1:35 pm
27. Gemini		27. Leo	1:20 am	27. Virgo	
28. Cancer	3:10 pm	28. Leo		28. Libra	7:15 pm
29. Cancer		29. Virgo	5:12 am	29. Libra	
30. Leo	5:48 pm	30. Virgo		30. Libra	
31. Leo				31. Scorp.	4:37 am

Summer time to be considered where applicable.

1999 PHASES OF THE MOON— NEW YORK TIME

New Moon	First Quarter	Full Moon	Last Quarter
Dec. 18 ('98)	Dec. 26 ('98)	Jan. 1	Jan. 9
Jan. 17	Jan. 24	Jan. 31	Feb. 8
Feb. 16	Feb. 22	March 2	March 10
March 17	March 24	March 31	April 8
April 15	April 22	April 30	May 8
May 15	May 22	May 30	June 6
June 13	June 20	June 28	July 6
July 12	July 20	July 28	Aug. 4
Aug. 11	Aug. 18	Aug. 26	Sept. 2
Sept. 9	Sept. 17	Sept. 25	Oct. 1
Oct. 9	Oct. 17	Oct. 24	Oct. 31
Nov. 7	Nov. 16	Nov. 23	Nov. 29
Dec. 7	Dec. 15	Dec. 22	Dec. 29

Each phase of the Moon lasts approximately seven to eight days, during which the Moon's shape gradually changes as it comes out of one phase and goes into the next.

There will be a partial solar eclipse during the New Moon phase on February 16 and August 11.

There will be a lunar eclipse during the Full Moon phase on July 28.

1999 FISHING GUIDE

	Good	Best
January	3-4-5-17-24-28-30-31	1-2-9-29
February	1-2-3-16-23-27-28	8
March	1-2-3-10-28-29-30	4-5-17-24-31
April	16-22	1-2-3-9-27-28-29-30
May	2-3-8-15-22-29-30-31	1-27-28
June	13-20-25-26-27-30	1-2-7-28-29
July	1-6-13-25-28-29-30	20-26-27-31
August	11-19-23-24-25-26-29	4-27-28
September	2-9-17-22-25-26	23-24-27-28
October	22-23-24-26-27-31	2-9-17-21-25
November	16-20-23-24-29	8-21-22-25-26
December	7-16-20-21-22-24-25	19-23

1999 PLANTING GUIDE

	Aboveground Crops	Root Crops
January	1-20-21-25-29	2-8-9-10-11-12-16
February	17-21-25-26	4-5-6-7-8-12-13
March	20-21-24-25-31	4-5-6-7-11-12-16
April	17-21-27-28-29	1-2-3-4-8-9-12-13
May	18-19-25-26-27-28	1-5-6-10-14
June	14-15-21-22-23-24	1-2-6-7-10-11-29
July	18-19-20-21-22-26-27	3-4-8-12-31
August	15-16-17-18-22-23	4-5-8-9-27-28-31
September	11-12-13-14-18-19-23-24	1-4-5-27-28
October	10-11-12-16-17-21	2-8-25-29-30
November	8-12-13-17-18-21-22	5-6-7-25-26
December	9-10-14-15-19	2-3-4-5-23-29-30-31

	Pruning	Weeds and Pests
January	2-11-12	4-5-6-7-13-14
February	7-8	1-2-3-9-10-14-15
March	6-7-16	2-9-10-14
April	3-4-12-13	5-6-10-11-15
May	1-10	2-3-7-8-12-30-31
June	6-7	4-5-8-9-12
July	3-4-12-31	1-2-6-10-29
August	8-9-27-28	2-6-7-10-29-30
September	4-5	2-3-7-8-9-26-30
October	2-29-30	4-5-6-7-27-31
November	7-25-26	1-2-3-23-24-27-28-29-30
December	4-5-23-31	7-25-26-27-28

MOON'S INFLUENCE OVER PLANTS

Centuries ago it was established that seeds planted when the Moon is in signs and phases called Fruitful will produce more growth than seeds planted when the Moon is in a Barren sign.

Fruitful Signs: Taurus, Cancer, Libra, Scorpio, Capricorn, Pisces
Barren Signs: Aries, Gemini, Leo, Virgo, Sagittarius, Aquarius
Dry Signs: Aries, Gemini, Sagittarius, Aquarius

Activity	Moon In
Mow lawn, trim plants	**Fruitful sign:** 1st & 2nd quarter
Plant flowers	**Fruitful sign:** 2nd quarter; best in Cancer and Libra
Prune	**Fruitful sign:** 3rd & 4th quarter
Destroy pests; spray	**Barren sign:** 4th quarter
Harvest potatoes, root crops	**Dry sign:** 3rd & 4th quarter; Taurus, Leo, and Aquarius

MOON'S INFLUENCE OVER YOUR HEALTH

ARIES	Head, brain, face, upper jaw
TAURUS	Throat, neck, lower jaw
GEMINI	Hands, arms, lungs, shoulders, nervous system
CANCER	Esophagus, stomach, breasts, womb, liver
LEO	Heart, spine
VIRGO	Intestines, liver
LIBRA	Kidneys, lower back
SCORPIO	Sex and eliminative organs
SAGITTARIUS	Hips, thighs, liver
CAPRICORN	Skin, bones, teeth, knees
AQUARIUS	Circulatory system, lower legs
PISCES	Feet, tone of being

Try to avoid work being done on that part of the body when the Moon is in the sign governing that part.

MOON'S INFLUENCE OVER DAILY AFFAIRS

The Moon makes a complete transit of the Zodiac every 27 days 7 hours and 43 minutes. In making this transit the Moon forms different aspects with the planets and consequently has favorable or unfavorable bearings on affairs and events for persons according to the sign of the Zodiac under which they were born.

When the Moon is in conjunction with the Sun it is called a New Moon; when the Moon and Sun are in opposition it is called a Full Moon. From New Moon to Full Moon, first and second quarter—which takes about two weeks—the Moon is increasing or waxing. From Full Moon to New Moon, third and fourth quarter, the Moon is decreasing or waning.

Activity	Moon In
Business: buying and selling new, requiring public support	Sagittarius, Aries, Gemini, Virgo 1st and 2nd quarter
meant to be kept quiet	3rd and 4th quarter
Investigation	3rd and 4th quarter
Signing documents	1st & 2nd quarter, Cancer, Scorpio, Pisces
Advertising	2nd quarter, Sagittarius
Journeys and trips	1st & 2nd quarter, Gemini, Virgo
Renting offices, etc.	Taurus, Leo, Scorpio, Aquarius
Painting of house/apartment	3rd & 4th quarter, Taurus, Scorpio, Aquarius
Decorating	Gemini, Libra, Aquarius
Buying clothes and accessories	Taurus, Virgo
Beauty salon or barber shop visit	1st & 2nd quarter, Taurus, Leo, Libra, Scorpio, Aquarius
Weddings	1st & 2nd quarter

GEMINI

GEMINI

Character Analysis

People born under this third sign of the Zodiac are generally known for their versatility, their duality. Quite often they are able to manage several things at the same time. Some of them have two or more sides to their personalities. At one moment they can be happy and fun-loving, the next they can be sullen and morose. For the outsider, this sudden change may be difficult to understand or appreciate.

The Gemini man or woman is interested in all sorts of things and in different ways. Many of the subjects that attract them seem contrary and dissimilar. To Gemini, they're not.

The person born under the sign of the Twins has a mercurial nature. He can fly into a rage one moment, then be absolutely lovable the next. Chances are he won't remember what all the fuss was about after a few moments have passed.

The Gemini man or woman is spiritual in nature. Intellectual challenges whet his appetite. He's a sensitive person. His mind is active, alert. He could even be described as idea-hungry, always on the lookout for new concepts, new ways of doing things. He is always moving along with the times. On the whole, Gemini is very energetic. However, he is apt to bite off more than he can chew at times. He may begin a dozen different projects at once—and never finish any. It's often the doing—starting something—that he finds interesting. As soon as something becomes too familiar or humdrum, he may drop it like a hot coal and begin something else. The cultivated Gemini, however, does not have this problem. He has learned by experience that constancy pays off. He knows how to limit his interests—no matter how great the temptation may be to take on more—and how to finish the work that he has begun. It's a hard lesson for the natural Gemini to learn, but it can be done.

In school, the Twins are quite popular and often at the top of their class. They learn quickly, and when they apply themselves, they can make good use of their powers of concentration. Many do well in languages. They are clever conversationalists; they can keep an audience entranced for hours. Still and all, the depth of their knowledge may be slight. They know how to phrase things well, and this gives the impression of deep learning. They read things too quickly at times and often miss important points. Sometimes they will insist that something is right when in fact it isn't.

Generally, Gemini has a good sense of humor. He knows how to appreciate a good joke, which is apt to make him popular. He seldom fails to see the humorous side of life. In fact, he may irritate others by not acknowledging the serious side of a situation when it is necessary.

All in all, Gemini is open-minded. He is tolerant of others no matter what their views are. He can get along well with various types of people. He's a great mixer. He never has much trouble understanding another's viewpoint.

It is held that the Gemini person is one who prefers to work with concrete things. To him, facts are more important than fantasy. He's practical—or at least attempts to be. He can be quite goal-directed; there is always a reason for what he does. An ambitious person, on the whole, he is never short on projects; there is always something that he has to get done. He could be described as restless; he doesn't like sitting still for long periods of time. He's got to be on the go.

Health

Gemini usually is an active person. He has plenty of energy stored up. Still, he has to be careful at times because he is apt to strain himself emotionally. He gets too wound up and finds it difficult to relax. Troubles, small and large, can turn him into a high-strung person, if he doesn't look out for himself. Weak points of his body are his lungs, arms, and nervous system. During the winter months, some Twins develop one cold after another. Sore throats are sometimes a common Gemini complaint.

On the whole, however, Gemini has a pretty good constitution. He's healthy, but he has to learn how to take care of his health. People often think of Gemini as being weak and sickly, but this isn't so. His physique is often thin and wiry. He may not look like he can endure too much pressure, but his powers for endurance are amazing. He is not delicate, by any stretch of the imagination.

Although the Twins may be bothered by one minor ailment or another, they seldom contract serious illnesses—if they take proper care of themselves. The wise Gemini acknowledges his limits and never tries to exceed them. He will never take on more work than he can comfortably handle. It is important that the Gemini man or woman learns how to relax. Sleep is also an important ingredient for good health. Some Twins feel they have to be constantly on the go; it is as if they were on a treadmill. Of course, they can only keep it up for a short while, then they have to pay the consequences.

The Gemini man or woman is often gifted with handsome looks. Others find them winsome and attractive. Their faces are very lively and expressive, their smiles charming. Most of them tend to be on the slim side. They may seem restless or fidgety from time to time.

Occupation

Geminis are ambitious; they have plenty of drive. They like to keep busy. Most of them do well in jobs that give them a chance to make full use of their intellects. They like to use their minds more than their hands. They are good talkers, generally, and do well in positions where they have to deal directly with the public. They are clever with words and are persuasive in their arguments. Also, they know how to make people feel at ease by making use of their sense of humor. A well-placed joke can work wonders when dealing with the public.

The Twins know how to turn a disadvantage to advantage. They know how to bargain. They are seldom made fools of when it comes to trading. Some of them make excellent salespeople and it is little wonder. Because they can juggle words so well and they have a deep interest in facts, they often become capable journalists. Some of them make good theater or film critics. Writing is one of their chief talents. They generally do well in the arts.

Anything to do with negotiating or bargaining is something in which Gemini is apt to excel. They know how to phrase things, to put them in a favorable light. The Twins fit in almost anywhere in business or profession.

One also finds Geminis in such professions as dentistry, medicine, law, engineering. They excel at logic and reasoning. Some of them have a head for mathematics and make good accountants.

When working with others, they will do what is necessary to make the project successful. However, they do like to go their own way. They do not like someone looking over their shoulder constantly, advising them how something should be done. They like to move around; nothing pleases them more than a job where they are free to come and go as they please. They generally find it difficult to sit at a desk for long stretches at a time. Geminis like movement for its own sake. They are not particularly interested in destinations. It's getting there that absorbs their interest.

They are generally not contented being busy with just one thing. They are apt to try to hold down two jobs at the same time just to be active. Their hobbies are varied; some they manage to develop into side occupations. They abhor dull routine and are creative in their approach to a familiar scheme. They will do what they can to make their work interesting. If they are placed in the wrong position—that is, a position that does not coincide with their interests—they can be grumpy and difficult to get along with.

They like to be attached to a modern, progressive concern that provides a chance to learn new technology. They dislike job situations that are old-fashioned and tiresome.

Geminis aren't money-hungry, generally, but somehow or other they always manage to find jobs that are well-paying. They are not willing to work for nothing. They value their own skills and know how much they are worth.

Money interests the Gemini man or woman because it represents security. The uncultivated Gemini, however, spends his earnings carelessly. He doesn't run out of money, but he mismanages what he has. When he has learned how to economize, he does quite well. He's always looking for a way to better his financial situation. Some Geminis are job hoppers; they are never satisfied with the position they have and they go from one job to another looking for their "proper niche," they think. It is the Gemini who knows how to make the best out of a job situation he already has who wins the day. Job hopping never seems to stop, and in the end the job hopper has nothing to show for all the changing.

People born under this sign usually know how to win the sympathy of influential people. The Twins are often helped, advised, and encouraged by people who hold important positions. People find it easy to believe in Gemini.

The Gemini man or woman is generous with what he has; he does not mind sharing. He can be expansive and doesn't mind paying for others if he can afford it. Once in a while, he may do something unwise with his finances, but, all in all, he manages to keep his financial head above water.

Home and Family

Gemini is adaptable. He is willing to do without if it is necessary. But if he can have his own way, he likes to be surrounded by comfortable and harmonious things. Home is important to him. He likes a house that radiates beauty and calm.

He likes to invite people to his home; he likes entertaining. It is important to Gemini that people feel at home while visiting him. Because he is such a ready host, his house is often full of people— of all description. Although he may be at a loss how he should handle some household matters, he always seems to manage in one way or another. His home is likely to be modern—equipped with the latest conveniences and appliances. He is often amused by gadgets.

Although his home may be important to him, he also likes to pick up and go somewhere whenever the mood strikes. He doesn't like the feeling of being tied down. Home is where he hangs his hat, he likes to think. A Gemini is apt to change his address more than once in his lifetime. This may or may not upset family ties to a certain extent. Still, if they understand him, they will give in to his plans. No one is more difficult to live with than a dissatisfied Gemini. Still, more than likely Gemini has his family conditioned to his moods and there is enough understanding to make life together possible. The cultivated Gemini learns to stay put and make the most of the home he has.

The Gemini man or woman is a great fixer. He likes to make minor repairs, changing appliances, painting, wallpapering, and so on. He will do many things to make improvements on his home. Sometimes he will go ahead and make changes without consulting those he lives with, which can cause discord.

Outsiders may not think of Gemini as the ideal parent or family man. In fact, they may be open in their criticism. Gemini might resent this strongly because he feels it just isn't true. Children may get on the Gemini man or woman's nerves now and again. They like the kids to be expressive and creative. But the Twins do enjoy moments of peace and quiet. Generally, they know how to get along well with their children. This may be because they do have a youthful streak themselves. They understand the ups and downs of childhood, the trials and tribulations of growing up—also the joys. They may scold once in a while, but children who know them will never pay too much attention to them. The Gemini parent is generally a pushover for the willful child.

Gemini children are usually filled with restless, nervous energy. It comes from their minds, which are like delicately tuned electronic instruments. Mercury, Gemini's planet, is the planet of mind and communication, which bestows the ability to think, speak, write, and observe. So these young sons and daughters of Mercury cannot keep still, mentally or physically. They must be constantly engaged in something that interests them.

Young Gemini is an exceptionally bright child. He or she learns almost instantaneously and has an alert, inquiring mind that demands to know the reason behind anything that catches his or her attention. Parents and teachers of Geminis may find this an exhausting business, mainly because these lovable imps lose interest more quickly than most children. When that happens, and no one is around, their capacity for mischief is unbelievable.

Gemini children are sometimes difficult to manage. They usually don't like to be hampered by parental guidance. They like to be allowed to do as they please when they please. They often show signs of artistic ability at a very early age. The perceptive parent knows how to encourage them and to help them develop the characteristics that will help them later on in life.

Social Relationships

Gemini is usually easy to get along with. He likes people and knows how to make them like him. He seldom has serious enemies; he's too friendly for that. Because of his lighthearted ways many people are drawn to him. He is generally sincere in his friendships and expects that sincerity to be reciprocated. A sensitive person, he never forgets or forgives an offense.

The Twins like to be in a crowd—a friendly crowd. They seldom like to be alone for long stretches. They like their friends to be as active and as enthusiastic as they are. Social involvement is important to them. They are apt to throw a party at the drop of a hat. The Gemini man or woman enjoys making others feel good. They are excellent hosts and try to anticipate their guests' needs. Gemini could never be called inhospitable.

Their friends are apt be very different from each other. Gemini gets along well with all types of people. Their social needs may seem contradictory to someone who does not understand the Gemini nature. The cultivated person born under this sign knows how to keep apart those friends who are not likely to get along. He'll avoid social conflict among his friends at all costs.

Meeting new people is important to the man or woman born under the third sign of the Zodiac. He thrives on social activities. He likes exchanging views and ideas.

Gemini does not demand that his friends be his intellectual equal. He can be content discussing trivial matters as well as profound ones. He likes people he can relax with.

Friends may like Gemini but find him hard to understand. The Twins seem to have so many different personas at the same time. They are difficult to pin down.

People are always inviting Geminis to parties; any social affair would seem incomplete without them. Their charm and liveliness are contagious. People enjoy being around them. They can be loose-tongued at social gatherings, and sometimes divulge information about themselves or others that they shouldn't. They can be severe, too, in their criticisms. A Gemini's sharp tongue has cut many a social tie.

Love and Marriage

Gemini longs for affection and understanding. He doesn't always find it, though. Although he's honest in his search, Gemini is apt to be too critical. Once he's won someone, he finds fault with them. The cultivated Gemini learns to take the bitter with the sweet. He realizes that no one is perfect, and he accepts the love of his life for what she is.

It is quite possible for Gemini to have many love relationships before he ever thinks of settling down with one person. He may not be an intense lover. He loves being affectionate, however. Flattery can turn his head.

Gemini does not like to feel that he is tied down. He likes someone who will give him the freedom he needs. He doesn't like to feel imprisoned by love. He is often attracted to someone who is as independent in spirit as he is. He likes a witty and intelligent companion, someone who can discuss things rationally.

It is sometimes difficult for the natural Gemini to give himself to any one person. He does not like being limited in his affections. He flirts just for the pleasure of flirting. He enjoys attention and at times will go to great lengths to get it. He likes variety in romance. The same love diet is apt to bore him after a while.

In spite of his changeability, the intelligent Gemini can settle down to one partner, once he puts his mind to it. The person who wins a Gemini is usually gifted and clever, someone adaptable who knows how to change with his moods. Gemini is not difficult to get along with. He is pleasant and gentle, for the most part. He likes people who are responsive to his moods. If he really loves someone, he sees to it that his demands are not too unreasonable. He's willing to make compromises.

Even after he's married, the average Gemini is given to flirting, but it's nothing for his mate to be concerned about. He'll keep it at a harmless level. He will not risk a love relationship that contains the benefits he appreciates.

Marriage for Gemini is a relationship that should be lively and exciting. He's not the kind of person who accepts a humdrum home life. He wants a family that is as active as he is.

Romance and the Gemini Woman

The Gemini woman has no trouble attracting members of the opposite sex. They find her dazzling and glamorous. Her disposition is almost always gay and fun-loving. She knows how to make her suitors feel appreciated and wanted. However, she is restless and easily changes from one mood to another. This often mystifies and disappoints admirers. Sometimes she seems easy to please, other times not. People who don't understand her think she is difficult and egocentric.

The Gemini woman likes variety in her love relationships. She may go through many romances before she thinks of marrying and settling down. She admires a man who can accept her as an equal, intellectually and emotionally. She is not too fond of domestic duties. After marriage, she wants to pursue her various interests just as she did when she was single.

An intellectual man is apt to appeal to her when she is interested in a serious love relationship. A man who can win her mind can win her heart. Gemini seldom marries someone she considers her inferior intellectually. She wants someone she can respect.

The single Gemini woman can be quite flirtatious. She may even toy with the affections of someone she is not seriously interested in. When she feels a romance has come to an end, she'll say so bluntly and move on. She likes her love relationships to be an adventure—full of amusement and excitement. Men looking for a housekeeper instead of a partner are wasting their time when courting a Gemini woman. She'll never tie herself to the kitchen for the love of a man. She is interested in too many other things.

The considerate Gemini woman, however, will cut down on her interests and confine most of her activities to the home if she feels the love of her man is worth the sacrifice.

The Gemini woman has good taste in decorating a home. She knows how to arrange rooms and how to use color tastefully. She can become a good homemaker once she puts her mind to it. She likes things tidy and neat but is not too fond of domestic chores. If possible, she will see to it that she has some help in carrying out household duties.

Romance and the Gemini Man

The Gemini man is interested in change and adventure in his romantic activities. The woman who desires to keep up with him has to be quick on her feet. His restlessness is apt to puzzle even those who love him. He is quick-witted and fond of challenge. Someone who is likely to drag him into a life of humdrum domesticity will not win him.

In spite of the fact that he may go from romance to romance quite easily, the Gemini man is really in search of a true and lasting love relationship. He is popular with women. They like him because of his charm and intelligence. If he cares for a woman, he can make her feel like the most important person in his life.

He is capable of steadfastness in his affections, but there is no guarantee how long this will last.

A girl interested in home and a family—and nothing else—is not one who will appeal to him. He wants someone who is a good companion, someone who can share his interests as well as his moods. He wants someone he can talk with as an equal, someone whose interests go beyond the trivial.

In love, he can be either passionate or mild; it depends on his partner and the circumstances. Some Geminis are easily distracted in romance, and their interests travel from one woman to the other with appalling ease.

When he does meet the ideal mate, Gemini proves himself to be loving and responsible. He does his best to protect the interests of his family and is willing to make the sacrifices necessary to keep his home life in order. He may flirt occasionally after marriage, but it seldom goes beyond that. The woman who marries him must allow him his romantic fantasies. He can become unreasonable if he is reproached for flirting harmlessly.

He will be faithful to the woman who allows him his freedom— the woman who is not suspicious and trusts him.

Life with a Gemini man can be a happy one indeed, but the woman who plans to go through life at his side has to be as adaptable and active as he is.

Woman—Man

GEMINI WOMAN
ARIES MAN

The man born under the sign of Aries is often attracted to the Gemini woman. In you he can find that mixture of intellect and charm that is so often difficult to find in a woman. Like you, he has many interests and is always seeking one adventure after another. He has an insatiable thirst for knowledge of all kinds.

He can do with a woman like you—someone attractive, quick-witted, and intelligent. He'll admire you for your independence. He's not interested in a clinging vine. He wants someone who is there when he needs her; someone who listens and understands what he says; someone who can give advice if he should ever happen to ask for it, which is not likely to be often.

The Aries man wants a woman who is a good companion and a good sport. He is looking for a woman who will look good on his arm without hanging on it too heavily. He is looking for a woman who has both feet on the ground and yet is mysterious and enticing, a modern Helen of Troy whose face or fine speech can launch a thousand business deals, if need be. That woman he is in search of sounds a little like you. If the shoe fits, put it on. You won't be sorry.

The Aries man makes a good husband. He is faithful and attentive. He is an affectionate man. He'll make you feel needed and loved. Love is a serious matter for Aries. He does not believe in flirting or playing the field—especially after he's found the woman of his dreams. He'll expect you to be as constant in your affection as he is in his. Try to curb your bent for harmless flirting if you have your heart set on an Aries. He'll expect you to be a hundred percent his; he won't put up with any nonsense while romancing you.

The Aries man may be progressive and modern about many things, but when it comes to pants wearing, he's downright conventional: it's strictly male attire. The best role you can take in the relationship is a supporting one. He's the boss and that's that. If you can accept it, you'll find the going easy.

The Aries man, with his endless energy and drive, likes to relax in comfort at the end of the day. The Gemini woman who is a good homemaker can be sure of his undying affection. If you see to it that everything in the house is where he expects to find it, you'll have no difficulty keeping the relationship on an even keel.

Aries is generally a good provider. He'll see to it that you never want. Although he is interested in security, he's a man who is not afraid to take risks. Often his gambling pays off.

Aries fathers, while affectionate and playful, sometimes have trouble seeing things through the eyes of a child. Your innate understanding of youth will always come in handy.

GEMINI WOMAN
TAURUS MAN

If your heart is set on a man born under the sign of Taurus, you'll have to learn the art of being patient. Taurus take their time about everything—even love.

The steady and deliberate Taurus is a little slow on the draw; it may take him quite a while before he gets around to popping that question. For the Gemini woman who is adaptable, the waiting and anticipating almost always pays off in the end. Taurus men want to make sure that every step they take is right, especially if the path they're on could lead to the altar.

If you are in the mood for a whirlwind romance, better cast your net in shallower waters. Moreover, most Taurus prefer to do the angling themselves. They are not keen on women taking the lead. Once she does, he may drop her immediately. If the Gemini woman lets herself get caught on his terms, she'll find that her Taurus has fallen for her—hook, line, and sinker.

The Taurus man is fond of a comfortable home life. It is very important to him. If you keep those home fires burning you will have no trouble keeping that flame in the Taurus heart aglow. You have a talent for homemaking. You are an old hand at harmony and color. Your taste in furnishings is excellent. Perhaps, with your moodiness, sense of adventure, and love of change, you could turn out to be a challenging mate for the strong, steady, and protective Bull. Perhaps he could be the anchor for your dreams and plans. He could help you acquire a more balanced outlook and approach to your life. Not one for wild schemes, himself, Taurus can help you to curb your impulsiveness. He's the man who is always there when you need him.

The Taurus man is steady—the kind of man the Gemini woman often needs.

When you tie the knot with a Bull, you can put away fears about creditors pounding on the front door. Taurus is practical about everything including bill paying. When he carries you over the threshold, you can be certain the entire house is paid for.

Married to a Taurus man, you need not worry about having to put aside your many interests for the sake of back-breaking household chores. He'll see to it that you have all the latest time-saving appliances and comforts.

You also can forget about acquiring premature gray hairs due to unruly, ruckus-raising children under your feet. Papa Taurus is a master at keeping youngsters in line. He's crazy about kids but he also knows what's good for them.

GEMINI WOMAN
GEMINI MAN

The Gemini man and the Gemini woman are a couple who understand each other. They are so much alike. Both are intelligent, witty, outgoing, and versatile. The Gemini man could easily turn out to be your better half. One thing that causes a Twin's mind and affection to wander is a bore, and it's highly unlikely that an active Gemini woman would ever allow herself to be accused of that.

The Gemini man who has caught your heart will admire you for your ideas and intellect—perhaps even more than for your good cooking and flawless talent for homemaking. The Gemini woman needn't feel that once she's made her marriage vows she'll have to put her interests and ambition in storage. The Gemini man will admire you for your zeal and liveliness. He's the kind of guy who won't pout and scowl if you let him shift for himself in the kitchen once in a while. In fact, he'll enjoy the challenge of wrestling with pots and pans for a change. Chances are, too, that he might turn out to be a better cook than you—that is, if he isn't already.

The man born under the sign of the Twins is very active. There aren't many women who have enough pep to keep up with him. But this doesn't set a problem for the spry Gemini woman. You are both dreamers, planners, and idealists. The strong Gemini woman can easily fill the role of rudder for her Gemini man's ship-without-a-sail. If you happen to be a cultivated Gemini, he won't mind it too much. The intelligent Twin is often aware of his shortcomings. He doesn't resent it if someone with better bearings gives him a shove in the right direction. The average Gemini does not have serious ego hang-ups and will gracefully accept a well-deserved chewing out from his mate.

When you and your Gemini man team up, you'll probably always have a houseful of people to entertain—interesting people, too. Geminis find it hard to tolerate sluggish minds.

Gemini men are always attractive to the opposite sex. You'll perhaps have to allow him an occasional harmless flirt. It will seldom amount to more than that if you're his proper mate. It will help keep his spirits up. A Twin out of sorts, as you well know, is capable of brewing up a whirlwind of trouble. Better tolerate his flirting—within eyeshot, of course—than lose your cool.

As far as children go, you are both pushovers. One of you will have to learn to fill the role of house disciplinarian, otherwise chaos will reign.

GEMINI WOMAN
CANCER MAN

Chances are you won't hit it off too well with the man born under Cancer, but then Cupid has been known to do some pretty unlikely things. Cancer is a very sensitive man, thin-skinned and occasionally moody. You've got to keep on your toes, and not step on his if you're determined to make a go of the relationship.

The Cancer man may be lacking in many of the qualities you seek in a man, but when it comes to being faithful and being a good provider, he's hard to beat.

It is the perceptive Gemini woman who will not mistake the Crab's quietness for sullenness or his thriftiness for penny-pinching. In some respects he can be like the wise old owl out on a limb; he may look like he's dozing but actually he hasn't missed a thing. Moon Children often possess a well of knowledge about human behavior; they can deliver very helpful advice to those in trouble or in need. Cancer certainly can keep you from making unwise investments in time and especially money. He may not say much, but he's always got his wits about him.

The Crab may not be the match or catch for many a Gemini

woman. In fact, he may seem dull to on-the-move Gemini. True to his sign, he can be cranky and crabby when handled the wrong way. He is perhaps more sensitive than he should be.

Geminis are usually as smart as a whip. If you're clever you will never, in any way, convey the idea that you consider your Cancer a little short on brain power. Browbeating is a surefire way of sending the Crab angrily scurrying back to his shell. It's possible all of that lost ground may never be recovered.

The Crab is most comfortable at home. Once settled in for the night or for the weekend, wild horses couldn't drag him away unless those wild horses were dispatched by his mother. The Crab is sometimes a Mama's boy. If his mate does not put her foot down, he will see to it that his mother comes first whenever possible. No self-respecting Gemini would ever allow herself to play second fiddle to her mother-in-law. If she's a tactful Gemini, she may find that slipping into number-one position can be as easy as pie (that legendary apple pie his mother used to make).

If you take enough time to pamper your Cancer man with good cooking and comfort, you'll find that "Mother" turns up less and less—at the front door as well as in conversations.

Cancers make protective, proud, and patient fathers, but they may resent a youngster's bid for freedom.

GEMINI WOMAN
LEO MAN

For the Gemini woman who enjoys being swept off her feet in a romantic whirlwind, Leo is the sign of love. When the Lion puts his mind to romancing, he doesn't stint. It's all wining, dining, and dancing till the wee hours of the morning.

Leo is all heart and knows how to make his woman feel like a woman. The Gemini in constant search of a man she can look up to need go no farther. Leo is ten-feet tall—in spirit if not in stature. He's a man in full control of his faculties, and he also manages to have full control of just about any situation he finds himself in. He's a winner.

The Leo man may not look like Tarzan, but he knows how to roar and beat his chest if he has to. The Gemini woman who has had her fill of weak-kneed men finds in a Leo someone she can at last lean upon. He can support you physically as well as encourage your plans and projects. He's good at giving advice that pays off. Leos are direct. They don't believe in wasting time or effort. They almost never make unwise investments—something a Gemini often does.

Many Leos rise to the top of their profession and through their example prove to be a great inspiration to others.

Although he's a ladies' man, Leo is very particular about his ladies. His standards are high when it comes to love interests. The idealistic and cultivated Gemini should have no trouble keeping her balance on the pedestal the Lion sets her on. Leo believes that romance should be played on a fair give-and-take basis. He won't stand for any monkey business in a love relationship. It's all or nothing.

You'll find him a frank, straight-from-the-shoulder person; he generally says what is on his mind.

The Gemini woman who does decide upon a Leo for a mate must be prepared to stand squarely behind her man. He expects it—and usually deserves it. He's the head of the house and can handle that position without a hitch. He knows how to go about breadwinning and, if he has his way (and most Leos do have their own way), he'll see to it that you'll have all the luxuries you crave and the comforts you need.

It's likely that the romance in your marriage will stay alive. Lions need love like flowers need sunshine. They're ever amorous and generally expect similar attention and affection from their mate. Lions are fond of going out on the town; they love to give parties. You should encounter no difficulties in sharing his interest in this direction.

Leos make strict fathers, generally. You'll have to smooth over your children's roughed-up feelings.

GEMINI WOMAN
VIRGO MAN

The Virgo man is all business—or he may seem so to you. He is usually cool, calm, and collected. He's perhaps too much of a fuss-budget to wake up deep romantic interests in a Gemini. Torrid romancing to him is just so much sentimental mush. He can do without it and can make that evident in short order.

He's keen on chastity. If necessary, he can lead a sedentary, sexless life without caring too much about the fun others think he is missing. You may find him a first-class dud. His lack of imagination and dislike for flights of fancy can grate on a Gemini woman's nerves. He is always correct and likes to be handled correctly. Almost everything about him is orderly.

He does have an honest-to-goodness heart, believe it or not. The Gemini who finds herself strangely attracted to his feet-flat-on-the-ground ways will discover that his is a constant heart, not one that goes in for flings or sordid affairs. Virgos take an awfully long time to warm up to someone. A practical man, even in matters of the heart, he wants to know just what kind of a person you are before he takes a chance on love.

The impulsive Gemini had better not make the mistake of kissing her Virgo friend on the street, even if it's only a peck on the cheek. He's not at all demonstrative and hates public displays of affection. Love, according to him, should be kept within the confines of one's home—with the curtains drawn. Once he believes you are on the level with him as far as your love is concerned, you'll see how fast he loses his cool. Virgos are considerate, gentle lovers. He'll spend a long time, though, getting to know you. He'll like you before he loves you.

A Gemini-Virgo romance can be a sometime—or a one-time—thing. If the bottom ever falls out, don't bother to pick up the pieces. Nine times out of ten, he won't care about patching up. He's a once-burnt-twice-shy guy. When he crosses your phone number out of his address book, he's crossing you out of his life—for good.

Neat as a pin, he's thumbs-down on what he considers sloppy housekeeping. An ashtry with just one stubbed-out cigarette in it can be annoying to him, even if it's just two seconds old. Glassware should always sparkle and shine.

If you wind up marrying a Virgo man, keep your kids spic-and-span, at least by the time he gets home from work. Train the children to be kind, respectful, and courteous. He'll expect it.

GEMINI WOMAN
LIBRA MAN

If there's a Libra in your life, you are most likely a very happy woman. Men born under this sign of the Lawgiver have a way with impulsive, intelligent women. You'll always feel at ease in his company; you can always be yourself with him.

Like you, he's given to occasional fits of impulsiveness. His moods can change rapidly. One moment he comes on hard and strong with "I love you", and next moment he's left you like yesterday's mashed potatoes. He'll come back to you, though; don't worry. Libras are like that. Deep down inside he really knows what he wants even though he may not appear to.

You'll appreciate his admiration of beauty and harmony. If you're dressed to the teeth and never looked better in your life, you'll get a ready compliment—and one that's really deserved. Libras don't indulge in idle flattery. If they don't like something, they are tactful enough to remain silent.

Libras will go to great lengths to preserve peace and harmony—even tell a fat lie if necessary. They don't like showdowns or disagreeable confrontations. But the frank Gemini woman is usually impelled to air grievances and get resentments out into the open, even if it comes out all wrong. To Libra, making a clean breast of everything sometimes seems like sheer folly.

You may lose your patience while waiting for your Libra friend to make up his mind. It takes him ages to make a decision. He weighs both sides carefully before committing himself to anything. You seldom dillydally—at least about small things—and so you will find it difficult to see eye-to-eye with a hesitating Libra when it comes to decision-making methods.

All in all, though, he is a kind, gentle, and fair person. He is interested in the "real" truth. He'll try to balance everything out until he has all the correct answers. It is not difficult for him to see both sides of the story.

Libras don't pose or prance to get attention like a Leo might do. They're not show-offs. Generally, they are well-balanced people. Honest, wholesome, and affectionate, they are serious about every love entanglement they have. If he should find that his date is not really suited to him, he will end the relationship in such a tactful manner that no hard feelings will come about.

He never lets money burn holes in his pockets. You don't have to worry about him throwing his money all over the place, though. Most likely he'll spend it all on you—lavishly.

The Libra father can teach youngsters fairness and tolerance in a gentle, patient way. A peace-loving man, he encourages discussion and debate but frowns on physical fighting. He teaches the children how to play by the rules.

GEMINI WOMAN
SCORPIO MAN

Many find the Scorpio's sting a fate worse than death. The Gemini woman quite often is no exception. When his anger breaks loose, you had better clear out of the vicinity.

The average Scorpio man may strike the Gemini woman as being a brute. He'll stick pins into the balloons of your plans and dreams if they don't line up with what he thinks is right. If you do anything to irritate him—just anything—you'll wish you hadn't. He'll give you a sounding out that would make you pack your bags and vow never to go back.

The Scorpio man hates being tied down to home life—and so do you to a certain extent. Instead of wrestling with pots and pans, you'd rather be out and about, devoting plenty of time to your many interests. The Scorpio man would rather be out on the battlefield of life, belting away at whatever he feels is a just and worthy cause, instead of staying home nestled in a comfortable armchair with the evening paper. If you're a Gemini with a strong homemaking streak, don't keep those home fires burning too brightly too long; you may run out of firewood.

As passionate as he is in business and politics, the Scorpio man has plenty of pep and ginger stored away for lovemaking. Most women are easily attracted to him. The Gemini woman is no exception—at least before she is really aware of what she might be getting into. Those who allow a Scorpio to sweep them off their feet soon find that they're dealing with a pepperpot of seething excitement. The Scorpio man is passionate with a capital P, you can be sure of that.

But even while he is providing so much pleasure to his lover, he can deliver a knockout emotional blow. He can wound on a deep level, and you may not know if he really means it. Scorpio is blunt and can be as cutting as a razor blade. An insult can whiz out even more quickly than a compliment.

If you're a Gemini who can keep a stiff upper lip, take it on the chin, turn a deaf ear because you feel you are still under his love spell in spite of everything—lots of luck.

If you have decided to take the bitter with the sweet, prepare yourself for a lot of ups and downs. Chances are you won't have as much time for your own affairs and interests as you'd like. The Scorpio's love of power may cause you to be at his constant beck and call.

Scorpios like fathering large families, but they seldom give youngsters the attention they need.

GEMINI WOMAN
SAGITTARIUS MAN

The Gemini woman who has set her cap for a man born under the sign of Sagittarius may have to apply a lot of strategy before she can get him to say "Will you marry me?" Although some Archers may be marriage-shy, they're not ones to skitter away from romance. A Gemini woman may find a relationship with a Sagittarius—whether a fling or the real thing—a very enjoyable experience.

As a rule, Sagittarius are bright, happy, and healthy people. They have a strong sense of fair play. Often they're a source of inspirations to others. They're full of ideas and drive.

You'll be taken by the Archer's infectious grin and his light-hearted friendly nature. If you do wind up being the woman in his life, you'll find that he's apt to treat you more like a buddy than the love of his life. It's just his way. Sagittarius is often chummy instead of romantic.

You'll admire his broad-mindedness in most matters—including that of the heart. If, while dating you, he claims that he still wants to play the field, he'll expect you to enjoy the same liberty. Once he's promised to love, honor, and obey, however, he does just that. Marriage for him, once he's taken that big step, is very serious business. The Gemini woman with her keen imagination and love of freedom will not be disappointed if she does tie up with an Archer. The Sagittarius man is quick-witted—but not as quick-witted as you sometimes. Generally, men of this sign have a genuine interest in equality. They hate prejudice and injustice.

If he insists on a night out with the boys once a week, he won't scowl if you decide to let him shift for himself in the kitchen once a week while you go out with the girls.

He's not much of a homebody. Quite often he's occupied with faraway places either in his dreams or in reality. He enjoys—just as you do—being on the go or on the move. He's got ants in his pants and refuses to sit still for long stretches at a time. Humdrum routine—especially at home—bores him. At the drop of a hat, he may ask you to pack your traveling bag for a quick jaunt. He'll take great pride in showing you off to his friends. He'll always be a considerate mate; he will never embarrass or disappoint you intentionally.

His friendly, sunshiny nature is capable of attracting many people. Like you, he's very tolerant when it comes to friends, and you'll most likely spend a great deal of time entertaining.

Sagittarius are all thumbs when it comes to little shavers. He'll develop an interest in youngsters when they get older.

GEMINI WOMAN
CAPRICORN MAN

The with-it Gemini woman is likely to find the average Capricorn man a bit of a drag. The man born under the sign of the Goat is often a closed person and difficult to get to know. Even if you do get to know him, you may not find him very interesting.

In romance, Capricorn men are a little on the rusty side. You'll probably have to make all the passes.

You may find his plodding manner irritating, and his conservative, traditional ways maddening. He's not one to take chances on anything. "If it was good enough for my father, it's good enough for me" may be his motto. He follows a way that is tried and true.

Whenever adventure rears its tantalizing head, the Goat will turn the other way; he's just not interested.

He may be just as ambitious as you are—perhaps even more so. But his ways of accomplishing his aims are more subterranean; at least they seem so. He operates from the background a good deal of the time. At a gathering you may never even notice him, but he's there, taking in everything and sizing up everyone, planning his next careful move.

Although Capricorns may be intellectual, it is generally not the kind of intelligence a Gemini appreciates. He may not be as bright or as quick as you are; it may take ages for him to understand a joke.

The Gemini woman who does take up with a man born under this sign must be pretty good in the cheering up department. The Capricorn man in her love life may act as though he's constantly being followed by a cloud of gloom.

The Capricorn is happiest in the comfort and privacy of his own home. The security possible within four walls can make him a happy man. He'll spend as much time as he can at home. If he is loaded down with extra work, he'll bring it home instead of staying at the office.

You'll most likely find yourself frequently confronted by his relatives. Family is very important to the Capricorn—his family, not yours. They had better take an important place in your life, too, if you want to keep your home a happy one.

Although his caution in most matters may drive you up the wall, you'll find his concerned way with money justified most of the time. He is no squanderer. Everything is planned right down to the last red cent. He'll see to it that you never want.

He can be quite a scold when it comes to disciplining children. You'll have to step in and smooth things over when he goes too far.

GEMINI WOMAN
AQUARIUS MAN

You've never known love unless you've known a man born under the sign of Aquarius. The Gemini woman is likely to find an Aquarius dazzling.

As a rule, Aquarius are extremely friendly and open. Of all the signs, they are perhaps the most tolerant. In the thinking department, they are often miles ahead of others.

The Gemini woman will find her Aquarius man intriguing and interesting. She'll also find the relationship a challenging one. Your high respect for intelligence and imagination may be reason enough for you to settle your heart on a Water Bearer. You can learn a lot from him.

Aquarius love everybody—even their worst enemies, sometimes. Through your relationship with an Aquarius you will run into all sorts of people, ranging from near-genius to downright insane—and they're all friends of his.

In the holding-hands phase of your romance, you may find that your Water Bearer friend has cold feet. Aquarius take quite a bit of warming up before they're ready to come across with that first goodnight kiss. More than likely, he'll just want to be your pal in the beginning. For him, that's an important first step in any relationship—love, included. The poetry and flowers stage—if it ever comes—will come much later. Aquarius is all heart. Still, when it comes to tying himself down to one person and for keeps, he may hesitate. He may even try to get out of it if you breathe down his neck too hard.

The Aquarius man is no Valentino and wouldn't want to be. The Gemini woman is likely to be more impressed by his broadmindedness and high moral standards than by his feeble attempts at romance.

You won't find it difficult to look up to a man born under the sign of the Water Bearer, but you may find the challenge of trying to keep up with him dizzying. He can pierce through the most complicated problem as if it were a matter of simple math. You may find him a little too lofty and high-minded. But don't judge him too harshly if that's the case; he's way ahead of his time—your time, too, most likely.

If you marry this man, he'll stay true to you. He'll certainly admire you for your intelligence and wit. Don't think that, once you're married, he'll keep you chained to the kitchen sink. He'll encourage you to go ahead in your pursuit of knowledge. You'll most likely have a minor tiff with him every now and again but never anything serious.

Kids love him and vice versa. He'll be as tolerant with them as he is with adults.

GEMINI WOMAN
PISCES MAN

The man born under Pisces is a dreamer. Sometimes he's so wrapped up in his dreams that he's difficult to reach. To the average Gemini woman, he may seem a little passive.

He's easygoing most of the time. He seems to take things in his stride. He'll entertain all kinds of views and opinions from just about anyone, nodding or smiling vaguely, giving the impression that he's with them one hundred percent while that may not be the case at all. His attitude may be "why bother" when he is confronted with someone wrong who thinks he's right. The Pisces man will seldom speak his mind if he thinks he'll be rigidly opposed.

The Pisces man is oversensitive at times—he's afraid of getting his feelings hurt. He'll sometimes imagine a personal injury when none's been made. Chances are you'll find this maddening; at times you may feel like giving him a swift kick where it hurts the most. It wouldn't do any good, though. It would just add fuel to the fire of his persecution complex.

One thing you'll admire about Pisces is his concern for people who are sick or troubled. He'll make his shoulder available to anyone in the mood for a good cry. He can listen to one hard-luck story after another without seeming to tire. When his advice is asked, he is capable of coming across with words of wisdom. He often knows what is paining someone before that person is aware of it himself. It's almost intuitive with Pisces, it seems. Still, at the end of the day, this man will want some peace and quiet. If you've got a problem on your mind when he comes home, don't unload it in his lap. If you do, you may find him short-tempered. He's a good listener, but he can only take so much.

Pisces are not aimless although they may seem so at times. The positive Pisces man is often successful in his profession and is likely to wind up rich and influential. Material gain, however, is not a direct goal for a man born under the sign of the Fishes.

The weaker Pisces are usually content to stay put on the level where they find themselves. They won't complain too much if the roof leaks and the fence is in need of repair. They can evade any responsibility if they feel like it.

Because of their seemingly laissez-faire manner, Pisces are immensely popular with children. For tots the Pisces father plays the double role of confidant and playmate. It will never enter his mind to discipline a child, no matter how spoiled or incorrigible that child becomes.

Man—Woman

GEMINI MAN
ARIES WOMAN

The Aries woman is a charmer. When she tugs at your heart, you'll know it. She's a woman in search of a knight in shining armor. She is a very particular person with very high ideals. She won't accept anyone other than the man of her dreams.

The Aries woman never plays around with passion; she means business when it comes to love.

Don't get the idea that she's dewy-eyed. She isn't. In fact, she can be practical and to the point when she wants to be. She's a gal with plenty of drive and ambition. With an Aries woman behind you, you can go far in life. She knows how to help her man get ahead. She's full of wise advice; you only have to ask. In some cases, Aries women have a keen business sense; many of them become successful career women. There is nothing passive or re-tiring about her. She is equipped with a good brain and she knows how to use it.

An Aries-Gemini union could be something strong, secure, and romantic. If both of you have your sights fixed in the same direction, there is almost nothing you could not accomplish.

The Gemini man will have to give up flirting if he decides to settle for an Aries partner or wife. The Aries woman is proud, and capable of being quite jealous. While you're with her, never cast your eye in another woman's direction. It could spell disaster for your relationship. The Aries woman won't put up with romantic nonsense even if it's done only in fun.

If the Aries woman backs you up in your business affairs, you can be sure of succeeding. However, if she is only interested in advancing her own career and puts her own interests before yours, she can be sure of rocking the boat. It will put a strain on the relationship. The overambitious Aries woman can be a pain in the neck and make you forget you were once in love with her.

The cultivated Aries woman makes a wonderful wife and mother. She has a natural talent for homemaking. With a pot of paint and some wallpaper she can transform the dreariest domicile into an abode of beauty and snug comfort. The perfect hostess—even when friends just happen by—she knows how to make guests feel at home.

You'll admire your Aries, too, because she knows how to stand on her own two feet. Hers is an independent nature. She won't break down and cry when things go wrong. She'll pick herself up and try to patch things up.

Like you she's social-minded. In the wit department, she can run you a close second. She'll love you as long as she can look forward to a good intellectual challenge.

She makes a fine, affectionate mother and will encourage her children to develop a wide range of talents and skills.

GEMINI MAN
TAURUS WOMAN

The woman born under the sign of Taurus may lack a little of the sparkle and bubble you like. The Taurus woman is generally down to earth and never flighty. It's important to her that she keep both feet flat on the ground. She may fail to appreciate your willingness to run here and there, especially if she's under the impression that there's no profit in it.

On the other hand, if you hit it off with a Taurus woman, you won't be disappointed at all in the romance area. She is all woman, and proud of it, too. She can be very devoted and loving once she decides that her relationship with you is no fly-by-night romance. Basically, she's a passionate person. In sex, she's direct and to the point. If she really loves you, she'll let you know that she's yours—and without reservations. Better not flirt with other women once you've committed yourself to her. She can be jealous and possessive.

She'll stick by you through thick and thin. It's almost certain that if the going ever gets rough, she won't go running home to Mother. She can adjust to hard times just as graciously as she can to good times.

Taurus women are, on the whole, even-tempered. They like to be treated with kindness. Pretty things and soft things make them purr like kittens.

With your quick wit and itchy feet, you may find yourself miles ahead of your Taurus woman. At times you are likely to find this distressing. But if you've developed a talent for patience, you won't mind waiting for her to catch up. Never try grabbing her hand and pulling her along at your normal speed; it won't work. It could lead to a fireworks display that would put Independence Day to shame. The Taurus woman doesn't anger readily but when prodded often enough, she's capable of letting loose with a cyclone of ill will. If you treat her correctly, you'll have no cause for complaint.

Taurus loves doing things for her man. She's a whiz in the kitchen and can whip up feasts fit for a king if she thinks they'll be appreciated. She may not fully understand you, but she'll adore you and be faithful if she feels you're worthy of it.

The woman born under Taurus will make a wonderful mother for your children. She knows how to keep her children loved, cuddled, and warm. She may not be too sympathetic toward them when they reach the teenage stage, however. Their changeability might irk her steadfast ways.

GEMINI MAN
GEMINI WOMAN

Although you and your Gemini woman may be as alike as peas in a pod, there will be certain barriers to overcome in order to make your relationship a smooth-running one. Before settling on anything definite, it would be wise for you both to get to know each other as you really are—without the sparkling veneer, the wit, the irresistible charm that Geminis are so well known for. You're both talkers and if you don't understand each other well enough you can have serious arguments. Get to know each other well; learn what it is that makes you tick. Two Geminis without real knowledge of themselves and their relationship can easily wind up behind the eight ball. But two cultivated, positive Geminis can make a love relationship or marriage work.

You are likely to find a romance with another Twin a many-splendored thing. In her you can find the intellectual companionship you crave and so seldom find. A Gemini woman can appreciate your aims and desires because she travels much the same road as you do, intellectually and emotionally. You'll admire her for her liveliness and mental agility. You'll be attracted by her warmth and grace.

While she's on your arm, you'll probably notice that many male eyes are drawn to her; she may even return a gaze or two, but don't let that worry you. Women born under this sign (the men, too) have nothing against a harmless flirtation; they enjoy the attention. If she feels she's already spoken for, she'll never let it get out of hand.

Although she may not be very handy in the kitchen, you'll never go hungry for a filling and tasty meal. She's in as much a hurry as you are most of the time, and won't feel like she's cheating by breaking out the instant mashed potatoes. She may not feel totally at home at the kitchen range, but she can be clever; with a dash of this and a little bit of that, she can make an uninteresting TV dinner taste like a gourmet meal. Then again, there are some Geminis who find complicated recipes a challenge to their intellect. Every meal they prepare turns out to be a tantalizing and mouth-watering surprise.

The Gemini woman loves people as much as you do—all kinds of people. Together you'll throw some very interesting and successful parties. Geminis do well in organizing social affairs. Everyone invited is bound to have the time of their life.

People may have the impression that your Gemini wife is not the best of mothers. But the children themselves seldom have reason to complain. Gemini women get along with their kids well because they, too, possess a childlike quality.

GEMINI MAN
CANCER WOMAN
If you fall in love with a Cancer woman, be prepared for anything. Moon Children are sometimes difficult to understand when it comes to love. In one hour, she can unravel a range of emotions that will leave you dizzy. She'll keep you guessing for sure.

You may find her a little too uncertain and sensitive for your tastes. You'll spend a lot of time encouraging her—helping her to erase her foolish fears. Tell her she's a living doll a dozen times a day and you'll be well loved in return.

Be careful of the jokes you make when in her company. Don't let them revolve around her, her personal interests, or her family. If you do, you'll most likely reduce her to tears. She can't stand being made fun of. It will take bushels of roses and tons of chocolates to get her to emerge from her shell.

In matters of money managing, she may not easily come around to your way of thinking. Geminis rarely let money burn a hole in their pockets. Cancers are just the opposite. You may get the notion that your Cancer sweetheart or mate is a direct descendent of Scrooge. If she has her way, she'll hang onto that first dollar you earned. She's that way not only with money but with everything from bakery string to jelly jars. She's a saver; she never throws anything away, no matter how trivial.

Once she returns your "I love you," you'll have a very loving, self-sacrificing, and devoted friend. Her love for you will never alter. She'll put you high on a pedestal and will do everything— even if it's against your will—to keep you up there.

Cancer women love home life. For them, marriage is an easy step. They're domestic with a capital D. She'll do her best to make your home comfortable and cozy. She feels more at ease home than anywhere else. She is an excellent hostess.

Cancer women make the best mothers of all the signs of the Zodiac. She'll consider every minor complaint of her child a major catastrophe. She's not the kind of mother who will do anything to get the children off her hands. With her, kids come first. If you are lucky, you'll run a close second. You'll perhaps see her as too devoted to the children; you may have a hard time convincing her to untie her apron strongs. When Junior or Sis is ready for that first date, you have to prevent your Cancer wife from going along.

GEMINI MAN
LEO WOMAN

If you can manage a girl who likes to kick up her heels every now and again, then Leo is for you. You'll have to learn to put away jealous fears when you take up with a Lioness. She makes heads turn and tongues wag. You don't have to believe any of what you hear—it's most likely jealous gossip or wishful thinking.

The Leo woman has more than a fair share of grace and glamour. She knows it, and knows how to put it to good use. Needless to say, other women turn green with envy and will try anything to put her out of the running.

If she's captured your heart and fancy, woo her full force if your intention is to win her. Shower her with expensive gifts and promise her the moon—if you're in a position to go that far—then you'll find her resistance weakening. It's not that she's such a difficult cookie. She'll probably fuss over you once she's decided you're the man for her. But she does enjoy a lot of attention. What's more, she feels she's entitled to it. Her mild arrogance, though, is becoming. The Leo woman knows how to transform the crime of excessive pride into a very charming misdemeanor. It sweeps most men right off their feet. Those who do not succumb to her leonine charm are few and far between.

If you've got an important business deal to clinch and you have doubts as to whether or not it will go over well, bring your Leo partner along to the business luncheon or cocktail party. It will be a cinch that you'll have the contract in your pocket before the meeting is over. She won't have to say or do anything, just be there at your side. The grouchiest oil magnate can be transformed into a gushing, obedient schoolboy if there's a Leo woman in the room.

If you're a rich Gemini, you may have to see to it that your Leo mate doesn't get too heavy-handed with the charge accounts and credit cards. When it comes to spending, Leos tend to overdo. They're even worse than Geminis. If you're a poor Gemini man, you'll have nothing to worry about because a Leo, with her love of luxury, will most likely never give you the time of day, let alone consent to be your wife.

As a mother, she can be both strict and easygoing. She can pal around with her children and still see to it that they know their places. She won't be so apt to spoil them as you will. Still, she'll be a loving and devoted parent.

GEMINI MAN
VIRGO WOMAN

The Virgo woman may be a little too difficult for you to understand at first. Her waters run deep. Even when you think you do know her, don't take any bets on it. She's capable of keeping things hidden in the deep recesses of her womanly soul—things she'll only release when she's sure that you're the man she's been looking for. It may take her some time to come around to this decision. Virgo women are finicky about almost everything; everything has to be letter-perfect before they're satisfied. Many believe that only Virgos can do things correctly.

Nothing offends a Virgo woman more than slovenly dress,

sloppy character, or a careless display of affection. Make sure your tie is straight and that your shoes sport a bright shine before you go calling on this lady. Save your off-color jokes for the locker room; she'll have none of that. Take her arm when crossing the street.

Don't rush the romance. Trying to corner her in the back of a cab may be one way of striking out. Never criticize the way she looks. The best policy would be to agree with her as much as possible. Still, you're an impulsive, direct Gemini; all those dos and don'ts you'll have to observe if you want to get to first base with a Virgo may be too much to ask of you. After a few dates, you may come to the conclusion that she just isn't worth all that trouble. However, the Virgo woman is mysterious enough to keep her men running back for more. Chances are you'll be intrigued by her airs and graces.

Lovemaking means a lot to you. You may be disappointed at first in her cool Virgo ways. However, under her glacial facade there lies a hot cauldron of seething excitement. If you're patient and artful in your romantic approach, you'll find that all the caution was well worth the trouble. When Virgos really love, they don't stint. It's all or nothing. Once they're convinced that they love you, they go all the way, tossing all cares to the wind.

One thing a Virgo woman can't stand in love is hypocrisy. They don't give a hoot about what the neighbors might say if their hearts tell them go ahead. They're very concerned with human truths. So if their hearts stumble upon another fancy, they will be true to that new heartthrob and leave you standing in the rain. She's that honest—to her heart, at any rate. But if you are honest about your interest in her, she'll know and she'll respect and reciprocate your interest. Do her wrong once, however, and you can be sure she'll put an end to the relationship for good.

The Virgo mother has high expectations for her children, and she strives to bring out the very best in them. She is both tender and strict, but always devoted. The youngsters sense her unconditional love for them and are quick to respond.

GEMINI MAN
LIBRA WOMAN

Gemini and Libra combine the airy qualities basic to both your zodiacal signs, so there should be an instant rapport between you. A breezy, chatty friendliness could soon lead to love.

You'll find that a woman born under the sign of Libra is worth more than her weight in gold. She's a woman after your own heart.

With her, you'll always come first—make no mistake about that. She'll always support you 100 percent, no matter what you do. When you ask her advice about almost anything, you'll get a very balanced and realistic opinion. She is good at thinking things out and never lets her emotions run away with her when clear logic is called for.

As a homemaker she is hard to beat. She is very concerned with harmony and balance. You can be sure she'll make your house a joy to live in; she'll see to it that the house is tastefully furnished and decorated. A Libra cannot stand filth or disarray— it gives her goose bumps. Anything that does not radiate harmony, in fact, runs against her orderly grain.

She is chock-full of charm and womanly ways. She can sweep just about any man off his feet with one winning smile. When it comes to using her brains, she can outthink almost anyone and, sometimes, with half the effort. She is diplomatic enough, though, never to let this become glaringly apparent. She may even turn the conversation around so that you think you were the one who thought things up. She couldn't care less, really, just as long as you end up doing what is right.

The Libra woman will put you on a high pedestal. You are her man and her idol. She'll leave all the decision making, large or small, up to you. She's not interested in running things and will only offer her assistance if she feels you really need it.

Some find her approach to reason masculine. However, in the areas of love and affection the Libra woman is all woman. She'll shower you with love and kisses during your romance with her. She doesn't believe in holding out. You shouldn't, either, if you want to hang on to her.

She likes to snuggle up to you in front of the fire on chilly autumn nights. She will bring you breakfast in bed Sunday mornings. She'll be very thoughtful about anything that concerns you. If anyone dares suggest you're not the grandest guy in the world, your Libra is bound to defend you. When she makes those marriage vows, she means every word she says.

The Libra woman will be everything you want her to be. As a wife and mother, her mate as well as her children will never lack for anything that could make their lives easier and richer.

The Libra mother is moderate, even-tempered, and balanced. She creates a gracious, refined family life in which the children grow up to be equal partners in terms of responsibility and privilege. The Libra mother knows that youngsters need both guidance and encouragement in an environment that is harmonious.

GEMINI MAN
SCORPIO WOMAN

The Scorpio woman can be a whirlwind of passion—perhaps too much passion to really suit you. When her temper erupts, you'd better lock up the family heirlooms and take cover from flying objects. But when she chooses to be sweet, her magic is sure to put you under the spell of love.

The Scorpio woman can be as hot as a tamale or as cool as a cucumber. But whatever mood she's in, she's in it for real. She does not believe in poses or putting on airs.

The Scorpio woman is often sultry and seductive—her femme fatale charm can pierce the hardest of hearts like a laser ray. She may not look like Mata Hari (quite often Scorpios resemble the tomboy next door) but once she's fixed you with her tantalizing eyes, you're a goner.

Life with the Scorpio woman will not be all smiles and smooth sailing; when prompted, she can unleash a gale of venom. Generally, she'll have the good grace to keep family battles within the walls of your home. When company visits, she's apt to give the impression that married life with you is one great big joyride. It's just one of her ways of expressing her loyalty to you—at least in front of others. She may fight you tooth and nail in the confines of your home. But during an evening out, she'll hang on your arm and have stars in her eyes.

Scorpio woman are good at keeping secrets. She may even keep a few buried from you if she feels like it.

Never cross her up on even the smallest thing. When it comes to revenge, she's an eye-for-eye woman. She's not too keen on forgiveness—especially when she feels she's been wronged. You'd be well-advised not to give her any cause to be jealous, as difficult as that may sound to Gemini ears. When the Scorpio woman sees green, your life will be made far from rosy. Once she's put you in the doghouse, you can be sure you're going to stay there an awfully long time.

You may find life with the Scorpio woman too draining. Although she may be full of spice, she may not be the kind of partner you'd like to spend the rest of your natural life with. You'd prefer someone gentler and not so hot-tempered; someone who can take the highs with the lows and not bellyache; someone who is flexible and understanding. If you've got your sights set on a shapely Scorpion, forget about that angel of your dreams. A woman born under Scorpio can be heavenly, but she can also be the very devil when she chooses.

As a mother, a Scorpio is protective yet encouraging. She will defend her children against any threat or abuse. Although she adores her children, she will not put them on a pedestal. She is devoted to developing their talents. Under her skillful guidance the youngsters learn how to cope with adversity.

GEMINI MAN
SAGITTARIUS WOMAN

In the astrological scheme of things Sagittarius is the true zodiacal mate of Gemini, but also your zodiacal opposite. With your youthful, adventurous streaks the two of you should be able to experience all the variety of life to the full.

You probably have not encountered a more good-natured woman than the one born under the sign of Sagittarius. They're full of bounce and good cheer. Their sunny dispositions seem permanent and can be relied upon even on the rainiest days.

Women Archers are almost never malicious. If ever they seem to be, it is probably due to the fact that they are often a little short on tact. Sagittarius say literally anything that comes into their heads—no matter what the occasion. Sometimes the words that tumble out of their mouths seem downright cutting and cruel. Still, no matter what she says, she means well. The Sagittarius woman is capable of losing some of her friends—and perhaps even some of yours—through a careless slip of the lip.

On the other hand, you appreciate her honesty and good intentions. To you, qualities of this sort play an important part in life. With a little patience and practice, you can probably help cure your Sagittarius of her loose tongue. In most cases, she'll give in to your better judgment and try to follow your advice to the letter.

Chances are, she'll be the outdoors type. Long hikes, fishing trips, and white-water canoeing will appeal to her. She's a busy person; no one could ever call her a slouch. She sets great store in mobility. Like you, she possesses a pair of itchy feet. She won't sit still for a minute if she doesn't have to.

She is great company most of the time and, generally, lots of fun. Even if your buddies drop by for poker and beer, she won't have any trouble fitting in.

On the whole, she is kind and sympathetic. If she feels she's made a mistake, she'll be the first to call your attention to it. She's not afraid to own up to her faults and shortcomings.

You might lose your patience once or twice with her. After she's seen how upset her shortsightedness or tendency to blabbermouth has made you, she'll do her best to straighten up.

The Sagittarius woman is not the kind who will pry into your business affairs. But she'll always be there, ready to offer advice if you need it. If you come home from a night out with the boys and you tell your Sagittarius wife that the red stains on your collar came from cranberry sauce and not lipstick, she'll believe you. She'll seldom be suspicious; your word will almost always be good enough for her.

The Sagittarius mother is a wonderful and loving friend to her children. She is always a lively playmate and certainly an encouraging guide. She urges youngsters to study and learn, everything from sociology to sports. She wants the children to have a well-rounded education, the best money can buy.

GEMINI MAN
CAPRICORN WOMAN

If you are not a successful business man, or at least on your way to success, it's possible that a Capricorn woman will have no interest in entering your life. Generally, she's a very security-minded female; she'll see to it that she invests her time only in sure things. Men who whittle away their time with one unsuccessful scheme or another seldom attract a Capricorn. Men who are interested in getting somewhere in life and keep their noses close to the grindstone often have a Capricorn woman behind them, helping them to get ahead.

Although the Goat may be a social climber, she is not what you could call cruel or hard-hearted. Beneath that cool, seemingly calculating exterior there's a warm and desirable woman. She happens to think it is just as easy to fall in love with a rich or ambitious man as it is with a poor or lazy one. She's practical.

The Capricorn woman may be interested in rising to the top, but she'll never be aggressive about it. She'll seldom step on someone's feet or nudge competitors away with her elbows. She's quiet about her desires. She sits, waits, and watches. When an opening or opportunity does appear, she'll latch on to it. For an on-the-move Gemini, an ambitious Capricorn wife or partner can be quite an asset. She can probably give you some very good advice about business. When you invite the boss and his wife for dinner, she'll charm them both.

The Capricorn woman is thorough in whatever she does: cooking, cleaning, making a success out of life. Capricorns are excellent hostesses as well as guests. Generally, they are very well-mannered and gracious, no matter what their backgrounds are. They have a built-in sense of what is right. Crude behavior or a careless faux pas can offend them no end.

If you should marry a Goat you need never worry about her going on a wild shopping spree. Capricorns are very careful about every cent that comes into their hands. They understand the value of money better than most women and have no room in their lives for careless spending. If you turn over your paycheck to her at the end of the week, you can be sure that a good part of it will wind up in the bank.

Capricorn women are generally very fond of family—their own, that is. With them, family ties run very deep. Don't make jokes about her relatives—close or distant. She won't stand for it. It would be good for you to check out her family before you decide to get down on bended knee. After your marriage, you'll undoubtedly be seeing lots of them.

The Capricorn mother is very ambitious for her children. She wants them to have every advantage and to benefit from things she perhaps lacked as a child. She will teach the youngsters to be polite and kind, and to honor traditional codes of conduct. A Capricorn mother can be correct to a fault. But through her loving devotion, the children are so thoroughly taught that they have an edge when they are out in the world.

GEMINI MAN
AQUARIUS WOMAN

If you've fallen head over heels for a woman born under the sign of the Water Bearer, you'd better fasten your safety belt. It may take you quite a while to actually discover what this dame is like—and even then, you may have nothing to go on but a string of vague hunches. Aquarius is like a rainbow, full of bright and shining hues; she is like no other woman you've ever known. There is something elusive about her, something delightfully mysterious. You'll never be able to put your finger on it. It's nothing calculated, either. An Aquarius doesn't believe in phony charm.

There will never be a dull moment in your life with this Water Bearer woman; she seems to radiate adventure and magic. She'll most likely be the most open-minded and tolerant woman you've ever met. She has a strong dislike for injustice and prejudice. Narrow-mindedness runs against her grain.

She is very independent by nature and capable of shifting for herself. She may receive many proposals for marriage from all sorts of people without ever really taking them seriously. Marriage is a very big step for her; she wants to be sure she knows what she's getting into. If she thinks it will seriously curb her independence, she'll return the engagement ring—if indeed she's let the romance get that far.

The line between friendship and romance is a fuzzy one for an Aquarius. It's not difficult for her to remain buddy-buddy with someone with whom she's just broken off. She's tolerant, remember? So if you should ever see her on the arm of an ex-lover, don't jump to any hasty conclusions.

She's not a jealous person herself and doesn't expect you to be, either. You'll find her pretty much of a free spirit most of the time. Just when you think you know her inside out, you'll discover that you don't really know her at all.

She's a very sympathetic and warm person; she can be helpful to people in need of assistance and advice.

The Aquarius woman is like a chameleon in some respects; she can fit in anywhere without looking like she doesn't belong.

She'll seldom be suspicious even if she has every right to be. If the man she loves allows himself a little fling, chances are she'll just turn her head the other way and pretend not to notice that the gleam in his eye is not meant for her. That's pretty understanding! Still, a man married to an Aquarius should never press his luck. Her tolerance does have its limits.

The Aquarius mother is generous and seldom refuses her children anything. Being an air sign like your mate, you both might spoil the children with too much of everything. But the Aquarius mother knows how to prepare the youngsters to get along in life. Her tolerant, open-minded attitude will rub off on the children.

GEMINI MAN
PISCES WOMAN

Many a man dreams of a Pisces lover. You're perhaps no exception. She's alluring and exotic yet capable of total commitment to her man. She's full of imagination and emotion, while at the same time being soft, cuddly, and domestic.

She'll let you be the brains of the family; she's contented to play a behind the scenes role in order to help you achieve your goals. The illusion that you are the master of the household is the kind of magic that the Pisces woman is adept at creating.

She can be very ladylike and proper. Your business associates and friends will be dazzled by her warmth and femininity. Although she's a charmer, there is a lot more to her than just a pretty exterior. There is a brain ticking away behind that soft, womanly facade. You may never become aware of it—that is, until you're married to her. It's no cause for alarm because she'll most likely never use it against you, only to help you and possibly set you on a more successful path.

If she feels you're botching up your married life through careless behavior or if she feels you could be earning more money than you do, she'll tell you about it. But any wife would, really. She will never try to usurp your position as head and breadwinner of the family.

No one had better dare say one uncomplimentary word about you in her presence. It's likely to cause her to break into tears. Pisces women are usually very sensitive beings. Their reaction to adversity, frustration, or anger is just a plain, good, old-fashioned cry. They can weep buckets when inclined.

She can do wonders with a house. She is very fond of dramatic and beautiful things. There will always be plenty of fresh-cut flowers around the house. She will choose charming artwork and antiques, if they are affordable. She'll see to it that the house is decorated in a dazzling yet welcoming style.

She'll have an extra special dinner prepared for you when you come home from an important business meeting. Don't dwell on the boring details of the meeting, though. But if you need that grand vision, the big idea, to seal a contract or make a conquest, your Pisces woman is sure to confide a secret that will guarantee your success. She is canny and shrewd with money, and once you are on her wavelength you can manage the intricacies on your own.

Treat her with tenderness and generosity and your relationship will be an enjoyable one. She's most likely fond of chocolates. A bunch of beautiful flowers will never fail to make her eyes light up. See to it that you never forget her birthday or your anniversary. These things are very important to her. If you let them slip your mind, you'll send her into a crying fit that could last a considerable length of time.

If you are patient and kind, you can keep a Pisces woman happy for a lifetime. She, however, is not without her faults. Her sensitivity may get on your nerves after a while. You may even feel that she uses her tears as a method of getting her own way.

The Pisces mother totally believes in her children, and that faith never wavers. Her unconditional love for them makes her a strong, self-sacrificing mother. That means she can deny herself in order to fulfill their needs. She will teach her youngsters the value of service to the community while not letting them lose their individuality.

GEMINI
LUCKY NUMBERS 1999

Lucky numbers and astrology can be linked through the movements of the Moon. Each phase of the thirteen Moon cycles vibrates with a sequence of numbers for your Sign of the Zodiac over the course of the year. Using your lucky numbers is a fun system that connects you with tradition.

New Moon	First Quarter	Full Moon	Last Quarter
Dec. 18 ('98)	Dec. 26 ('98)	Jan. 1	Jan. 9
5 2 4 8	2 9 8 9	7 7 3 1	5 9 1 7
Jan. 17	Jan. 24	Jan. 31	Feb. 8
4 8 4 7	5 0 4 2	8 8 1 0	5 6 3 9
Feb. 16	Feb. 22	March 2	March 10
4 7 1 8	8 5 6 2	4 4 8 9	9 6 3 7
March 17	March 24	March 31	April 8
1 8 1 0	7 8 4 6	6 1 2 8	8 5 9 3
April 15	April 22	April 30	May 8
1 0 7 4	5 1 0 3	1 8 5 2	2 6 9 7
May 15	May 22	May 30	June 6
6 4 5 4	9 2 6 7	2 4 1 0	5 8 6 6
June 13	June 20	June 28	July 6
5 3 4 9	2 8 3 4	8 7 2 5	5 3 2 3
July 12	July 20	July 28	August 4
9 1 6 8	3 4 3 9	5 1 0 4	2 1 2 8
August 11	August 18	August 26	Sept. 2
9 5 7 2	3 9 4 1	9 8 6 0	5 3 4 9
Sept. 9	Sept. 17	Sept. 25	Oct. 1
9 2 6 7	7 3 5 6	3 7 6 7	4 5 1 0
Oct. 9	Oct. 17	Oct. 24	Oct. 31
3 7 8 5	2 6 9 3	1 1 0 7	8 4 6 1
Nov. 7	Nov. 16	Nov. 23	Nov. 29
1 2 8 5	9 3 1 4	0 1 1 2	7 9 4 5
Dec. 7	Dec. 15	Dec. 22	Dec. 29
5 2 8 3	6 4 0 9	8 7 3 5	5 9 1 0

GEMINI
YEARLY FORECAST 1999

*Forecast for 1999 Concerning Business
and Financial Affairs, Job Prospects,
Travel, Health, Romance and Marriage
for Those Born with the Sun
in the Zodiacal Sign of Gemini.
May 21–June 20*

For those born under the influence of the Sun in the zodiacal sign
of Gemini, ruled by Mercury, planet of communication and wit,
the year ahead promises strengthened relationships and career
progress. You may have to work hard to establish new friendships
and contacts. The people who move into your circle are likely to
become the backbone of life for you throughout the year. Opportunities for expansion in your career are plentiful this year.
Your status is apt to increase as well as your pay. This is the ideal
year for making your mark and establishing an excellent reputation. Where business matters are concerned, doors that were previously closed to you are likely to begin to open. If you are
interested in expanding into a different area, it is worth considering business interests which involve travel or the transportation
of goods by sea. You should be able to make your overall financial
situation more secure this year. Greater opportunities to move up
in your career are likely to ease your cash-flow situation. However, you may be tempted to spend more on private pleasures
simply because you have more. Whether or not your security ex-
tends into the future depends on how you handle what you gain.
Routine occupational affairs are likely to be hectic this year as
you take on more and more overall responsibilities. Analytical
research is likely to increase as part of your daily routine. In relation to travel, you might receive invitations or come across opportunities to travel to unusual, exotic destinations. Your health
needs to be guarded all through the year. It is important to program in periods of rest so that you have a chance to properly relax

and recharge your batteries, thus avoiding potential burnout and exhaustion. Where romance and marriage are concerned, this year is likely to be intense. The expression of negative feelings within the relationship needs to be carefully directed if there is to be continuing harmony between you.

For professional Gemini men and women, a whole world of opportunity is ready and waiting this year. There is much more room for expansion than before, either within your chosen area of interest or into other, completely new territory. One of the best areas for making new strides in business this year is in trade and commerce related to the sea. The acquisition and sale of sea-related products is worth exploring. Business finance and investment needs to be handled within your preplanned and preapproved budget, yet also be flexible enough to allow you to take advantage of new opportunities as they arise. If you can manage to hold back some of your resources, rather than reinvest everything into your existing business, you should have more opportunity to invest in golden new enterprises that come along. Travel and tourism may be lucrative this year. If you are not already involved in these areas, long-term contacts from the past could come to you with propositions which appeal. While expansion is both possible and favorable, this is also a year when you are likely to feel the need for a certain degree of caution. While it may be wise to take your time in weighing both the viability of any new enterprise you are interested in developing, too much procrastination could mean that you lose out on an important deal. Stay aware at all times of what the competition is doing. Guarantees of a successful outcome will be hard to obtain. Some degree of uncertainty is inevitable. Calculated risk is the best solution, where you are neither potentially jeopardizing everything with a shot in the dark, nor suffering a form of paralysis in decision-making and initiative-taking, therefore missing the boat entirely. Clever judgment combined with faith in the possibility of a good outcome should help ensure your long-term success. The best period for beginning business expansion is right from the start of the year until February 13.

Financially, this is a year when the past is likely to creep up on you in unexpected, yet positive ways. If you are coming to the end of a series of repayments for a loan you took out a long time ago, the monthly sum may have become so automatic that you temporarily forget that they will eventually end, and that this end is now very close. An unexpected source of money is likely via efforts you have made to help somebody in the past, most likely when you never expected any material reward. Personal spending can be your downfall, however, unless you make an effort to consolidate your gains. Avoid splurging on items you have wanted for a long time but could not afford to buy. You may have the means to do so this year, but do not overdo it. Try to maintain financial equilibrium long term in order to ensure your future security. Clearing away debts which have continued to be quite a drain on your cash-flow situation and establishing regular savings should be your priority. Also be prepared for unexpected repairs which need to be done on your property over the summer months. Keep looking ahead. If you are thinking of selling your property in the winter, then the fall or summer will be ideal times for any major work that needs to be done. Prepare ahead for the period between October 18 and November 26 when bills may be heavier than usual.

You are in for a very active and busy year with routine occupational affairs. Throw yourself wholeheartedly into fulfilling your role, even though your job specification may change more than once during the course of this year. There are likely to be fewer lax periods when you are able to sit back and plan, so make a point of planning your overall strategy early in the year. If filing systems are inefficient, restructure them, before you get into new projects. It is possible that you will be under an obligation to take on more than your fair share of tasks on a daily basis. Although you may resent this, it is in your best interests to ensure that no area is subject to total neglect. Grim determination and a willingness to be patient are your allies in attending to detailed tasks, including research work, where a high degree of accuracy is essential.

Where travel is concerned, there will be possibilities for overseas trips, yet not all of these will come to fruition. Most likely, when you end up traveling abroad the opportunity will come out of the blue, almost overnight. Communication-related work or enterprise could lead to such opportunities. If you are planning a major vacation this year, sea and air travel is more favorable than an overland trip of any kind, unless you intend to travel as part of a large group or with friends who are familiar with the territory. Travel to mystical and magical places is quite possible. The opportunity to go to such a destination may appear in a roundabout way. If you are intending to travel early in the year, schedule free days at the end of a short trip since unexpected delays are quite possible. The period between June 29 and August 4 is the best time for a family vacation.

Your overall health should be good. Minor rather than major irritations are the prime problem. You can do much to prevent the onset of illness due to stress and accidents caused through carelessness. Make a conscious effort to slow down and plan your moves conscientiously. Because this is a very busy year, especially where work and business matters are concerned, it is important to plan rest periods in your daily routine so that you allow yourself a chance to recuperate physically and reflect mentally. Be extra careful when handling sharp or hot items at home; you could be more prone to cut or burn yourself in a minor way. As a Gemini you tend to do two or three things all at once much of the time. Your best tactic is to concentrate fully on each individual task.

Romance and marriage are apt to be more intense. For single Gemini men and women who link up with someone new this year, the feelings between you are likely to be ardent and passionate. There is a possibility that there will be more than one romantic relationship since very intense pairings sometimes burn out quickly. This is by no means inevitable, however. In marriage or a more settled relationship, it is important to reignite the passion of previous years. There could be much friction between you due to pressures on you individually in other areas of life. A cold-war type of situation may develop if you are not careful to channel your feelings constructively toward one another. Developing a shared interest can be good therapy for keeping the relationship in prime form.

GEMINI
DAILY FORECAST

January–December 1999

JANUARY

1. FRIDAY. Mixed. Turn to friends and family members for any advice that you need. It is likely that they will be able to come up with some useful insights regarding your situation based on their own personal experience. You soon must make a decision in relation to your personal aims and ambitions. Think about the future. Consider taking up a new interest which is appealing and important to you. If there is tension in a particular partnership, you are probably not the one instigating it. However, there is no point in pretending that hurtful remarks do not offend you. Accepting unfair criticism only fuels the other person's sense of self-righteousness while secretly irritating you.

2. SATURDAY. Challenging. You have reached an important moment in relation to your financial situation. Now is the time to get your priorities in order. Concentrate on settling accounts and clearing debts out of the way before taking on any new commitments. If you are short of money at the moment, now is the time to come up with a plan to improve the situation. An opportunity to take on new or additional work may be available. Figure out if you have sufficient resources, especially time and energy, to include evening or weekend work as part your regular routine. It can solve your problems in the long term, but do not risk your health. If you already have more than enough to do, find a way to cut expenses instead.

3. SUNDAY. Frustrating. Although you are trying hard to sort out a complicated financial situation, it is going to take quite some time to resolve the problem overall. Whether or not you are actively earning income, having a particular financial goal to work toward should inspire you to make any necessary sacrifices. Obtaining additional work may not appeal to you unless it means a substantial raise in your take-home pay. Consider what kind of occupation might bring you the salary or commissions you require. The type of work, rather than the amount of it, is the key to your success. Do not undersell yourself or the services you offer. Hold out for what you know you are worth.

4. MONDAY. Rewarding. Expect to stay on your toes throughout the day. Your working life is likely to be particularly hectic. A certain degree of restlessness is not unusual for Geminis. You should be happier if you have a good variety of work as well as fun activities. Where close personal relationships are concerned, greater passion and intensity is foreseen. For single Gemini people, group social activity can lead to meeting someone new with whom you feel immediate rapport. If you are going on a date, suggest a venue with which you are familiar so that you feel comfortable and relaxed right from the start. Gemini parents may have to spend more time helping with homework or conferring with a teacher or principal.

5. TUESDAY. Sparkling. This should be another active and diverse day, with plenty going on all around you. There is also opportunity to concentrate on your personal affairs. Now is a good time to get your priorities in order. Do not hesitate becoming involved in something new, although it is probably a good idea to find out more about it before you make a firm commitment. Someone with specific training or experience can be an ideal adviser. Spend some time socially with one or more friends this evening. There is sure to be some pleasant and stimulating conversation. Single Gemini men and women may receive an interesting invitation; accept it without a second thought even though it may be rather costly.

6. WEDNESDAY. Rewarding. This is not a day for staying in and moping around the house. If you have nothing specific to do, call friends and suggest going out. This is especially true if you live with a roommate. There could be an overcrowded atmosphere due to their guests. Get out for a change of scene. Life with a loved one may be rather strained. If you are planning to move, do not expect to see eye-to-eye on the kind of home you are interested in or even on the area where you want to live. It is likely that a move will require much in-depth discussion over a period of time before you can agree on anything. Where joint finances are concerned, you can reach an agreement about a new budget by hammering out your priorities first.

7. THURSDAY. Manageable. If you are thinking about redecorating your home, spend some time planning carefully in advance. Work out exactly what you need to buy new and what you can recycle. Decide what new materials and supplies you need as well as how long the job is likely to take. Decide between wallpapering or painting, and whether to do it yourself or hire a professional. For restless Gemini people who want to be on the move, this should be a helpful day for searching out a potential new home. Take time to look over property with an eagle eye. If you spot some imperfections, you may be able to haggle successfully for a considerably lower price. If you need a mortgage, consult several agents for the best interest terms.

8. FRIDAY. Favorable. If you are single, someone special may walk into your life and romance will ensue. For Gemini men and women already involved in a love relationship, passion should certainly not be lacking. Take advantage of the good rapport between you; think of a reason to celebrate. If you want to stage a surprise, prepare a favorite dinner for your loved one or make reservations at a four-star restaurant. Or it may be even more exciting to sample the fare of a new or unusual restaurant that has been recommended to you. Words are probably best left unspoken in relation to money matters at the moment, especially if you have been overspending but intend to repay the money very soon.

9. SATURDAY. Disquieting. This is one of those days when you will probably feel happier if someone else takes care of routine chores. If you are taking care of more than one child, expect a few squabbles. Your youngster may resent sharing your time and attention. Disappointing news that you have to deliver is likely to put a cloud on the family mood. Think of something pleasant to suggest before dropping the bomb. You should have a very pleasant time if you are planning to go out this evening. The cost involved could worry you, however, especially if you also have to pay a babysitter. Try to cut back in another area so that you can enjoy the evening without guilt.

10. SUNDAY. Enjoyable. Spend more time enjoying your hobbies and private interests. You have more artistic and creative flair than usual, which can be put to good use. Take your time with any work of art or intricate task. It is unlikely that you can finish a project in one day. Noisy children around your home may be a distraction. If they do not want to go out, you may decide to do so for a short while. Family opinion may force you to reverse a recent decision. It is easier to give in and keep the peace at home rather than demand your own way. Be as courteous with loved ones as you are with virtual strangers.

11. MONDAY. Favorable. It is a favorable day for pressing on with routine tasks. You should be able to charge ahead of schedule if you put your mind to it. Make hay while the sun shines. If you need to make meeting and social arrangements, spend some time calling the people you hope will be able to attend. You should have a lot settled by the end of the day. Colleagues are cooperative and eager to join forces with you. It is likely that you can inaugurate new work methods or begin a team effort. For Gemini people who have been temporarily out of work, this is a key day for contacting employment offices and sending out resumes.

12. TUESDAY. Fortunate. This is another day when you can make excellent progress with work and routine matters. Some of your colleagues or the boss may have been rejecting your ideas for some time. Now, however, they tend to be more broad-minded and willing to try something new. Your innovative efforts are sure to be appreciated. If you are attending an important meeting, do not be afraid to speak out. You have useful ideas to offer, and they are likely to be accepted. In fact, you may be influential in creating major change in your work environment or your community. Aim to spend more time sharing activities with your mate or partner this evening, talking or listening to music together.

13. WEDNESDAY. Satisfactory. This is an exciting day for your relationship with your spouse or partner. There is an opportunity to go on an adventure of some kind. If you have both been in a rut lately, now is the time for instigating a new routine or at least scrapping the old one. Be more enterprising; try a new activity together, such as ballroom dancing or motorcycling. For single Gemini people, new love is more easily found in new places. Do not stick to your usual haunts. Be open to getting to know a whole range of different people socially. Someone with an unusual name could turn out to be the love of your life. Keep your plans and options as flexible as possible.

14. THURSDAY. Successful. There should be a favorable outcome involving a legal matter. It is important to be totally truthful about your side of the story, particularly if your honor is at stake.

Any gaps in an account are likely to be picked up by a shrewd attorney. This is a very promising day for romance. Single Gemini men and women may be surprised by an invitation from someone new on the scene who has everyone talking. In the business world, hard work is likely to pay off. You may be in for an unexpected financial bonus in acknowledgment of your recent efforts. Try out a new idea in a small way before investing a lot of time and effort.

15. FRIDAY. Demanding. Be prepared for difficult negotiations with an authority figure at work. There may an awkward or even stressful atmosphere because your boss is under a lot of pressure. Be sensitive to clever timing. This is not the best time to be making new suggestions, even if you feel you have very sound, helpful ideas. Be prepared to toe the line, at least temporarily. This is a favorable day for concentrating on your own individual projects. Take advantage of a burst of creativity energy. The quicker you get through practical tasks, the happier everyone is likely to be with your results. Stay home tonight, or leave a gathering early if you promised to attend.

16. SATURDAY. Cautious. This is a starred day for key conversations involving money matters. If you are thinking of buying property, discuss your mortgage requirements with more than one agent. It is possible that better rates are being offered by one company as a special promotion. At home you may need to revise the family budget. If you go out shopping, beware of bargains which are not quite as good as they are advertised to be. You may be tempted to impulse buy, but it is wiser not to do so, particularly if you have other people and commitments to consider. Aim to clear debts rather than create new ones. Use your credit card sparingly; keep it for an emergency situation only.

17. SUNDAY. Difficult. This is another important day for discussions about money, savings, and budgeting. If you are struggling with your financial situation, it is a good idea to talk the situation over with someone who has good judgment. Either a close friend with experience or a professional adviser should be helpful. An offer of new or additional work could come your way. Be sure to check the terms and conditions of this employment carefully. The hours involved may be longer than you expect, and the pay perhaps not as high. This is no time to sign documents without reading them thoroughly. The small print could later lead to a legal hassle.

18. MONDAY. Deceptive. A change of scene is apt to be highly beneficial. There may be an opportunity to visit a place you have never visited before. The journey may be long but is likely to be well worth the effort. Special experiences, which you will remember for years, are indicated today. Do not travel without first making careful preparations for all eventualities. Bad weather conditions could force an overnight stay that you have not banked on. Your love life is likely to be fiery. This evening is a particularly passionate and intense time for Gemini lovers, old and new. Go out of your way to please that special person in your life.

19. TUESDAY. Profitable. If you are trying to expand your business interests, consider overseas markets. It is possible that someone will come to you with a proposition that makes this possible without a great deal of effort on your part. Take advantage of links that are being provided. If you work for yourself, you may be able to enter a new sector, such as the mail order market, with considerable success. This evening is favorable for hosting a mixed gathering of both single and attached guests. If you are single but looking, a friend may introduce you to someone new. A passionate relationship could soon develop, perhaps even leading to marriage before the end of the year.

20. WEDNESDAY. Slow. Take your time sorting out complicated or detailed matters relating to your professional life. Rushed efforts are likely to produce negative results. You may end up having to go back and retrace your steps. Completion of a contact, deal, or agreement may not be possible until the matter has been looked at and discussed in greater depth. People tend to be less reliable than usual, perhaps because they are involved in a lot all at once. Be prepared to struggle in your effort to tie them down to exact times or costs. It might be best to stick to just handling practical tasks, postponing making key arrangements until a more favorable day. Get to bed early tonight.

21. THURSDAY. Useful. This is a much better day than yesterday for sorting out business matters. Negotiations should lead to agreements being made and contracts being drawn up. It should also be possible to get in touch with people and tie them down to specific arrangements. Concentrate some of your time and effort on research which needs attention sooner or later. You should be able to make good progress. Useful information is likely to come your way simply by conversing casually with various associates, especially in the business world. Do not hesitate to ask delving questions if you are trying to obtain more information from someone in the know.

22. FRIDAY. Buoyant. This is a particularly busy and active day. Professional matters should be moving right along. Certain individuals are eager for you to take on more duties and obligations. First, however, sit down and assess just where you stand with current commitments before agreeing to anything new. Getting overloaded could be your downfall. Ensure that you are not neglecting key areas of your life, particularly your family members. There may be an introduction to someone very interesting in your social life. An important new friendship or love relationship could ensue in the future between you. Play up to a person's strengths while overlooking obvious weaknesses.

23. SATURDAY. Easygoing. You should be able to make good progress with personal affairs. Concentrate on your most private and cherished dreams and schemes. Rely more on other people to help you along. Your mate or partner may be instrumental in helping you create positive changes if you give them half a chance. People tend to be more resourceful than you expect. Try to find time to get out to enjoy a different environment, especially if the weather is decent. A change of location is apt to rejuvenate you, particularly if you usually spend time indoors. Act naturally when meeting someone new; you can impress without even trying.

24. SUNDAY. Productive. You need to be more discriminating in accepting social invitations. There are apt to be a number from which to choose. Some events cost more than others; take this expense into account. If you are concerned about offending a friend by turning down an invitation, just be honest and they will probably understand. Time is another important issue for you. Although you may feel the need for a change of scene, weigh whether you can spare the time for a long journey. Opt for those events or activities which are likely to have the most beneficial effect on you overall. Exercise can improve your energy level more than an afternoon nap.

25. MONDAY. Disconcerting. You need peace and quiet in order to make progress with complex, detailed matters, but do not expect to get it. You will probably have to go off somewhere quiet, or at least unplug the telephone. Get your priorities in order. If you do not have a moment to spare, be more reticent about taking telephone calls, especially if you sense that a conversation could end up being very long-winded. Unexpected guests are another possibility, ether at home or on the work scene. Although you probably cannot just dismiss these people, make it obvious if you are involved with other matters. If they do not get the hint, suggest getting together later in the week.

26. TUESDAY. Fair. Today is more productive overall than yesterday. It is likely that you will be left alone to do your work in peace and quiet. If higher-ups are aware that you are under pressure, they will probably do whatever is possible to assist you in completing an urgent matter. You may be able to use someone else's office if yours is too noisy or frantic. Forget the social scene this evening if you are feeling tired. Sitting down with your feet up, then going to bed early, is a better alternative. Time alone should give you a chance to get your personal priorities in perspective and make plans for advancing your ideas.

27. WEDNESDAY. Mixed. If you have some money to spare at the moment, this is a favorable day for hunting out bargains for yourself or for your home. Beware of buying on credit, however, if there is a shortage of hard cash in your bank account. Your mate or partner may not be amused if you get carried away with spending. Concentrate on joint plans to create more security for the future. It is better to work at clearing debts rather than increasing them. Avoid a change of scene if it might detract too much from current priorities. Be prepared for a surprise visit from someone you have not seen in a long time. Reminiscing about the past can be very enjoyable this evening.

28. THURSDAY. Manageable. A careful juggling act is required if you are to fulfill work obligations as well as your personal aims. You may have to put one before the other, at least temporarily. Conflict with a boss or other authority figure is likely. It is best not to be too willful or to lose your temper; doing either could end up jeopardizing your position. Toeing the line, even if it irritates you, is in your better interests. A new friendship is moving from strength to strength. Specific actions on the other person's part probably signal that this person can be relied on for fun and companionship, but do not neglect longtime friends.

29. FRIDAY. Lucky. This is a propitious day for making progress in the world of work. Relationships with colleagues and higher-ups should be harmonious. Your time is likely to be tightly scheduled, but your efforts should be highly rewarding. Your more personal life may be less simple. Family members are apt to be intense and demanding. There should not be any hard feelings between you, however, if you are willing to put as much effort into the relationship as you put into work and business affairs. A passionate, intense encounter is foreseen for single Gemini men and women out in search of companionship this evening. Someone new may take you completely by surprise.

30. SATURDAY. Changeable. If you have been out of work, take heart. A favorable opportunity is likely to come your way, with optimum pay. For Gemini people whose work is not bringing in enough earnings overall, it may be possible to increase income by taking on extra work or turning a creative talent to lucrative ends. A financial bonus is likely for efforts beyond the call of duty. Your social life may be less favorable in relation to money matters. An unreliable friend could call on you to bail them out of an awkward situation. Help if you can, but make it clear that you expect to be repaid in full.

31. SUNDAY. Disquieting. There is so much going on in your social life at the moment that it may be difficult to make a choice. It might be best just to toss a coin, so long as you are willing to stick to the decision based on this. If you have not planned a summer vacation, this is a good time to start thinking about where you want to go. Spend more time with your partner this evening. You are sure to thoroughly enjoy each other's company. For single Gemini men and women, tonight is likely to bring a powerful meeting of minds and physical energy with someone relatively new on the scene. Love at first sight should not be ruled out.

FEBRUARY

1. MONDAY. Fair. This is a favorable day for getting down to some serious business with both colleagues and acquaintances. Aim to make firm plans for a future heart-to-heart talk. A pleasant and productive atmosphere permeates the workplace. Make more of an effort to attend and be seen at local events; the publicity and the chance to network with other people should prove useful. If you are in sales or marketing, you should be able to boost your profits handsomely through more aggressive tactics coupled with personal presentations. One thing to watch is that you do not take on too many additional responsibilities. Strive for greater balance between work, rest, and play periods.

2. TUESDAY. Unsettling. Put more effort into tidying up your work and home personal space. If you have a basic aversion to carrying out routine chores, think about paying someone else to do them for you. Neighbors and colleagues who have hired help are likely to be a good source of references. In your personal relationships it is important to discuss basic matters such as expenditures and budgeting. Sit down and discuss the details of your current financial situation so that you both know where you stand. This is especially important if you are considering making major changes together which will significantly affect your bank balance and outstanding debt.

3. WEDNESDAY. Sensitive. Expect the unexpected. A last-minute change of plan is likely. Your routine may be pleasantly interrupted, or it may be an unwelcome intrusion. Take advantage of opportunities to train in another area of your current work. Additional skills can be a boon in the future if you look for another job as well as a help in your present position. An overseas trip is also possible. Vacation plans may need to be changed based on new information you receive today. Do not panic; it is possible that a better option will be offered in compensation for any disappointment you feel. A change in your basic perspective is likely to help you adjust to the inevitable.

4. THURSDAY. Variable. If you are applying for a loan do not get your hopes up too high. Authority figures may not be as willing to lend as it appears from their advertisements. Whatever is decided, however, is actually likely to be in your best interests. A contract which is due to be signed needs to be read over once again, especially the fine print. Expect delays. All the individuals required to be present at a meeting where key decisions are to be made may not be available. Make an effort to settle outstanding accounts if you have the funds available. Loose budgeting in relation to buying a new car, home, or other costly purchase must be avoided.

5. FRIDAY. Satisfactory. This is a propitious day for focusing on more personal interests and pastimes. You may be surprised at how good you are at a new sport or hobby which you try for the first time. Business and pleasure can be easily mixed. If you have creative or artistic talents, you may be able to find a way to turn them into a profitable business undertaking. A change of scene is sure to be refreshing and revitalizing. Your sense of adventure may lead you to an interesting place known to very few travelers. Restless children are bound to appreciate the opportunity to get out. Enjoy dinner at a restaurant you have never frequented before.

6. SATURDAY. Tedious. The temptation today is to go your own way without much consideration for how others feel or react to you. Be careful; you are at risk of upsetting someone very close to you. If you have promised to do something specific, go out of your way to keep your word. This evening is a favorable time for hosting a party. Do not rely on friends to help much with preparations. Be considerate of your neighbors. Either invite them, or warn them of what you are doing. Otherwise you could end up with an angry telephone call late at night that breaks up the party just when it is getting into full swing.

7. SUNDAY. Deceptive. Although this is a traditional day of rest, you are likely to be quite busy. There are a lot of routine tasks to get out of the way. It is a good idea to also plan a change of scene. If you spend too much time cooped up inside you may start to experience cabin fever! If you need help getting basic tasks completed, active elders may be able to lend a hand because they have some free time. An unexpected opportunity is likely to come your way. Although you may not feel too sure about it, trust your good Gemini instincts. There could be some deception going on, which is not obvious, but you should quickly spot it and be able to defuse it.

8. MONDAY. Frustrating. Make more effort to take care of your health. Avoid doing anything that tends to stress you. Aim to keep everything in balance. Too much drinking, eating, or even driving may affect you more than you expect. If you have been getting too little sleep lately, make sure you go to bed early. Discussions about work matters are likely to get out of hand if nobody steps in and takes charge. Try to guide a meeting with colleagues back to the main issues; otherwise little is going to be achieved or settled. Delays are likely on the highways, making even short trips a hassle. Try to avoid any type of travel as much as possible.

9. TUESDAY. Productive. This should be a much better day for getting things done on the professional scene. People are willing to get down to details rather than beating around the bush. If you are seeking a promotion, this is a propitious time to talk to your boss about the possibilities that may be opening up. Aim for a good pay package which includes travel costs or relocation expenses if you will be required to move. The key thing to remember is that the early bird usually does get the worm. Be on time for an important meeting. Arrive a little earlier than expected for job and sales options where there is an open invitation to the general public.

10. WEDNESDAY. Disquieting. This is a day when close personal relationships are marked by greater intensity. Be careful that you do not say anything negative about an issue that, for your partner, is extremely sensitive. For single Gemini men and women, subtlety is the best approach with someone who is a potential love partner. A business relationship which has become stale and nonproductive can be moved to another level, but be sure to be tactful in the suggestions that you make. If higher-ups are difficult, it may be due to their own personal problems. Do not expect to be the person they choose to confide in about their dilemma, but be willing to help if asked.

11. THURSDAY. Rewarding. A new relationship that you recently become involved in may move to a deeper level today. The feeling between you is likely to lead to making permanent plans. For Gemini men and women in long-established relationships or married, this is a propitious day for discussing key matters relating to the future. If you both have the time to spare, it might be worth planning a weekend break so that you can discuss all that is on your mind without interruptions from the outside. Spend some time talking about your vacation preferences if you have not already made any reservations.

12. FRIDAY. Profitable. Additional income is coming your way through extra work that you take on. This should be a particularly helpful day for Geminis who have been out of work. It is likely that a welcome opportunity is coming your way. Now is the time to make important changes. Strive to clear away or throw away anything that is no longer useful to you. Make your work space, as well as your home, tidier than is usual for you. Ambitious Gemini people should start to feel more sure about the next step up the career ladder. The key to success involves sorting the wheat from the chaff, discarding possibilities which do not seem quite right and quickly accepting new opportunity.

13. SATURDAY. Easygoing. Make more time to rest and relax. If you have an important event to attend this evening, do not worry too much about it. So long as you are wearing what is appropriate and have time to prepare in a relaxed frame of mind, all should be well. There are likely to be a lot of people attending who you know, giving you the chance to chat and catch up with news. For Gemini men and women who share their life with a partner but do not live under the same roof, it might be more fun to get ready to go out together either at your place or theirs. A friend may be a better organizer of any function you are hosting. Take advantage of their offer to help or even to take over.

14. SUNDAY. Confusing. You may start to wonder about the integrity of certain people you know. Unless you are directly involved, it may not really be your place to judge their actions or decisions. Chances are, however, that the situation will somehow affect you. Someone you consider a friend or a casual associate may start to flirt with you or with your loved one. This is apt to be more embarrassing than threatening. It is probably best to make a joke out of it rather than ignore it or become angry. Try to get away for a change of routine if you have the opportunity to do so. Fresh air should do you a lot of good physically and mentally, but avoid getting chilled.

15. MONDAY. Variable. A loved one may make you feel on top of the world. Your relationship is likely to contain more passion and intensity, creating a potentially very romantic evening. Share unusual activities together. Going somewhere a little out of the ordinary should make the day very special. You may be changing your perspective significantly in regard to one or two major issues, mostly as a result of the company you are keeping. This is a favorable day for property hunting if you want to move. If you are hoping to sell your current residence, it is likely that you have to be a little more patient and advertise more aggressively.

16. TUESDAY. Pleasant. Be on the lookout for a new way to broaden your horizons. There should be a sense that the world is your oyster at the moment. Take advantage of this optimistic mood to make telephone calls you have put off and generally get back in contact with the world at large. Many doors that were previously shut are likely to start opening up for you. This is a propitious time for making plans relating to your educational and academic ambitions. Explore the possibility of evening classes; there may be more options than you expect. Keep an open mind about everyone and everything. The suggestion of a family member may make you want to drop everything and join them.

17. WEDNESDAY. Mixed. Expect your life to be moving at a fast pace. Important meetings and discussions that are about to take place will mark a turning point for you. Although there may be controversy over particular matters concerning clients or proposals, it is possible to bring about a creative conclusion. Being able to discuss issues in all their complexity is part of the answer to any problem. Although career matters have top priority, make sure that you are not neglecting your home life. Your partner and family members may start to feel left out of your life if you hardly ever have time to spend alone with them.

18. THURSDAY. Fair. An interesting social invitation is likely that will probably involve a little effort on your part. Perhaps the dress will be formal or a creative gift will be suggested. Do not worry; this is sure to be quite enjoyable. There should be good rapport in your relationships with friends. If you need help or favors, turn to the people you know best. In discussing problems you should find more than a simple solution. Quite possibly, you may begin to change your overall perspective on life in general. Any change of scene or environment is apt to be beneficial, especially if you have been feeling tired and a little overwhelmed by all that is going on.

19. FRIDAY. Exciting. The past is likely to be important in your life. You may be reminded of people whose company you used to enjoy. Take this as a signal to get in touch again. There may be reason to travel back to a place you used to know well. If you are hosting a party, try to bring different kinds of people together. Singles and couples are likely to mix better than you expect. Your partner may hit it off right away with certain friends of yours who can be quite critical. Do not neglect to include one or more professional acquaintances on your guest list. A buffet meal can be easier and more fun for you than a sit-down meal.

20. SATURDAY. Tricky. Make time to relax and unwind. If you can get out of a long-distance trip, so much the better. If you absolutely have to travel a long way, you may find it very tiring. This is not a day to predict exactly what will happen next. If people catch you unaware, particularly unexpected guests, do not feel that you necessarily must accommodate them. It is only polite for others to make a point of warning you if they intend to visit. If you feel run-down, guard against a panic attack. If at all possible, avoid taking on extra work or responsibilities. Be willing to delegate tasks you usually enjoy.

21. SUNDAY. Tense. A busy day is likely, even though this is usually a day of rest. You will feel better if you get a few neglected, practical tasks out of the way. At the same time, it would be a mistake not to find time to simply rest and relax. If you plan carefully you can get the best of both worlds. Avoid accepting obligations connected with other people or you could end up overloading yourself. It is likely that there will be changes to advance arrangements over which you have no control. Either go with the flow or opt out altogether. Try to get prepared for the week ahead by washing and ironing the clothes you will wear each day of the week.

22. MONDAY. Variable. This is a day for concentrating on your own affairs. Do not hesitate to be more self-indulgent in regard to matters that really are important to you. Your friends are likely to support your most important aims and ambitions. A little extra moral support and encouragement can do much to help you to put your plans into action. If you have an important business or social engagement coming up, it might be worth investing in a new outfit or special haircut. Alternative health therapies could be good for helping you relax and unwind. If you are constantly tired, spiritual healing could help you put all that is going on in better perspective.

23. TUESDAY. Satisfactory. Focus once again on your more personal affairs and ambitions. It is important to think about the future. If you have been under a lot of stress for a long time, consider a weekend away at a retreat where you can really unwind. If this is not financially feasible, come up with some restful alternative. Think of someone who lives far away from you who has issued an open invitation for you to visit. Just a change of scene for a few days might be a great help to you. More exercise can also be an energizer. Walk partway to work, or use stairs instead of an elevator. Joining a health club could give you new incentive to exercise your frustrations.

24. WEDNESDAY. Stressful. You are likely to have to give a lot of yourself in the business environment. Key meetings and negotiations are foreseen. You may start to wonder if there is a world outside because you are so cooped up all day. Try to find time to get out of the environment just to clear your mind. Everything on your agenda may not be so major that it cannot be handled satisfactorily by someone else. Delegation is one of your keys to success at the moment. Take advantage of various resources available to you which are there to make your life easier. If you can find a shortcut, take it. Meeting a deadline is more important than achieving perfection.

25. THURSDAY. Changeable. If there is someone for whom you want to buy a special gift, expect to have to shop around. Local stores may not have sufficient stock to include the type or quality of item you desire. There are likely to be bargains advertised in large stores, but question whether they really are bargains. This is a favorable day for beginning to save for something specific, such as a major item for the home. Interest-free credit promotions may be helpful. Before making any commitment, check that the regular repayments are affordable for you and that they will be due at the right time of the month for you. Save for what you really want rather than settling for second best.

26. FRIDAY. Useful. This should be a productive day for Gemini people interested in finding new work or an additional job. Make the most of your various contacts, particularly people you have worked with in other capacities in the past. An employment agency doing business in your local area may also be a helpful source. It is possible that a new agency will try harder than established companies to obtain work on your behalf. If you are hoping to increase business profits, focus on the array of advertising, marketing, and promotion options currently being offered at favorable rates. Go out tonight with your mate or partner but not with a group.

27. SATURDAY. Enjoyable. If you feel as though you are in a rut where your social life is concerned, perhaps it is time to cancel a regular weekly event and try something new. A new club, if you are not happy with the one in which you are currently a member, might be worthwhile. It is quite possible that alternative clubs offer better rates as well. If you have to make a choice between a local event and one which will require long-distance travel, think carefully. The latter alternative may offer more, but carefully make the decision about whether you want to do the extra traveling. A new person on the scene could be a casual flirt; do not take their words seriously.

28. SUNDAY. Disconcerting. People are likely to change their individual plans to help you out, but they may only let you know about it at the last minute. The problem is that their arrangements may not coincide with yours any better than they did before. Stick to arrangements you have committed yourself to if you are otherwise at risk of upsetting someone. An invitation is likely to a pleasant local event. If you are concerned about not knowing many people there, invite along one of your own work associates or friends for company. Be wary of bickering with a family member. What is unimportant to you could be a threat to them. Be especially gentle with children.

MARCH

1. MONDAY. Rewarding. This promises to be a particularly optimistic and productive day, an especially favorable time for attending to matters which have been totally neglected or left half done. Much can be achieved both at home and at work. It is likely that the past is going to impact the present more than usual. Nostalgic feelings may lead you to get in touch with someone you used to know; there could be a happy reunion later this month. You may unexpectedly end up in a place that you used to know well. Although a lot will probably have changed, it should be good to see the old sights again. Where business matters are concerned, reward good work but watch out for subterfuge.

2. TUESDAY. Demanding. It is best if you and your mate or partner go your separate ways for a while today. Spending a lot of time cooped up together doing the same old things can make your relationship stale and stressful. If other people get on your nerves, likewise opt for a change of scene. They will probably be less difficult if they have something new to occupy their minds. For Gemini people who share living arrangements, lack of space may be a long-term problem. Things could now come to a head, prompting you to start looking at other alternatives. Good progress with practical matters is likely, particularly at work. Prioritize and delegate; you do not have to do everything yourself.

3. WEDNESDAY. Stressful. Focus on doing your own thing. You do not need to be told what is important. In fact, you may get quite annoyed with anyone who tries to do so. Relatives or friends are apt to toss their opinions around too freely. You may not want to become embroiled in an argument, but you will be wise to stand by what you believe in. Someone making plans on your behalf is sure to irritate you, and you have every right to be annoyed unless this person genuinely was thinking of your best interests. If anger wells up inside you, try releasing it via vigorous sports or independent physical exercise. A good book is your best bedtime companion.

4. THURSDAY. Variable. A strongly creative and imaginative streak in your Gemini nature is likely to take over all of your activities today. This is a very favorable time for artistic endeavors. Keep your work to yourself while you are in the creative phase, however. Friends or associates may not offer the right kind of encouragement if they see the unfinished work, perhaps because they lack imagination or have not done much creative work themselves. Romance is in the air this evening, particularly if you and your loved one try out a new restaurant or club. Single Gemini men and women may have a problem keeping an admirer at bay but still on the hook.

5. FRIDAY. Manageable. You should have a productive day at work if you get more involved in a team effort. Where your social life is concerned, plan on going out with good friends to somewhere quiet enough to talk so that you can catch up on their news. People you have not seen in a while may surprise you with their recent activities. A different point of view on a matter which is troubling you should be helpful, so talk about any problems. If there is an opportunity to go somewhere other than your usual haunts, take it up. This is especially vital for single Gemini men and women hoping to meet someone new. An instant mutual attraction is possible if you are both new on the scene.

6. SATURDAY. Satisfactory. Be careful not to take on more than you can comfortably handle, especially if you are working on projects around the home. Practical work which requires a lot of physical effort or mental concentration may be quite tiring. Set some time aside simply to rest and relax. If you are trying to solve a dilemma, you can expect to have more success if you allow plenty of time to ponder the matter. There is little point fretting about anything that cannot be changed, or which is not within your control. Take extra care if using sharp tools or fast-moving machinery. Be sure to follow all safety rules precisely.

7. SUNDAY. Successful. This is an excellent day for getting down to basic, practical tasks so long as you feel up to the job. Devote some time to working in the garden; this should be relaxing as well as useful. If coping with certain technical matters has so far eluded you, do not give up entirely; you might have a breakthrough today. Although you are likely to be going great guns with whatever you undertake, be sure not to get too carried away. Total exhaustion is not the best idea on a Sunday night. If you are going out socially, be prepared for a possible change of arrangements at the last minute.

8. MONDAY. Quiet. This promises to be an easygoing, peaceful day. Nobody should get on your case about problems, errors, or deadlines. You can make good progress with complex matters which require intense concentration because there should be less noise and distractions around you. If you are thinking about a possible new project you want to begin soon, now is the time to do some serious planning. If there are neglected matters to attend to, you should be able to find time for them. In fact, you could actually get ahead of yourself today. Use spare time at home to complete a crafts project or a complex puzzle just for the fun of it. Leave the TV screen blank and enjoy your own company.

9. TUESDAY. Fair. You should enjoy a greater closeness with your mate, partner, or friends. Take advantage of this opportunity to discuss matters which are close to your heart. Openly expressing your feelings is likely to lead to a particularly romantic interlude. You may feel the urge to revisit a place that has been important to both of you in the past. This could be where you first met, or where you went on your first date. Single Gemini men and women may have a chance meeting with someone you feel very close to right from the start, particularly in a new place. Trust your good Gemini instincts and intuition; they are a reliable guide. If you must cancel a date, be sure your excuse rings true.

10. WEDNESDAY. Mixed. If your loved one wants to take on more work at home, do not resist. This is an opportunity that might not come along again in a hurry. If you simply must be in control, carry on as usual. However, you probably will not be doing yourself any favor. The key to your success in handling both your personal and work relationships is to make sure that you are not the one who does all the work or has all of the ultimate responsibility. Gemini men and women starting to get involved with someone new may be having trouble finding a good balance. This is not unusual in any new relationship. Be patient, giving yourselves time to get in sync with each other and establish a firm foundation.

11. THURSDAY. Slow. Spend time sorting out financial matters which have become quite confused or which you have temporarily neglected. You should be able to establish an amicable new set of terms with your partner. Aim to settle accounts which are outstanding. If people owe you money to your business, send out reminder letters or make telephone calls. Set a time limit to receive payment. Advice on loans, mortgages, and other financial services is likely to be helpful if you are thinking of significantly altering your financial setup. Some matters are so sensitive that you will probably feel more comfortable dealing with an expert rather than asking a friend or family member.

12. FRIDAY. Fortunate. This is a helpful day for finalizing financial arrangements. If you are interested in taking out a loan of some kind, apply for it now; it is likely that you will receive a favorable response. If you are filling out important applications or documents, make more effort to read exactly what is required. Even professionals may not take the time to spell everything out to you. If you are signing anything, it is vital that you understand what you are committing yourself to. Time spent with friends this evening should be inspiring. You have much to discuss, and plans can be made for a joint vacation or other activity.

13. SATURDAY. Frustrating. Be careful how you spend your money. There may be apparent bargains on sale, but closer inspection could reveal that the workmanship is shoddy or that there are other quality problems. Small shops may be the best places for certain items but not for others. Check carefully what you are given if you do not select items yourself. If you get carried away with spending, your mate or partner is not going to be too pleased. Think forward to the future. If you overspend now, you will probably have to compensate for it by cutting back later on. A friend may need your help and support, particularly a listening ear and a few pats on the back.

14. SUNDAY. Tricky. A change of environment should be particularly refreshing. An opportunity to travel may arise through your association with a group of local people. Friends and acquaintances generally are likely to be good company. Schedule some time to sit around talking to people whose company you enjoy. A fun time is likely to be had by all on a day trip. Where close personal relationships are concerned, this evening is likely to be a passionate time with your love partner. Single Gemini men and women may be spellbound by someone met in a distant destination, but do not start making wedding plans right away.

15. MONDAY. Satisfactory. This is a key day for getting into new surroundings. It is possible that change at work may take you into a different environment. If you have been concerned about conditions at work, now is the time to arbitrate on behalf of yourself and other staff. You are likely to receive a favorable response. You can do much to cheer up your environment both at home and in the office. More greenery should be appealing, not least because plants tend to be a healthy addition for cleaner air. At home, consider making cost-free changes which could have quite a dramatic effect, such as rearranging furniture or just sitting at a different place around the dining room table.

16. TUESDAY. Rewarding. There may be a privileged opportunity to work with key figures in your professional life. You can learn a lot from these individuals, but be prepared to have to make more effort and perhaps work longer hours. You will tend to get as much from the opportunity as you put in. With routine matters, strive to get up to date. The more organized you are, the better. In your more personal life do not expect a particularly easy time. Your mate or partner may be holding a grudge, perhaps without realizing how damaging this can be in the long term. An apology on your part might help open the door to better communications. Time is probably the real answer.

17. WEDNESDAY. Successful. You will soon be moving to another level in your career. Recent events may be prompting you to start considering an entirely different path. Now is the time to begin to make careful preparations. If changes are already going on at work, you could be offered greater responsibility. If a new job would necessitate a move to another office or branch of the company, a handsome relocation package may be offered to you. This is a favorable time for Gemini people who have been temporarily out of work to make a fresh start seeking a job. Be sure your resume is as positive as possible.

18. THURSDAY. Useful. Make the effort to contact friends and spend more time discussing life in all its complexities. Stimulating conversations are likely to lead to making positive changes in your own everyday affairs. It is likely that a close associate may need to confide a sensitive matter to you. Be sure to keep this to yourself. This is a starred day for intimate discussions with people who you know care about you deeply. There may be some matters which you do not feel able to discuss with your love partner but you can with a close friend. If you need encouragement, turn to a friend for moral support. Even someone you do not know too well may have useful ideas for you to consider.

19. FRIDAY. Enjoyable. You should be able to expand your social circle. New friends are likely to come into your life. In following up an unusual interest you could meet particularly interesting people. As a Gemini you are good at networking, and this should really pay off now. If you are looking for more excitement or a change of routine, try a different kind of hobby.

Give free rein to your creativity. Public discussions and lectures on current subjects are likely to be stimulating. Where professional matters are concerned, this is a time for key meetings. Some important decisions can be made that will have a positive effect on your future.

20. SATURDAY. Demanding. Although this is a busy day, it should be fairly quiet. You ought to be left alone to get on with private projects. Solitude suits you now since you do not want the distractions that other people around you tend to create. If you want help or advice on a particular matter, turn to someone older and wiser. A relative a generation or two ahead of you may understand your problem better than a contemporary friend. Try to do something charitable today. It is probably best to take your time with matters which require intense concentration. Avoid making mistakes that force you to go over everything twice; proofread and calculate carefully the first time around.

21. SUNDAY. Disquieting. What you most want to happen is not likely to occur, so do not waste time building up your hopes. It is best to just get on with routine matters. If it seems difficult to pick yourself up after a disappointment, think of some pleasant alternative activity to improve your state of mind. Sometimes sleep is the best way of getting over feelings that are difficult to bear. Older members of your family are especially understanding at the moment. Avoid long-distance travel if possible. A lengthy journey is apt to wear you out and have a negative effect on the workweek ahead.

22. MONDAY. Fair. Spend more time concentrating on your own personal affairs. You can benefit from meditating on what you want to create for the future. You should be able to take more initiative in both work and social affairs. Other people are going to respond positively to your clear sense of purpose. If a specific problem is getting you down, or if things seem to be going wrong in one particular area, discuss the matter with someone whose judgment you trust. Stay away from people who tend to tell you only what you want to hear. A friend with a good sense of humor is likely to cheer you up, inspiring you to push on with your special aims and ambitions.

23. TUESDAY. Variable. This is another day to focus on your own personal concerns. Some people tend to consider it wrong to be self-centered. However, if you never spend time analyzing yourself, it is unlikely that you can manage to direct your life very effectively. Do not worry about being self-indulgent with the best possible intentions. It is probably worth acting out a desire to be slightly outrageous in your own way. There is a side to your character which is seeking expression. This could be the more creative and artistic element, so set it free. Consider going on a trip to a place you have never visited but find intriguing because of its historical connection.

24. WEDNESDAY. Challenging. Focus on long-range financial matters. A sense that time is slipping through your fingers may be very much with you. You are likely to feel a need to start saving for the future if you are not already doing so. If you do not participate in a pension plan, this is the time to investigate what is on offer. If you simply want to save for an important purchase which will take quite some time to afford, begin now. It might be worth seeking some expert advice on long-range investments. Try to keep away from friends who tend to be a drain on your physical and emotional energy.

25. THURSDAY. Profitable. Current conditions allow you to make excellent, fast progress with all sorts of professional matters. You may even be able to get ahead of a deadline. Additional earnings may come your way because you have more time available to handle some extra work. If you have been out of work, an offer may come up now to at least carry you over this difficult period. All kinds of temporary options are well worth considering. Praise or other acknowledgment is likely if you have been putting in that extra bit of effort at work. Take advantage of this by negotiating a pay raise or discussing a future promotion.

26. FRIDAY. Exciting. It is not unusual for Gemini people to have more than one pot on the boil. You should be happier today if you have the freedom to handle a number of different tasks. Variety tends to keep your energy level high. When you get bored with one task, immediately switch to another. If you have to travel a long distance, you may find the journey a chore even if you are not driving. If it is possible to put off such a trip, do so. If you must travel, take along a good book or tapes to keep you occupied. People at a distance will be welcoming; getting there is the problem.

27. SATURDAY. Demanding. Expect this to be a busy day demanding a lot of running around to look after other people's needs. Someone in the family may not be feeling well, or neighbors may need your help. Set aside some time for your social life.

A gathering of good friends should be particularly enjoyable. A large group probably suits you better than a cozy twosome. There is safety in numbers, and less intensity as well. Single Geminis should be able to get closer to someone who was once a friend or romantic partner. Beware, however, of jump-starting this relationship at this late date. You may both have changed too much.

28. SUNDAY. Happy. Make the most of the easygoing atmosphere of the domestic scene. This is a good day for sitting down with individual family members you have been meaning to speak to for some time about a problem. Greater intimacy is likely in your marriage or closest relationship. Your loved one is more sensitive to your needs than usual. If a friend needs to share a secret, be willing to lend a listening ear without making many harsh judgments. Take time to organize the week ahead. Plan meals and the grocery shopping that needs to be done. It is best to keep away from very spicy food. Keep plenty of fruit and vegetables on hand for healthful snacks.

29. MONDAY. Unsettling. The domestic scene may be less serene today than yesterday. People around you may have problems that they are trying to deal with on their own. It is doubtful whether your intervention will help at this point. It is probably best to keep your distance unless you feel able to handle an emotional scene. If family members are standoffish, it is possible that they are playing some sort of psychological game; try not to get caught up in it. Also strive to avoid saying anything that could provoke a strong response. If you are shopping for a major purchase, be wary of buying second hand. It is possible that the problems of the first owner will not be specified and just be passed on to you.

30. TUESDAY. Stressful. There may again be a difficult atmosphere on the domestic scene. It is probably best to bring an emotional issue out into the open to discuss. Anyone taking things to extremes, when all has been said or done, is probably quite unreasonable. Complicated emotional states are often an enigma to the logical, quick-thinking Gemini. Nobody can really blame you if you go off where there is less strife. Problems which are not absolutely major are apt to blow over later. If you stick around, you could end up being somewhat manipulated. Beware of making promises in the heat of the moment.

31. WEDNESDAY. Cautious. After recent upsets on the home front you may yearn to escape from the world of emotions. With a romantic streak running through you at the moment, try to get away to somewhere new to pick up your spirits. Sometimes a change of scene can be better medicine than a rest. For single Gemini people, there is a strong possibility of meeting someone romantically attractive. A distant place may be what brings you together. You may need to discuss dreams and wishes. Contrary to what you expect, a stranger may prove to be a better listener than someone you know all too well. Be wary of writing down your innermost thoughts; they could be read by prying eyes.

APRIL

1. THURSDAY. Fortunate. This is a particularly favorable day for single Gemini people to meet a possible new mate. It is likely that an attraction to this person will be very strongly charged right from the start. More involved Gemini should not have a dull life either. Your relationship with your partner is likely to be more exciting, especially if you do all that you can to encourage more togetherness. Children are apt to respond well to an outing to somewhere unusual. This does not have to an expensive destination, just a place that is a little bit different. On a more personal level, consider taking up a new pastime or hobby to add spark to your own life.

2. FRIDAY. Confusing. Be prepared for an on-the-go day where work matters are concerned. In order to meet an important deadline you may have to sit and plod through what needs to be done. Inspiring yourself by thinking about what you will be able to do once you are not so tied down should give you the incentive to press on. Do not forget to take occasional breaks even if you are very busy. A change of environment can help clear your thoughts and prevent a stress headache. It is possible that you will not find the answer to a problem until you stop thinking about it for a while. Relax your mind and the solution should come of its own accord.

3. SATURDAY. Stressful. Gear up to work at a quick pace throughout the day. You should be pleased with your progress because your thinking is clear and your insight good. Going on a long journey is likely to tire you out. Try to plan some rest at your destination before attending a meeting and driving back. The upheavals going on all around you can be disturbing. If you need to do some work from home, put on some headphones and play music that helps you concentrate. It is important to get your priorities in order. A flash of intuition about the future may leave you in no doubt about what needs to be done.

4. SUNDAY. Variable. It is best today if you do not have to undertake difficult tasks of any kind. You need some rest and relaxation. If you must attend to practical matters, try to do only the minimum. You can probably catch up tomorrow with whatever you cannot manage today. Physical work such as gardening may usually be quite relaxing, but today it is apt to just seem like hard work. If someone in your family is more in the mood to do some of this, do not stand in their way. Be especially kind to yourself this evening. A leisurely bath can help relax your whole body and relieve your aching limbs. Get to bed earlier than usual.

5. MONDAY. Happy. An exhilarating time is likely in your closest, personal relationship. If you recently met someone special, there may be an incredible sense of anticipation because you do not know this person well enough to know exactly what to expect. In a more established relationship it is up to you to provide some surprises. Think about the future; start preparing an exciting outing for the two of you, such as a special weekend trip. If your loved one is reaching a birthday milestone, arrange a surprise party. Single Geminis are likely to fall for someone from a different country or culture, or for someone considerably older.

6. TUESDAY. Manageable. You can count on a good general rapport at work and at home. Your partner can be a great asset to you, breaking the ice with strangers who you need to get to know. If you are in the mood for matchmaking, you should be quite successful. Your single friends are sure to thank you for your efforts. For single Gemini people, scholastic interests can lead to meeting a romantic potential. This is not a time to be rushing things, however; so take your time getting to know each other. Try not to take to heart anything that is said to you in a harshly critical or judgmental way at work.

7. WEDNESDAY. Profitable. There is likely to be a reassuring development in relation to your financial situation. This is a favorable time to plan for the future. Look for ways to create more long-term security for you and your family. If you do not have any life insurance or retirement savings, now is the time to act. If you do not know enough about these areas, seek advice from a reliable financial expert. A friend may be able to recommend a knowledgeable person to help you. In both business and finances, it is important to deal with people you feel you can depend on for confidential, professional assistance. The plan that is best for a friend may not be best for you.

8. THURSDAY. Mixed. An important contract may be drawn up today. Agreements should be easily negotiated without much hesitation. Nevertheless, it is in your best interests to read the small print on documents carefully before signing anything. Be sure that you understand exactly what is involved before you make any commitment. A friend may be curious to the point of intrusion. You are now more sensitive than usual to people intervening on your behalf or interfering in your personal affairs. It may be a case of too many cooks spoiling the broth where routine matters are concerned. Try to keep a low profile and do only what is necessary. Avoid volunteering for anything.

9. FRIDAY. Variable. It is a good idea to shop alone if you are intent on buying. If you go with a friend you are unlikely to have the same response, which could just end up being very confusing. This is a day of key meetings and discussions at work. Important conclusions can now be reached relating to promotions and business expansion. If you have been out of work, get back in touch with employment counselors and agencies who may be able to find you another job. Catch up on correspondence which has been piling up and pay bills before the ultimate due date. Keep evening plans simple; avoid crowds.

10. SATURDAY. Demanding. Ignore outside distractions and go more into your own world. You are unlikely to be very focused; all you may want to do is dream. Avoid complicated undertakings which require intense concentration. In thinking about all that is going on and is in the pipeline, you may come up with some interesting schemes which can be developed in the future. If there are important tasks awaiting you, a family member is likely to be helpful in seeing that they get done. Let other people take more of the load for a while. They are probably better than you at the moment at organizing.

11. SUNDAY. Changeable. Try to get away for a change of scene, perhaps to visit a friend who lives at a distance or an older family member. A trip by train or bus may be more enjoyable than driving. A group outing can also be fun and a good break for you. If you are going to be studying with or negotiating with committee members, you should get your way by persevering and refusing to give in. If you do not have much chance to speak to these people, this is likely to be a great opportunity for catching up on their personal news as well. Friendship generally tends to be uplifting. Someone you know well may encourage you to get involved in a new and rather unusual activity far different from your usual interests.

12. MONDAY. Unsettling. A magazine article, news report, or movie may upset you than you realize at first. This is a day when you are especially sensitive to images. Be more discriminating in what you choose to become involved in. Souvenirs from your past which are stored away in a trunk are probably best left there, even though you may feel a desire to look at them. Many of your memories are happy, but not all of them. Think twice before poring through old letters or viewing photographs of times gone by. A lack of money or qualifications for what you want to do may force you to adjust your aspirations. Focus on what you can manage with your current skills.

13. TUESDAY. Disquieting. Someone who is competing with you at work may be playing a little dirty. This person may not actually be able to do much in practical terms but could make your life difficult at an emotional level. If you sense that professional jealousy is involved, consider what you may be able to do to smooth over the situation. Do not get involved in an underhanded deal involving the boss or other authority figures. If your actions are discovered at a later date, you may be in for a difficult time. Play by the rules. If it is too late to stop what is already in the works, at least make more of an effort to be discreet and not draw attention to yourself.

14. WEDNESDAY. Buoyant. This is a productive day when it comes to expanding your business interests. Discussions which take place now should give you a clear idea of just what is going to be possible. There may be an opportunity for Gemini working people with an enterprising streak to become self-employed through partnership with another colleague. First, however, consider what you are letting yourself in for if this is intended to be a major, long-term career change. It is vital to set some ground rules between you and the other person, not just verbally but also in writing. Legal advice can be very important to be sure nothing is overlooked.

15. THURSDAY. Good. Friends may be brimming over with news about a recent personal or business success. Enjoy discussing everything over lunch or dinner, when you have the time to really listen. If an opportunity arises for you to go on a journey somewhere unusual, take it up. You can learn something especially interesting and useful from a foreigner. Gemini people are often right on target with hunches. Follow your intuition today; it is unlikely to steer you wrong. Where vacation plans are concerned, consider an adventure holiday of some kind rather than a sedentary setting. Do not neglect to return a phone message.

16. FRIDAY. Challenging. Be prepared to make a new beginning in several areas of your life. Friendships can be enhanced by a change of routine or approach. Where your more secret wishes and desires are concerned, reevaluate and be willing to alter your perspective. It is possible that a dream you put aside once upon a time, because it seemed impossible to turn into reality, can now be fulfilled. You have every reason to feel optimistic. A chance meeting may occur with someone who will become important in your life in the future. This is more likely to be a friendly relationship rather than a romance, but still of great significance for your happiness.

17. SATURDAY. Uncertain. Spend more time on behind-the-scenes matters. If you concentrate on influencing developments in the background of life, everyday needs will start to take care of themselves. A rather unusual opportunity could come your way, allowing you to spread your wings. Keep an open mind. It is sometimes surprising where the best opportunities come from. Nonetheless, be wary of areas that you are not familiar with or people you do not know well. Wait until you have a better sense of what is going on before setting your heart on any new course. A false start could set you back financially.

18. SUNDAY. Pleasant. This is another day to focus on personal aims and ambitions. Put your priorities in order. If you have not been very social lately, spend more time with friends to catch up on their news. Someone in your social circle may be influential in helping you develop some of your private plans. A change of scene can be good for you, especially if you need rest and relaxation. Try to get out to the country or at least to a park. If attending an important social function, make an effort to look your best. You may be introduced to somebody quite important; first impressions are apt to be lasting.

19. MONDAY. Fair. Expect to have no choice but to put some of your personal plans temporarily on the back burner. It is likely that your partner needs more of your time and energy. While you may feel it is your duty to help with problems, it is important not to get too involved. Ultimately, the responsibility lies with the person who is affected. It is just as well not to discuss private matters which touch on sensitive areas or which are still in the early stages of development. Much may change over a short space of time, and you could regret having created waves when you did not actually know all the facts. Be alert for favorable money-making options close to home.

20. TUESDAY. Stressful. Usually your friends are a blessing to have around, but today you may have other ideas. It is likely that one of them may try to get you involved in a business scheme which will benefit them more than you. Do not be fooled by promises of easy money. It is likely that you will have to work hard for any additional income. A business proposition which genuinely provides the opportunity to use your creative talents is well worth considering, however. Avoid buying anything that you do not really need. You could end up purchasing an item on sale just for the sake of it, then never use it.

21. WEDNESDAY. Variable. Smart salespeople are likely to have a number of ploys designed to get you to part with your money. Avoid shopping in large stores if you know that you easily get talked into buying what is state-of-the-art. Your partner may not be very pleased if you spend most of this week's family budget on an electronic gadget or new kitchen appliance. This is no time for trying to keep secrets from your loved one; you will probably be found out. Mail order catalogs are full of tempting offers, but be discriminating; additional gifts being offered with a purchase may not actually be worth very much. Do not buy anything by phone sight unseen.

22. THURSDAY. Frustrating. If you have been having problems with your car over a long period of time, the source of the difficulty may at last be discovered. Now is the time to try to solve a mechanical problem once and for all. Keep an eye on areas of rust or small dings and dents. Prompt repair measures can keep them from getting any worse and lowering your ultimate resale value. This is also true of mold around the house or loose tiles. Disillusion with the results your repairs have achieved so far may encourage you to get the job done by a professional. It could be necessary to spend money now in order to protect your future profit. Trying to help a friend can be frustrating if they refuse to take your advice.

23. FRIDAY. Exciting. This is a favorable day for a group get-together with relatives or neighbors. Siblings, in particular, are likely to be friendly and comforting. Discuss with them an issue which you find difficult to reveal to anyone else. The key to success in all matters is not to take on too much. Focus on what is most important. Evening events should be short-lived so that you can get a reasonable night's sleep. Although the weekend is ahead of you, it is going to be hectic. Get off on the right foot tonight by being in bed earlier than usual. Do not forget to set the alarm if you have a morning appointment.

24. SATURDAY. Sensitive. It is apt to be a battle to focus your mind on current responsibilities and priorities. Recent developments have given you a lot to think about in relation to the future. By all means mull over plans and ideas, but do not ignore urgent matters while you go off sailing in a dream world. If you are feeling below par physically, consider taking up a new form of exercise designed to stimulate your circulation and increase your energy level. Also consider changing your diet to some degree, perhaps by eating more raw food and avoiding dairy products and fried food for a while. Avoid spending a lot on evening entertainment; conversation can be more stimulating than a movie.

25. SUNDAY. Fair. This is a helpful day for handling routine tasks around the home and in the neighborhood. You should be able to get everything done in double-quick time. If you do not already recycle your newspapers and other items, begin to do so. Tidying up and clearing out around the home can also have the effect of clearing your mind. If there are items in your wardrobe which you never wear, give them away so that they do not clutter up your space. This is a favorable day for catching up on neglected matters. If you have something to hide from your mate or partner, be particularly discreet. Do not write anything you would not want a certain person to read.

26. MONDAY. Lucky. This is a day of discoveries for Gemini people eager to move. Consider even the most out of the way sources and possibilities when it comes to where you might live. A real estate agent you have not bothered to contact so far might be the one to come up with your dream property. Be sure to negotiate if the price is high; the seller may be more willing to haggle than you expect. This is one of those days when the desire to transform the way you look may be almost overwhelming. A change of image may give you a real lift if you feel that you are starting to look old. The changes you make are apt to reflect changes going on in your mind as well.

27. TUESDAY. Mixed. Enjoy the company of younger people. There may be an opportunity to take children out somewhere special, which you should enjoy as well. Follow your creative and artistic urges and you could discover a talent you did not even know you had. There is an emphasis on foreign links; you could hear from a friend overseas or get an offer from abroad. For single Gemini men and women it is worthwhile traveling further in order to meet new people. You could be introduced to someone sensitive and imaginative with whom you have immediate special rapport. Partnered Gemini people can also benefit from a stimulating change of scene.

28. WEDNESDAY. Variable. This is an ideal day for getting involved in spare time pursuits that include your mate or partner. You are likely to want to do more together, which can only improve the love between you. Someone you consider a good friend may surprise you with a rather harsh, sarcastic comment because you have upset this person without realizing it. The one you innocently hurt may only be able to communicate this indirectly. It is probably worth bringing the matter out into the open so that it can be cleared up. Turn a deaf ear to comments about other people, and be sure not to spread rumors or gossip about anyone.

29. THURSDAY. Stressful. This is a particularly intense and potentially stressful day where work matters are concerned. It is difficult not to feel under pressure. However, if you can manage to relax you should be able to produce more accurate and higher quality work. Work that is piling up could start to have a negative effect on your health. It might be a good idea to try to delegate some of your tasks. Your energy may get used up more quickly if you are working intensely. Try to eat more energy-giving food, such as grains and cereals, which should sustain you over a longer period of time. Do not skip a meal no matter how busy you are.

30. FRIDAY. Changeable. This is a day of ups and downs. Your usual routine could be disrupted, especially at work. Expect unexpected telephone calls and drop-in, unannounced visits. There is a chance that you may not make as much progress as you intend, but this may not matter as much as you think. With everything around you changing so quickly at the moment, it is possible that you will only be required to spend a limited time on a current project in the future. Try to concentrate on practical matters rather than on ideas and long-range planning. Your social life is likely to be more enjoyable if you go somewhere new and get to know someone different.

MAY

1. SATURDAY. Unpredictable. On this varied type of day you cannot be sure how anything is going to turn out. Expect a number of different distractions which keep you from making progress with your intended aims. A change of routine is not always bad, however, especially if you are secretly tired and bored with what you are doing. A pet that disappears for a while may worry you, particularly if this is a new animal, but try not to be overly concerned. If it has not returned after a day, call the animal shelter and post some notices. Like you, pets may be experiencing wanderlust and have no hesitation to act on it.

2. SUNDAY. Pleasant. Spend extra time with your loved one. This is a propitious time for sitting down together to discuss your mutual future plans. If you are currently away from home territory you should be able to discuss matters more openly. Broadening your horizons physically often seems to release you mentally from self-imposed boundaries. Do not worry if some of your notions lately have been rather hazy. It is likely that they will crystallize and be put in new perspective this weekend. For business-minded Gemini people, there is an opportunity to develop a creative partnership with someone whose abilities are along different lines than yours. Test out your compatibility in a small way first.

3. MONDAY. Happy. Developments in your love life are likely to be quite dramatic. The relationship between you and your partner is becoming so intense that you may wonder if it is about to end. Keep in mind, however, that for matters to be resolved and for you both to move on to a different level, problems usually have to come to a head. Do not be surprised if you end up discussing issues such as commitment and permanence. For single Gemini men and women who meet someone new, the attraction is likely to be spellbinding. Try to find out more about each other before you get very deeply involved. Remember that love can be blind, but you have to go into a permanent relationship with your eyes open.

4. TUESDAY. Variable. Someone you have had a falling out with is likely to make a gesture toward getting back together. Do not be too dubious. It is likely that this person is entirely sincere. An individual who has been antagonistic to you on the work scene could now turn over a new leaf. Perhaps this person is realizing that jealousy says more about them than about you. Take advantage of these channels of communication that are opening up between you. If there is anything important to say, now is the time to speak your mind in the most tactful way. If you have a date planned for this evening, relax beforehand rather than worrying about looking perfect. Focus on the interests of the other person rather than on yourself.

5. WEDNESDAY. Useful. If you have a dilemma to solve, look to the past and recollect the experiences you have had. It is likely that you already know the right answer simply from previous experience. This is a favorable time for research work of any kind. At a personal level, it is a propitious time for beginning a course if this is something you have been considering. If you have an interest in technology, this is a favorable day for experimenting on your own. Through trial-and-error you can learn a lot. Confidential discussions in your business life are likely to be encouraging but may not yet yield any definite results.

6. THURSDAY. Unsettling. Undercover dealings are likely where negotiations are concerned. Whether such involvement is a good idea is something you have to decide for yourself. If you are not aware of subterfuge at play, however, be alert for it. Figuratively speaking, a door which cannot be opened by you directly can probably be opened by someone you know who has influence or access. A rare opportunity may come your way to get involved in a golden business or financial plan. Do more research into any option which seems just a little too good to be true. This is no time for gambling with major investments and big money. Take a walk tonight to clear your mind and release stress.

7. FRIDAY. Disruptive. It is important to keep sensitive matters to yourself. A friend who just cannot help revealing confidential information, despite trying not to, may pass a secret on to someone else and start a chain reaction. This is likely to be an expensive day for matters relating to children or other younger family members. It may be necessary to cut back on personal spending in order to help out. If you have a hobby which is expensive, look for alternatives. You may be able to recycle supplies. If club membership is involved, there may be another club which offers more favorable options. Or you may be able to take advantage of an introductory membership rate. Focus on your long-term aims that can be accomplished on your own.

8. SATURDAY. Satisfactory. If you can manage to get away to a different environment this weekend, do so. It is likely that your relationship with your mate or partner will improve with a refreshing change of scene. For single Gemini men and women, opportunities to meet the right partner exist away from your home territory and regular haunts. Something you hear via the grapevine may make it obvious that an old enemy has stopped holding bad feelings about you. Although you no longer spend much time consciously worrying about this, a reconciliation should lift a burden from your mind as the slate is finally wiped clean. Give generously to a worthy cause.

9. SUNDAY. Favorable. Follow up on an urge to expand your academic or vocational horizons. Through your connection with a friend or acquaintance you may be inspired to study an interesting subject. This may be intended to improve your employment position or simply for your own pleasure. Either way, a course of study begun soon should be very stimulating. A summer school program may appeal. Register early to ensure a place. Single Gemini men and women may experience a true meeting of minds with a potential love partner through educational interests. There could be a surprise visit or phone call from someone who has been on your mind.

10. MONDAY. Buoyant. Take advantage of an opportunity to establish a stronger rapport in a new friendship. If you have a spare ticket to an enjoyable social event, invite this person to accompany you. If this is someone of the opposite sex, be sure that your motives are totally honorable. This is a key time for making new contacts in the business world as well as in your social life. If a problem has been consistently troubling you lately, discuss the matter with someone whose judgment and integrity you trust. Your love relationship is likely to be intense and passionate. That special person in your life wants to please you in every way. Enjoy being pampered.

11. TUESDAY. Useful. This should be a helpful day for handling neglected tasks and half-completed matters. You should be able to get a lot finished. There is a possibility that not everything will turn out in your favor. There could be a disappointment relating to business matters, but this is probably less significant than you now think. You are apt to be feeling more sensitive and vulnerable than usual. Any little criticism from the boss or some other authority figure is likely to be blown out of true proportion. Bear in mind that it may take a little while to clarify your perspective and see the situation in its true colors. Check that you have not exceeded your monthly budget; cut back if necessary.

12. WEDNESDAY. Fair. Spend time extending your personal interests. Explore options relating to local clubs and societies. Group interests may attract you. If you intend to go on a serious diet, consider joining a health club or a dieting group. You will probably find it easier to keep going with your diet if you have some moral support from people with the same aim in mind. Mail order catalogs offering additional incentive items if you order more than a certain amount are trying to get you to spend more. Keep this in mind if you generally find it hard to resist a so-called bargain. This is a day when all that glitters is not necessarily gold.

13. THURSDAY. Easygoing. Your close friends are likely to be an inspiration to you. Someone who has recently taken up a new interest is likely to be so enthusiastic that you want to join in with them. Accept an invitation to an unusual place or event. A change of scene and perspective is sure to be beneficial for you. Generally speaking, this is a day to be more adventurous. If you want to study something new, opt for a group class rather than individual tutoring, which may be rather costly and less exhilarating. A local school may offer evening classes in the subject. The library can also open up new worlds for you. Just be careful not to go off in too many new directions.

14. FRIDAY. Deceptive. This is a day for making future plans. It is a good idea to think over the past so that you do not repeat errors that you made back then. Try moving in a different direction or adopting a totally new approach in order to get more promising results this time around. Greater strength and clarity of vision is a bonus, especially in relation to business and financial matters. You are likely to benefit from greater solitude, giving you a chance to relax. There may be travel costs involved in getting to a place that makes you feel calm, but being in more pleasant surroundings should be highly beneficial as you struggle to make an important decision.

15. SATURDAY. Sensitive. If you must travel by car, try to share the driving with someone else. Otherwise it is probably better to cancel a long trip. You are at risk of falling asleep behind the wheel if you are tired or driving too aggressively if you are in a mad rush. Aim to delegate minor tasks to other people, especially household chores. Try to unburden yourself as much as possible so that you have more chance to relax and unwind. In planning for the future, aim to keep your aspirations on solid ground. Pie-in-the-sky ideas will probably never come to much. Focus on overcoming a bad habit by trying different approaches until you find the one that works best for you.

16. SUNDAY. Exciting. Make the most of this day. Focus on your personal plans and interests. You should be able to further one particular aim if you put your mind to it and get an early start. Concentrate on long-term as well as shorter term plans. If you truly desire success, it is important to strengthen and clarify your vision. There is a better chance of being able to turn dreams into realities if there is some solid ground to build on in the first place. Follow through on any artistic or creative desires and aspirations. It is possible that you can turn a clever talent into a money-making enterprise. Start small; try to build up an exclusive clientele.

17. MONDAY. Productive. This is a particularly helpful day where work matters are concerned. You should find it easier to obtain cooperation from colleagues and authority figures who have previously been difficult. Those who were once averse to your plans and ideas may now do a quick about-turn. You are more than usually popular both in your business and social life. Various associates are ready and willing to be more generous and helpful in providing you with needed resources. Socially, you are likely to be drawn to people with intellectual interests and strong philosophical views. One individual in particular may help expand your horizons while keeping discreetly in the background.

18. TUESDAY. Rewarding. You should be able to put business dealings on a firmer footing. If you have been debating new investment or budget plans, now is the time to commit yourself to a definite course of action. This is a favorable day for making future plans. Once again, rely on past experience as your best guide. If you are trying to bring an important plan to fruition, you may need the

help of someone in a powerful, influential position. Make your approach today; you are likely to receive a favorable response. Your
artistic and creative talents can be a greater strength than you realize. Make full use of your excellent Gemini intuition.

19. WEDNESDAY. Disquieting. It is best to be more discreet
and close-mouthed with all business and financial matters. If you
have new ideas, keep them to yourself for now. Someone who
tends to be quicker off the mark in initiating new projects may
snatch your idea from under your nose and use it for their own
ends. This is not such a threat if your own chances of success
remain intact. However, do not take that kind of risk. Behind-the-
scenes discussions should help move your plans forward. If you
are not in a position to disclose details to other people, nonetheless make sure that business dealings are kept aboveboard and as
free from intrigue as possible.

20. THURSDAY. Demanding. Expect a busy and demanding
day, especially where business matters are concerned. You may
become involved in a lot of meetings and negotiations. The outcome should be productive but will probably involve more work
for you. There is a need to be constantly on the move, running
errands both for yourself and for other people. A conversation
with a neighbor or relative could provide you with some important
information or new insight. If there have been difficulties with
neighbors recently, now is the time to sort the matter out amica-
bly. Allow your mate or partner to handle more domestic responsibilities. Divide household tasks on an equal basis.

21. FRIDAY. Changeable. Spend time socializing around your
neighborhood. There could be interesting and unusual activities
going on. News received now may temporarily stun you. If this
comes by mail, reread the letter later after you have had time to
absorb the shock. On second reading, the information may not
seem so surprising or disturbing. You may have to move quickly
to do something about a financial dilemma. Your partner or an
older family member should be able to help temporarily. Last-
minute changes of plan are likely in relation to your social life.
An unusual invitation may come from a neighbor; be quick to
accept or the offer could be withdrawn.

22. SATURDAY. Stressful. There is a lot to do on the domestic
scene. Try to get family members to help out more so that you
are not personally burdened. It is important to get an early start
so that you are left with time to do as you please. Some of your

major personal ambitions may have to be temporarily shelved, but not all of them. Make wise choices. Take advantage of your partner's energy and vitality to accomplish more around the home than usual. Your loved one is probably a better organizer than you at the moment. An idea that you rejected earlier in the month may now begin to appeal to you. Be willing to change your mind.

23. SUNDAY. Pleasant. You are likely to want to spend more money on your home, either because there are specific items which need to be replaced or because you want to brighten up the overall atmosphere. Seek out some bargains. If you want to redecorate but cannot really afford the time and money, consider minor overall changes. Slipcovering furniture in a different color could create a whole new theme. More, or even less, doodads scattered around could make a lot of difference to the sense of space. Some kind of visual change, whether you are adding or taking away, is likely to make you feel more at ease. Positioning furniture at an angle can also be visually stimulating.

24. MONDAY. Good. This is a day when you are likely to feel the need to spend more time with younger family members, particularly if you have not had much chance to be with them of late. Someone may turn to you for guidance on a specific matter, perhaps a subject that is difficult to raise. Initiate the conversation, particularly if the person seems moody. Sometimes young people, teenagers especially, feel too embarrassed to simply ask questions. They may benefit from more guidance based on your own principles, but be sure to listen to what they want. Try to combine various activities so that you still have time for your own personal priorities. If you go out for dinner, skip dessert.

25. TUESDAY. Excellent. Spend more time with your mate or partner, especially if you have shared interests. Time away from your usual routine should be stimulating and exciting. There is a possibility that you have to make an unexpected trip. It can save time if you have an overnight bag already packed. There may be an opportunity related to work matters to travel overseas in the not too distant future. Although business oriented, your loved one may be able to join you. Talk about your own plans, especially your desire to broaden your horizons. Being part of a group, such as a chorale or sports team, can spur you on to greater achievement.

26. WEDNESDAY. Mixed. Romance is in the air. Find new ways of expressing your feelings to your mate or partner. While a luxurious gift is almost always appreciated, you may not have the cash to spare. Look for an alternative which will not break the bank. If you are involved in a new relationship, a gift of flowers may be particularly appreciated. Sincerity is more important than extravagance. Try to avoid taking risks with financial affairs. It is generally not a good idea to commit yourself without knowing where the money will come from when it is time to pay up. Avoid buying anything on credit; pay cash or wait to make the purchase.

27. THURSDAY. Frustrating. Expect a busy time on the work scene. There is likely to be much new responsibility to handle as well as work to catch up on. Prioritize all of your tasks. It is possible that a new project will be more important than something you already have up and running. You may have difficulty pinning down individual people and obtaining important documents. Piles of paper stacked up in front of you are likely to be quite daunting. Finding the time to get them in order should make your job simpler now and also in the future. If you are blocked with creative work, do not panic; it should pass after a good night's sleep, thanks to a dream that opens your eyes to new possibilities.

28. FRIDAY. Demanding. This is another busy day. It is important to take greater care to protect your overall health. Too much running around, surviving only on coffee and snack food, is not good for you. If you have been putting on weight, a diet where weight loss is fast may appeal to you. However, be careful that you do not do anything too extreme. It is better to lose weight gradually over the longer term, adjusting your diet so that the pounds stay off. Try not to create too much of a change in your eating routine. If you really want to make faster progress, exercise more. Joining a health club or an organized walking group could be good incentive.

29. SATURDAY. Happy. You and your partner should feel closer today. It can be beneficial to get out of town for a change of scene. Away from routine and prying eyes, greater intimacy is likely. Give free rein to your sense of adventure. Do something different, or visit somewhere new. A trip to a country haunt or retreat is likely to be quite magical. If you get high up in the mountains you are likely to start seeing life from a different perspective inwardly as well as outwardly. Do not neglect to send someone who lives far away a card for a special occasion or just to let them know you are thinking about them.

30. SUNDAY. Disconcerting. This is a demanding day where partnership interests are concerned. At least temporarily, you may have to put your own private and personal affairs on the back burner and make a significant sacrifice. Oddly enough, this should not seem too difficult in the long term, although it may aggravate you temporarily. Harmony between you and others is likely to be stronger if you are willing to compromise. Deep-seated, angry feelings may surface and come to a head. This is probably not bad, for it should help clear the air. Just be careful not to say anything in the heat of the moment that you will regret later. Get to bed earlier than usual tonight.

31. MONDAY. Buoyant. This is a particularly romantic and passionate day. Spending extra time with your mate or partner should allow a free expression of feelings between you. The channels of communication are open once again, perhaps because you managed to clear the air between you yesterday. Concentrate on spending more spare time with one another. If you have shared interests, schedule related activities together. Sports, in particular, are likely to be uplifting. If you recently experienced a satisfying personal success, do not flaunt the fact. Someone close to you could feel irritated that you took the prize or achieved the recognition they hoped would be theirs. Be as gracious in winning as in coming in second best.

JUNE

1. TUESDAY. Calm. This is a favorable day for research and investigation of any kind. If someone is coming to survey or inspect your home or your property, do not worry. It is likely that the work will be carried out smoothly, quickly, and without too much disturbance to you personally. It can be helpful to pool your resources with other people in order to afford an expensive item you can all use or social activities. It is likely that you can save quite a lot of money in the long run by buying in bulk or a large quantity at a sale price. If you regularly drive to work along the same route as a colleague, consider the possibility of splitting the costs by carpooling at least a few times per week.

2. WEDNESDAY. Satisfactory. Conditions are ripe for getting to the bottom of a mystery. The pieces of a puzzle should start to fall in place. If you have been considering obtaining some counseling in order to better understand how you function in relationships or to pinpoint career objectives, this should be a favorable day for making a start. Other people are likely to be able to help you find the answers and identify your options. An important discovery is also likely to be made in either your business or personal life. With an extra push you can bring long-term financial negotiations to an end, reaching an amicable mutual agreement that allows you to plan for the future.

3. THURSDAY. Manageable. It is best to take your time with important matters which require some in-depth attention. This is one of those days when skipping over details may cause you to create problems for yourself in the future. Time spent with children may be more tiring than usual because they are likely to be restless and noisy. It might be a good idea to take them out in order for them to burn up some energy. Concerns about your relationship with someone you recently became romantically involved with may be playing on your mind. Try instead to focus your attention on something totally different and less stressful; worry will not resolve much and could just magnify the situation.

4. FRIDAY. Happy. Try to get away sometime today with your loved one for a break from routine. Leave the hustle and bustle of everyday life behind and travel where nobody can contact you. A log cabin retreat or a beachfront rental could be ideal. This is a key time for intimate conversation to bring you closer together. If you are not romantically involved with anyone, a greater closeness is still likely in an important friendship or other personal relationship. Be prepared for possible delays if traveling a long distance by car or public transportation. Plan on eating out tonight where the food is good and the atmosphere is even better.

5. SATURDAY. Good. If you are away from your usual haunts this weekend you should start to feel revitalized. A change of scene can bring about a change of overall mental perspective, which is bound to be refreshing. Children, too, are likely to appreciate a stay away from home, or a day trip. Because children usually love stimulating excitement, try to find a destination that will keep them happy. School or club trips can be ideal if you do not have much time to plan. There may be an opportunity for you to go on an outing to an unusual destination with members of a club or society that you belong to. The socializing can be as enjoyable as the planned activity.

6. SUNDAY. Mixed. Life may not be as easy and relaxing today as it was yesterday. This is a time of greater duties and responsibilities, even if it is supposedly a day of rest. It is likely that family members need your help more than usual. If you have to handle chores around the house, do not expect much support from others. It is likely to be a long, hard day, but at least try to make some time just for yourself this evening. If you want to concentrate your thoughts, you probably need to be alone. Redecorating or repairs being carried out on your home are likely to be messy and distracting but worth it in the long run.

7. MONDAY. Exciting. This is another day when you have to attend to duties and obligations, especially on the work scene. If you have been temporarily out of work, any benefits due you may take some time to come through. There may be a lot of paperwork to fill out before you see any money coming your way. It is likely that you will not have much time to pursue personal interests during the early part of the day, but there should be more opportunity to do so later. Try to keep your private and professional life completely separate. Bosses may not take too kindly to your using work time for private matters. Wait until this evening to make calls to friends.

8. TUESDAY. Tranquil. You should have some time to pursue your personal interests today. Get more involved in club and group activities. A change of activity is bound to be stimulating. If you have a specific interest which you would like to find out more about, consider taking a class in the subject. You might be able to learn new craft or cookery techniques. Courses on image, style, and color are likely to appeal and could save you money in the long term. If you want to know about the history of your local area or your family heritage, it may be possible to learn through an evening class at a local school or historical society.

9. WEDNESDAY. Variable. You are apt to enjoy group social activities. An opportunity may arise for you to travel somewhere interesting in connection with educational matters. If you are around children all day, it can be difficult to concentrate on any personal matters. They will probably be restless and demand more of your attention. Consider talking a relative or neighbor into looking after them for a while, especially if they have children who would be good company for yours. Social events this evening are likely to be more enjoyable if you leave the children with a reliable babysitter, especially an older family member.

10. THURSDAY. Pleasant. Spend time with close friends whose company you enjoy. Exchanging views about an area or activity you are interesting in getting involved in is likely to be helpful. Friends are apt to encourage you to expand your horizons. This is also an important day for having some time to yourself in order to think and plan. Rest and relaxation can sometimes do more to clear your mind than endlessly thinking and trying to mentally solve problems through logic and reasoning. There may be several social invitations awaiting your response. Be discriminating; there will probably not be time for all of them. Opt for a party where you may meet new people.

11. FRIDAY. Unsettling. This should be a fairly quiet day, though not necessarily straightforward. One of your schemes or plans is likely to come to nothing, which cannot help but make you feel a bit low. However, try not to get too down in the dumps. It is possible that this is only a temporary setback and that you can rejuvenate the plan at a later date. Pieces of a perplexing puzzle are just beginning to fall into place. For the time being, focus on something altogether different which is more easily attainable. For single Gemini men and women, someone you like a lot may not seem to feel the same way about you. Be willing to change your approach or to look for someone more compatible.

12. SATURDAY. Fair. This is a better day than yesterday all around. Encouraging news should start to make you feel increasingly optimistic. Focus on fresh new schemes and ideas. Broader horizons are opening up for you. Forge ahead with your personal initiatives. It is likely that a welcome social invitation is coming your way. Make the most of opportunities to enjoy yourself and clear your mind of self-defeating thoughts. The company of friends is sure to cheer you. Your mate or partner's strange mood may simply reveal the need for some time alone to sort out a problem. You probably cannot help by being inquisitive; wait to be asked for advice.

13. SUNDAY. Useful. Spend time working out your future plans. There should be time available to focus on all of your personal matters. You are at the start of an important new episode in your life. This is the time to bring private aims and ambitions into closer perspective. There are good opportunities to broaden your horizons, particularly in connection with friends, clubs, and societies. Gemini parents of young children should try to find time to take them somewhere special. They are likely to respond well to a change of scene. You, too, can probably benefit from a temporary change of environment to stimulate your senses. Do all that you can to avoid getting in a rut.

14. MONDAY. Rewarding. This is a favorable day to spend as much time as possible with your friends. It is quite possible that they have good ideas to help you expand your personal horizons. They may even be able to open a few doors for you. From a practical point of view, it is likely to be worthwhile joining a club which specializes in a particular interest of yours. For Gemini people who have recently moved to a new area, a club or a class might also be a way of meeting new friends locally. Greater involvement in a hobby or pastime is sure to be rewarding. This is a key day for both learning and strengthening your various skills; you could even turn it into a money-maker.

15. TUESDAY. Challenging. Encouraging news is on its way to you. If you have been concerned about a financial problem, there should be less cause to worry now. Perhaps a check is finally in the mail or a legal matter has been settled in your favor. Get more involved in behind-the-scenes activities. Efforts in this respect are likely to be rewarding. There are profits to be made through confidential undertakings. Look for a way to utilize your artistic or creative talents to earn extra income. It can be helpful to spend some time discussing self-employment potential with somebody who has a thorough knowledge of marketing and the current economic climate. Make plans, but take no hasty action.

16. WEDNESDAY. Frustrating. Be more careful with money matters. If a check has been paid to you recently, it may not clear through your bank in time to cover a bill you need to pay. The timing is all-important. Check your accounts and statements. You do not want to suddenly find that some kind of restriction shows on your credit card account when you go to buy something in a store. It is possible that your payment was late in reaching your credit card company, perhaps through no real fault of your own. It is best to avoid making any impulse purchases. Hold back on spending until you know where you stand. An older person can help you budget more effectively; ask for assistance.

17. THURSDAY. Changeable. This should be a pleasant day for your social interests. Several attractive invitations are likely to come your way. You should be feeling lively and able to face the world with your head held high. If you go out to a local gathering, you may end up the center of attention. This prospect should be especially appealing for single Gemini people eager to attract a new romantic partner. It is unlikely that you will be short of dates. Being pursued by a romantic admirer is bound to be flattering. If you feel tired toward the end of the evening, opt for an early night. Beware of driving when you can hardly keep your eyes open.

18. FRIDAY. Buoyant. Make more of an effort to get in touch with people you have not seen for a while or would like to see more frequently. This is a favorable day for reestablishing contact with somebody you broke off with in the past. Be the one to call and suggest social arrangements. Work meetings are likely to be spirited and industrious. A colleague may make a suggestion that you have more social outings or activities after work. If this appeals to you, do your best to encourage them. Do not hold back on matters of importance to you personally; the responses you get should be favorable. Increased sports activities can help keep you in shape and also expand your social horizons. Join a team, or offer to coach one.

19. SATURDAY. Stressful. Expect a rather stressful atmosphere in your home. It is likely that your mate or partner is in a moody frame of mind. It is in your interests to just ignore any outburst. If the atmosphere is unbearable, however, it might be better to confront the person. Do aim to be subtle. You can benefit from spending time quietly on your own. Concentration is likely to be difficult to sustain if others are moping around you. Hide away in your room or out in the yard, and keep a low profile. If you own a car, it is possible that an old problem will reappear with the vehicle. Be prepared to work on it yourself or to pay a trained mechanic.

20. SUNDAY. Enjoyable. This should be a much happier day on the domestic scene. Your mate or partner may seem to have turned over a new leaf after being depressed about a problem or overtired recently. After a little rest, the world generally looks brighter to most people. This is a helpful day for discussing money matters and new investment ideas. It may be necessary to sit down and go over each item of the family budget. Reassuring news is on the way from a neighbor or relative. Aim for balance in all of your activities. Use the earlier part of the day to handle general interests and the latter part to focus on your own personal affairs. Break away from routine tonight and enjoy yourself.

21. MONDAY. Fortunate. Be more supportive with a family member interested in broadening their experiences. If you are too protective they may never manage to establish the needed degree of self-confidence. Trips on offer may be expensive. If you cannot really afford the extra money, think of a safe way to raise the money by yourself or with a group of friends. If you have some ideas, suggest them. If not, brainstorming could lead to a profitable scheme. If you do not belong to a sports team or hobby club, this is the right time to join. Do not limit yourself in any way; look past the known to the wider world.

22. TUESDAY. Changeable. Try to become more involved in spare time pursuits. Sports and games are likely to be particularly stimulating and enjoyable. This is no time to be sticking to dull routine. A whole range of social options is available to you. Make more of an effort to broaden your horizons. If there is an opportunity to travel a long distance, accept without delay. The change of scene will probably do you a world of good. A trip may come about through your work and business interests. For Geminis who are self-employed, it might be worth creating time to visit current trade shows and meetings. You could make some useful new contacts. Prove to yourself that you are perfectly capable of handling whatever comes your way.

23. WEDNESDAY. Lucky. If you want to get new social interests and arrangements off the ground, you probably have to take more personal initiative. Do not just wait for someone else to organize a party or other get-together. It could be that you want to do something different from what you are used to doing in a group. You may have to work at rallying interest and enthusiasm, but your efforts should be worthwhile when you manage to get people to finally agree. It is possible that you can increase your income by taking on additional work. This is a lucky day for Gemini people looking for a new job or hoping for a promotion or pay raise. Expect good news.

24. THURSDAY. Productive. Take better care of your general health and well-being. Be careful that you are not getting too stressed out. That run-down feeling may be caused as much by mental worries as by having overexerted yourself physically. In fact, stress is most likely to be the basic problem. Involvement in physical activities, such as a team sport, can help release tension and make you feel more in control overall. Be prepared for an up-and-down day and night. It could be quite difficult to concentrate on mental matters. Take a break and do something to help clear your mind, such as jogging or bicycle riding or even walking upstairs instead of using an elevator.

25. FRIDAY. Successful. This is a starred day for negotiations and meetings. You should be able to get a new project approved and then up and running. It is likely that you will have greater cooperation from colleagues who have recently been self-focused. There should be more team spirit. In general, this is a time when you can rely on others to live up to their promises. If a potentially profitable business proposition comes your way, look to the future; consider how it might benefit you over the longer term. It is important not to take on more commitments than you can comfortably manage, however. Do not divulge your intentions prematurely nor brag before results are in.

26. SATURDAY. Useful. Try to spend most of your free time with your mate or partner. You can resolve a lot if you discuss your future plans. Dreams and hopes can be furthered by talking them through. Also discuss any worries and fears, which should lead to receiving reassurance from those who matter most to you. Greater honesty in your close relationships is likely to benefit you. Concentrate on making solid plans for the future. You may have the opportunity to return to a place that was very significant to you in the past, perhaps where you and your loved one first met and fell in love. Enjoy reminiscing about the past even while looking ahead expectantly.

27. SUNDAY. Pleasant. This is likely to be a day of exciting developments in your love life. Single Gemini men and women may meet someone instantly appealing. The attraction may turn out to be more than purely physical once you get to know one another. People at or from a distance are particularly important in your life today. You could hear from a friend living overseas or a former schoolmate. Be willing to accept social invitations which will give you a break from routine. Going out on this Sunday evening could make the working week ahead seem less daunting, but do not stay out so late that your sleep pattern is disrupted.

28. MONDAY. Variable. Your love life is likely to be warmer and more passionate due to you taking the initiative. For single Gemini men and women there could be a romantic meeting with someone different whose background is quite foreign. If you are entertaining at home prepare a special meal to impress the most important guest, who may actually be your only guest. Go all out with candles and flowers to create a romantic setting. Try to find out what this person especially likes when it comes to planning the menu. There may be a cause for celebration today; if not, think of one. Do not let a family member feel ignored or a pet be neglected.

29. TUESDAY. Fortunate. Concentrate on financial matters. It is a good idea to ensure that your accounts are up to date. If you have been busy lately, you may have buried important paperwork under a pile of junk mail. Sort it all out. Negotiating a financial agreement or refinancing a loan should be easier than you expect. Joint financial matters generally are full of positive developments. Your mate or partner may get a raise or receive word of an inheritance. Work on getting more done behind the scenes. It is important to keep an eye on the future, particularly if you are considering reinvesting money that is now earning a low rate of interest.

30. WEDNESDAY. Demanding. There are apt to be more financial constraints placed on you than usual. If you have overspent the family budget, now is the time to tighten your belt. If your kitchen cabinets are well stocked, try to survive on what you already have. Leave more exotic meal planning until another time. If you are personally short of money for social pursuits, it is possible that your partner or an older family member can tide you over. Particularly expensive plans might have to be postponed until you have more available cash. Be sure not to overcommit yourself at work or in your community. Resist volunteering even for an interesting job.

JULY

1. THURSDAY. Disquieting. If you intend to make a long journey on the weekend, take along a map even if you know the route well. There is a possibility of detours and delays which send you on a very different route. If you have a friend or colleague traveling with you, so much the better; they are apt to have some useful insights. Life with your mate or partner should be very amiable. If you have personal or even professional problems to solve, it is likely that your loved one can help find a solution. Take advantage of their insight and coolheaded approach. Becoming emotional can blind you to the most useful options available to you.

2. FRIDAY. Challenging. Keep an overnight bag packed and ready for you. There is a possibility that you may need to travel a long distance without much warning. A taste of the unexpected should be welcome since you are likely to be feeling quite restless. Where work matters are concerned, do not expect your day to go according to plan. Telephone calls are likely to be important and lengthy, bringing news of changes which you must accommodate. Find time for new priorities. A social event may be appealing but may become less so if you are loaded down with greater responsibilities at work. Consider canceling out if you are pressed for time or too tired to be good company.

3. SATURDAY. Fair. This is a particularly favorable day for legal dealings. You are likely to receive reassuring news. All of your affairs are now beginning to pick up speed. A negotiated settlement may be the best solution for everyone involved. There is every reason to be optimistic. If you have to travel a long distance, the journey should be interesting and not as tiring as you expect because it is an unfamiliar route with interesting sights along the way. If you have estimated extra time to allow for the possibility of a delay, it is likely that you will end up arriving earlier than scheduled. Weekend traffic could be light for a change.

4. SUNDAY. Happy. Friends may be up to something behind the scenes. Do not worry; they may be planning a pleasant holiday surprise for you. An opportunity could arise to go on a spur-of-the-moment trip to an unusual place. This will probably appeal to your current sense of adventure and your desire for finding a deeper meaning. As a Gemini you are often happier bouncing along on the surface of life and not digging too deep, but today is an exception. Your curiosity is likely to be aroused, making this a more spiritual and philosophic day. What you discover could change your perspective quite radically and put you on a new track.

5. MONDAY. Mixed. There is opportunity to increase your earnings. You may be offered additional work at a good rate of pay. Overtime may not usually be easy to come by, but this could be an exception at the moment. If you have been out of work, a suggestion from a friend or former colleague is likely to bring a solution to your current financial situation. Do not overlook the possibility of temporary work options. Such a job could develop into something much longer term and permanent if you make a good impression. It is possible that a boss will congratulate you for your recent efforts, but ulterior motives may also be involved; stay alert and on guard.

6. TUESDAY. Changeable. Spend more time concentrating on your social and private interests. This is a favorable time for applying to join a club or society that interests you. You may be able to take advantage of special terms which are being offered as an incentive to attract more members. An invitations to a local event that comes your way may not seem all that exciting, but go anyway. It could turn out to be lot more interesting than you expect. For single Gemini men and women, getting together with strangers could be the route to meeting a new love partner. There should be good rapport with your mate or partner this evening. Go out of your way to show your love.

7. WEDNESDAY. Enjoyable. You probably have a number of different social invitations from which to choose, all of them quite appealing. You could suffer from the usual Gemini dilemma of finding it difficult to know what to do. It is likely that you will enjoy a large group gathering better than one-to-one pairings. Spend more time with friends. If you socialize in a group, you may be introduced to someone new with whom you immediately see eye-to-eye. For single Gemini men and women this could signal the start of a wonderful new romance. Someone could be secretly matchmaking on your behalf, or you may want to arrange to bring together two of your friends to see if they click.

8. THURSDAY. Misleading. Keep a low profile. What is going on behind the scenes can be rather worrisome. You may overhear something unpleasant or unnerving, perhaps a rumor that is being spread around. Before you start believing it, bear in mind that it is often easier to latch onto the negative and ignore the positive, perhaps because nobody wants to end up looking foolish. You could be the one with egg on your face, however, if you act on incorrect information or misguided advice. Stick with what you know based on personal experience. This is not time for allowing your imagination to get the better of you. Shy away from anything that is controversial.

9. FRIDAY. Disconcerting. This is another day when rumors and gossip are likely to be floated. You may hear unpleasant comments about someone you know. This time it may not be so easy, or advisable, to simply ignore the matter. If you feel that someone's honor is at stake, make it your business to speak up in their defense. Sometimes people say cruel things out of ignorance more than spite. Define and set your own personal plans for the future. Consulting an older member of the family on a personal issue which you are struggling to clarify or resolve is a good idea. You may be surprised by this person's insight. Pamper yourself this evening by doing what you enjoy most.

10. SATURDAY. Disquieting. In theory, this should be a favorable day for advancing your own personal aims and ambitions. However, conflict with your loved one or another family member is quite possible. This person may not appreciate how important a hobby is to you, or how much you need to get done. The basic problem is probably that you both need personal time and space at the moment. Being cooped up together can lead to getting on each other's nerves. Opt for a change of scene if possible. It is better if you each spend time in separate parts of the house or even away from home. Any kind of suspicion on your partner's part may highlight a basic insecurity; this is their problem, not yours.

11. SUNDAY. Rewarding. There is more opportunity to be single-minded about your own affairs. Sheer determination should mean that you can make good progress. It is particularly helpful that there is probably less chance of upsetting those close to you by doing your own thing away from them. Your mate or partner may come to realize that jealousy or suspicion is more their problem than yours, or that there is actually no problem at all. In general, expect people around you to be reasonable and cooperative. A social get-together with neighbors or relatives should be enjoyable. Be sure to include children in your social activity. Try to teach them manners and courtesy by your example.

12. MONDAY. Profitable. This is a positive day where financial matters are concerned. Something in your current situation is about to change, making you feel more secure about the future. You may be offered additional work which brings in welcome extra earnings over the longer term, perhaps providing a chance to save on a regular basis. Greater personal strength, even stubbornness, is an asset in dealing with strong-minded and well-seasoned business people. Because the general environment around you is calm and smooth, you should feel more emotionally stable. Conditions favor getting complicated matters settled once and for all. There is no time like the present to hammer out an agreement.

13. TUESDAY. Sensitive. A strong focus on money is once again likely. Focus on the long term. It is important to put your overall financial situation into clearer perspective. If you do not work by a strict budget, it might actually help to draw one up one now.

This should be especially useful if you have debts to clear. Set a time limit for when you intend to have them all paid in full, which should give you a greater sense of purpose in saving. You cannot aim well if you do not have a specific target in sight. Today marks the start of a fresh page of your life. Make good use of past contacts in arranging future activities.

14. WEDNESDAY. Confusing. Spend more time in your local area. There are apt to be some interesting events going on which are fun for both you and your mate or partner. If you are thinking of making changes around the home, focus on easier things you can do to brighten it up, such as a fresh coat of paint or a well-placed mirror. Different furniture, particularly antiques, could add a special touch. It is surprising what people sometimes want to get rid of; you can probably find some genuine bargains in a thrift shop if you have the time to root around. If you go out this evening to a party, arrive a little late or you may get roped into helping with the preparations.

15. THURSDAY. Easygoing. You should have more opportunity today to relax and unwind. Accept a social invitation which provides a chance to do something a little different. Breaking away from your usual routine should be beneficial, especially if you have been under a lot of pressure lately. An event hosted by relatives or neighbors should be well worth attending. Relax, soak up the atmosphere, and enjoy yourself. It is unlikely that you will have to lift a finger to help out. You could end speaking for a long time with someone quite interesting. There may be a romantic opportunity for single Gemini people to become better acquainted with someone you only know by reputation.

16. FRIDAY. Buoyant. Home and family life should be smooth and pleasant. This is a favorable day for indulging in family entertainment. Someone close to you is likely to share some good news. People around you are likely to seem happier than they were earlier in the week. If you are having guests over for dinner, aim for a relaxed affair. Make it easy on yourself by preparing a casserole, which does not have to be watched over while you want to entertain. Avoid flirting with anyone in front of your mate or partner even if it is just for fun. Your actions might be taken the wrong way. Be sure that someone who is shy is encouraged to participate in group activity.

17. SATURDAY. Good. You may receive reassuring news in relation to home or family matters. One of your relatives is likely to tell you about their recent success, which means that everyone can breathe a sigh of relief. They may have passed their examinations, given birth to a healthy baby, or received a promotion. There should be more opportunity to settle plans and arrangements involving other people. Spending more time with your loved ones should make you feel more united. If you intend to do some redecorating, try to get other members of the family involved in the planning as well as the actual work. Enjoy being with that special person in your life tonight; go out as a twosome.

18. SUNDAY. Easygoing. Plan to do more with your leisure time. This is a propitious day for beginning a new hobby or getting back into an old pastime you used to enjoy in your spare time. There are likely to be pleasant social options for you; choose carefully. If you have the opportunity to travel for a change of scene, take it up. A different environment is sure to be refreshing, especially if you and your mate or partner are away together for the weekend. The atmosphere between you is likely to be quite magical because of the environment you are in, or it may simply be that you are free of stress and strain and able to focus on one another totally.

19. MONDAY. Exciting. Focus on ways to broaden your social, mental, and personal horizons. You may have a desire to travel to exotic, faraway places. Or perhaps you want to get involved in a new hobby or work project. Follow your instincts and do something exciting. Other family members are also apt to benefit from a change of scene or routine. Plan a special trip to a place that you know they will enjoy. Do not worry if your imagination is limited at the moment; it is possible that neighbors or relatives will inspire you to come up with a good idea. There may be a local party going on, which will be fun for the whole family. If you cannot leave work on time, be sure to call home and let loved ones know when to expect you.

20. TUESDAY. Disappointing. This is another day when there are opportunities to expand your horizons. You have to keep a stronger hand on your budget, however. Where a new hobby is concerned, hold back from investing in very costly, specialized equipment right at the start. Borrow or rent what you need instead until you find out if you really like the activity. Guard against spending a lot of money which you may later regret. With work matters it is best to take your time. Be more thorough and exact when handling detailed work. Shortcuts may only lead to having to go over old ground in search of an obvious mistake. Do not stay out late tonight.

21. WEDNESDAY. Strenuous. This is a very productive day for work matters. You have the necessary positive energy to get things done early in the day. Take advantage of this. Try not to put off too much until later; your energy is apt to flag after a while. Unwelcome news later in the day could drain you of energy. If this happens, try to get into an environment for a short while where you can let your feelings out. Holding in anger or hurt can make it very difficult for you to maintain your focus. Do not panic if you experience a creative block; it should vanish as your emotions take a turn for the better this evening. Relax with a good book or video after dinner.

22. THURSDAY. Quiet. This is a better day overall for attending to complicated and detailed work matters. You should be able to concentrate easily and for a longer stretch of time without needing a break. Good organization is one of your main keys to success. If you have not got around to your filing lately, now is the time to do it. This is especially true if you are about to launch a new project. It is better to start with a clear desk and a clear mind. You may have a lot of paperwork to handle, perhaps due to a sudden flurry of communications. Pace yourself throughout the day. It is as important to look after your health as your work; eat light and right, and avoid alcohol.

23. FRIDAY. Variable. It is quite possible that you can turn a skill or talent toward profitable ends. Even a hobby you have only recently taken up can become a lucrative enterprise if you have the right contacts. It is likely to be helpful to speak to marketing people about the best strategies. Concentrate on ways to improve your general health and well-being. If you have lately overlooked your exercise program, plan to get back to it starting today. Perhaps a change of activity would suit you better, helping you adapt to changes going on in your life. If you need to discuss an important matter with your mate or partner, do so outside of the earshot of other people who are somehow involved.

24. SATURDAY. Enjoyable. This is a particularly favorable day for getting involved in shared interests and activities with your loved one. There should be an increased sense of companionship and rapport between you. Being more involved in the social scene is likely to bring an exciting romantic encounter for single Gemini men and women. Whatever you do, avoid sitting at home and moping around being lonely when you could be out meeting very interesting people. Someone you have not been able to get along with for a long time may surprise you by taking the initiative to mend the damage caused in your relationship in the past. Be quick to accept their apology, and perhaps offer one of your own as well.

25. SUNDAY. Excellent. You may have an urge to get more involved in educational and intellectual matters. Consider attending a public lecture on a subject that interests you. Being involved in discussion and debate should be stimulating. You could even end up seeing life from a whole new perspective. It is likely to be easier to understand complicated concepts if you are involved as part of a group and get to hear a number of different views on the matter. It could be a good idea for you and your mate or partner to get involved together in interests of the mind. As a Gemini you are curious and ready to try something new without worrying about whether you will be immediately successful.

26. MONDAY. Tricky. This is an important day where property and home matters are concerned. If you share your home with others, you may feel that you need to be with a different kind of people. Although as a Gemini you often go out socially, your home is still a very important part of your life overall. Not being content with your living arrangements is likely to mean that you are generally not content. Now is the time to be making key changes. If you are thinking of buying property, shop around for a favorable mortgage deal. Pooling resources should mean that you can afford a better home in a better neighborhood.

27. TUESDAY. Deceptive. It is a toss-up today whether you go to a local event or make more of an effort to travel to a more distant place. Both options have much to offer. The deciding factor may be whether you really have enough time to spare. Try to focus on your true priorities. Various distractions may make work difficult to handle. If you cannot concentrate where you are based, investigate the possibility of moving to another location temporarily. Noise, in particular, can interfere with your concentration more than usual. Do not fall for an offer that seems too good to be true; there is probably a catch to it.

28. WEDNESDAY. Disquieting. If you intend to travel a long distance today, find out as much as you can about traffic and general road conditions before you leave. It is still possible that you will be delayed, even if you listen to traffic bulletins and updates, but at least you will then be prepared for it. Unfortunately, not all of the problems are reported or even noticed. It is a good idea to consider alternative routes which you can switch to if you happen to spot a bottleneck ahead. You may have to make a major decision in relation to long-term plans. Trust your good Gemini instincts not to lead you astray. Postpone making a final decision until the end of the week.

29. THURSDAY. Unsettling. Spend more time working out interesting ways to broaden your horizons. A quite unusual subject may be brought to your attention and immediately appeal to you. Investigate what is available locally in terms of evening or part-time day classes. Your mind is apt to be especially restless. Unexpected news may make it difficult to settle down to any particular task you need to work on. A change of scene is likely to be the best cure for this. If you feel awkward about expressing your views at work, write a memo listing your reasons for the changes you want to see made. If you do nothing you have only yourself to blame.

30. FRIDAY. Successful. This should be a favorable day for making progress with behind-the-scenes work efforts. It is likely that you can work faster, although perhaps for shorter periods of time. Clarity of vision is one of your great strengths at the moment. Your more intense focus means that it is much easier to make plans, both in the present and for the future. Take advantage of this. Spend some time thinking about your overall career prospects. If you are self-employed, this is the right time to concentrate on business expansion. It is vital, however, to have a firm foundation from which to work. You may also want to consider a new partnership.

31. SATURDAY. Unsettling. No matter how well you actually know your relatives, there are times when they do things that make no sense to you. Probably the situation is mutual. Be careful not to be seen as interfering if you decide that a problem really needs to be aired. Be realistic about matters where it is obvious you will never be able to reach an agreement. Diplomacy is your key to getting what you want at the moment. Take more responsibility in terms of what you say. Certain sensitive individuals around you can be particularly hurt by words uttered in a flash of anger. Be careful rather than risk offending someone you love. Go out with a group of people tonight, not as a twosome.

AUGUST

1. SUNDAY. Positive. There is much to be looking forward to at the moment. Your future prospects in relation to work matters are excellent. A promotion or an opportunity to work on an exciting new project may be made available to you. If you know you will have to submit a resume, make sure that your current one is up to date. Important meetings with influential people are likely during the coming five days. Someone will want to discuss details of a potentially profitable job opening or business proposition. This is a day for looking into these matters in greater depth. Do not to take too much at face value; make up your own mind on the basis of your own in-depth analysis.

2. MONDAY. Favorable. There is an enviable opportunity to establish stronger links in a new friendship with someone you recently met or in a relationship which has previously been distant. For single Gemini men and women this may be a relationship that is going to turn into a full-fledged romance. For married Gemini people, an interest enjoyed by your partner could soon start to seem more attractive to you personally. If there is an opportunity for you to work together, do so. An evening social event could be quite rewarding, bringing someone new into your life. Accept an invitation from a neighbor; you are not likely to regret it.

3. TUESDAY. Confusing. Financial factors have to be fully taken into consideration in relation to your various social commitments. Increased membership fees to a club or society may make you think twice about whether to rejoin. On close examination, you may start to wonder if it is really worthwhile. One option is to look around for a less costly alternative. A competing group may welcome you with open arms as well as a reduced initiation fee. Or you may decide that it is time to opt out altogether and try something entirely different. The main thing is to get your priorities in order, both socially and financially. Try to make better use of your local library instead of buying one-read-only books.

4. WEDNESDAY. Disquieting. This is a day to just quietly move ahead with various personal and work tasks. While you may long for a lot more time and space, it may not be that easy to get. Various problems which occur are apt to be time consuming and involve contacting people at a distance. Inaccurate paperwork could also be a problem. Although this may not actually be your fault, you probably will have to deal with the matter and make the necessary adjustments. Today is likely to be less frustrating if you accept that you have to put on more of a public face than usual, masking your annoyance and be careful of what you say. Home life should be a comfort to you.

5. THURSDAY. Pleasant. You simply have to plod on gradually with work matters if you are to make some solid progress today. Although as a Gemini you are usually restless, this may not bother you very much at the moment. Keep in mind that steady effort should pay off eventually. Behind-the-scenes developments are particularly important, setting the stage for what is to come later in the year. It is possible that you will be involved in some secret negotiations in connection with your work or personal life. You could also receive a financial bonus or notification of a raise. The domestic scene should be peaceful, harmonious, and relaxing. Try to include younger people in your future plans and current activities.

6. FRIDAY. Variable. Aim to spend more time concentrating on your personal affairs and ambitions. This is a particularly favorable day for making moves to expand your career and social horizons. Significant developments are foreseen in relation to someone at or from a distance. A sense of the magical exists in your life at the moment. Make the most of opportunities to do something totally out of the usual. You may be drawn to deeper religious and spiritual involvement. This evening there could be an opportunity to attend a thought-provoking meeting or lecture. Put aside domestic plans in order to attend to these more important matters affecting your overall well-being as well as your family's.

7. SATURDAY. Challenging. There are likely to be obvious opportunities to expand your horizons and some that practically sneak up on you. Life is becoming more exciting, with a lot of doors starting to open up for you. The only real dilemma may be in making choices, which is often a problem for Gemini people. Try to be more discriminating without shrinking from what is new to you. Dabbling in one or two areas can give you an idea of their appeal. If you are seriously thinking of changing your focus in life, however, you have to develop a strong sense of commitment. What is said to you today in an offhand manner may end up changing your perspective quite significantly and helping you make up your mind.

8. SUNDAY. Enjoyable. Spending money is sure to be a happy pastime so long as you have it to spare. Focus on buying for your home, especially if you are not happy with the look of one or two rooms. This is a favorable time for redecorating a room which is overdue for an overhaul or which you never really put your personal stamp on in the first place. Purchasing one or two beautiful items may be enough if you are happy with the basic decor. A new rug, lamps, or curtains could make a world of difference. If you want to make a room look larger, or give it a strong focal point, consider purchasing a decorative mirror with an elaborate frame for the central wall area. Arranging furniture on an angle also makes good decorating sense.

9. MONDAY. Frustrating. A potentially profitable new work opportunity may come your way. As an enterprising Gemini you may be able to turn a special talent into a lucrative business enterprise. If you have been out of work, this is a good day for trying to sell yourself to new companies in your commuting area. Do not hide your light under a bushel; aggressively market your special talents. Put more effort into behind-the-scenes activities and you should achieve favorable results. It is best to turn a deaf ear to rumors which are being spread far and wide. Someone is probably exaggerating the facts or twisting them to suit their agenda. Be careful that you do not pass on incorrect information as unvarnished truth.

10. TUESDAY. Mixed. Focus your energies on financial planning for current expenses and the long term. If you have not really made any plans for the future, it is imperative to do so now. Investment schemes may need a very large influx of cash in order to build a reasonable retirement fund if you are starting to save later in life. Do not delay acting if you have been leaving the future to chance for many years. It is a good idea to discuss your needs with a financial planner or an accountant who can provide expert advice about finance and investing. Go into depth on matters which you do not really understand. Do not hesitate to ask even the most basic questions if you are in the dark.

11. WEDNESDAY. Difficult. This is one of those days when gossipy people tend to spread rumors around the office or neighborhood. They may not even consider that they are upsetting certain individuals and getting others into trouble. Although you may feel quite startled or unsettled by what is said, it is not a good idea to attach too much importance to anything that has not been proven. Instead, concentrate on known facts, particularly if you are about to make a key decision. This is a starred time to consider buying a new car, particularly if you have been having mechanical problems with it over a long period of time. Guard against paying so much in repairs that you could almost have bought another vehicle.

12. THURSDAY. Fair. Your home and family life should be especially happy and easygoing. A magazine on interior decorating may encourage you to start thinking about possible redecorating plans of your own. It might be worth investing in some useful how-to books, particularly if you are thinking about trying out an unusual paint effect or finish. Much can be achieved through paint, light, and furniture arrangement to make a room very special. Thoroughly consider all possibilities. If you can afford getting a professional designer involved, do not hesitate to do so. In the final analysis, they may be able to save you money by preventing poor choices in color or style. Find a way to display a special collection.

13. FRIDAY. Tranquil. This promises to be another peaceful, relaxing day. Continue to focus on developing plans to improve the look of your home. The general atmosphere around you should be particularly calm and soothing, which may inspire you to plan a special outing for your family. Also spend some time looking for interesting new recipes or checking out new restaurants. If you usually only eat specific kinds of food, it might be interesting to try another cuisine. Your working life should also be more peaceful than usual. This is an excellent day for planning and organizing. Look ahead with optimism; you are definitely on the right track.

14. SATURDAY. Happy. This particularly enjoyable, light-hearted weekend favors spending more time making the most of entertainment and amusements that are available locally. If you have not been to the movies in a while, perhaps catch up with the latest offering. A change of scene is likely to be highly beneficial. There may be an opportunity to take a day trip to visit a former neighbor or a friend who recently moved. For single Gemini men and women there is a strong possibility of being asked out unexpectedly by someone new on the scene. Married Gemini people should make time for romantic conversation as a prelude to a star-studded evening.

15. SUNDAY. Good. This is another day for taking a more light-hearted attitude toward life in all its aspects. Well-calculated risks can be taken now, without fear of failure. Try to do so in conjunction with other people; you are likely to have even greater luck if you operate as part of a pair. It is likely that an opportunity will arise for you to travel to a distant and perhaps exotic place. For single Gemini men and women, a romantic encounter in an unusual setting is foreseen. If you decide to participate in leisure pursuits that are unfamiliar to you, get a friend involved in teaching you the basics. Shared leisure activities are likely to be particularly enjoyable, whether in competition or just for the fun of them.

16. MONDAY. Unsettling. This is one of those days when you are apt to be tempted to take on more responsibilities than is good for you unless you are careful. Be sure to check what is already on your calendar before committing yourself to additional new obligations. Also avoid the tendency to make life all work and very little play. Try not to exhaust yourself at this early point in the week, especially if you have a lot of hard work ahead of you. Let other people wear themselves out if they choose, but avoid doing so yourself. Key meetings and negotiations that are about to take place should be as productive and helpful as you anticipate. Keep your expectations to yourself, however.

17. TUESDAY. Changeable. You should be able to achieve much in both your personal and professional life if you have your mind firmly set on a specific plan. However, if your thinking is hazy or incomplete, it could be difficult to get going because you cannot decide where to start or how to proceed. Solid preparation is essential to achieving favorable results. Do not rush into anything. Take the time to think matters through in depth. If your mind is on two things at once, as the Gemini mind often is, you risk weakening your resolve. Put other people's inquiries off until another day. Do not comment one way or another on a new proposal suggested to you.

18. WEDNESDAY. Sensitive. It is in your best interests to allow other people to organize on your behalf and take the lead. Aim to keep a fairly low profile. You should make better progress if you can be content with plodding away slowly behind the scenes. Maintaining your focus on immediate matters while listening to a lot of talk about the future may not be easy. It is important, however, to attend to immediate priorities first and foremost. The future is prone to flux and abrupt change. And there may be upsetting developments occurring more often than you expect. Try to make today's load as easy as possible on yourself by focusing on the here and now.

19. THURSDAY. Manageable. Get an earlier than usual start, and be sure to eat a good breakfast. There is a lot of work to get through early this morning. If you do not go out to work, it is still beneficial to run major errands before lunchtime when there are likely to be less people around. If you are planning a dinner party, you may find the best produce earlier in the day before it has been picked over. If you have any specific appointments, keep in mind that traffic or other delays may occur. It is best to stay within earshot of a telephone in case you receive word from clients, the boss, or friends of their late departure or want to warn them that you are running behind schedule.

20. FRIDAY. Pleasant. Much that is pleasant is likely today. A business or personal partnership is moving onto a new and more positive level. For single Gemini men and women, this is a key time for meeting someone who may have a transforming effect on your life. You could be changing the habits of a lifetime before you even realize exactly what is happening. Sometimes when you meet someone special it is no sacrifice to give up habits or even attitudes that they do not like. Someone who cares about you can give you the courage to give up a habit that you know is unhealthy. This is a favorable day for all kinds of negotiations. Hold out for a little more than you might actually be willing to take.

21. SATURDAY. Buoyant. Greater peace and harmony is indicated in all of your relationships. There should be particularly good rapport between you and your love partner. Take advantage of this; spend some time discussing your hopes and dreams in relation to the future. Be more open in expressing your feelings of love, which should draw you even closer together. For single Gemini people, this evening is a key time for meeting a compatible new partner. It is likely that you will immediately feel very comfortable with this person and that their response to you will be exactly the same.

22. SUNDAY. Rewarding. This is a favorable day for working on ways of increasing your resources. If the family budget is tight, it might be a good idea to apportion less to personal spending and put more toward basics which everyone can appreciate. Alternatively, you may want to start a systematic savings plan so that you can make important purchases for the home in the not too distant future, paying in cash instead of high-interest credit. It is a good idea to pool resources with other people in order to create more overall buying power among you. This is a propitious day for shopping with your mate or partner. Make joint decisions in regard to key purchases. Buying necessities in bulk can save you a lot in the long run.

23. MONDAY. Profitable. Look for ways to develop a joint enterprise along more positive lines. This is a starred time for starting a business with a partner if you have been thinking about becoming self-employed. New beginnings are indicated in relation to joint endeavors. Just be certain that your talents and skills complement each other. Spend time clearing up affairs which have dragged on for some time or which simply have been neglected in the press of other work. It is likely that extra efforts made on the job will be rewarded handsomely in a material way. There may be an extra bonus for getting a project done more quickly than scheduled.

24. TUESDAY. Interesting. An opportunity arises to take a trip away from your usual scene. Take advantage of this; it could turn out to be quite a magical excursion. This is a time for getting closer to people from a different country or culture and learning more about them. It is important to be discriminating, however, in terms of whom you decide to trust with your innermost secrets. One particular person may try to push you too far, to a point which makes you uncomfortable. Some people just do not know when to take no for an answer. It is up to you to draw the line. If you feel ill at ease in someone's company, leave the scene without delay. Never mind if this would seem impolite. Your personal safety and well-being is more vital than any possible offense you might cause.

25. WEDNESDAY. Satisfactory. There should be opportunity to broaden your horizons, especially in conjunction with other people. It is likely that team effort will bring much success. You can probably get everything done much more quickly through joining forces with others. If you are involved in legal negotiations of any kind, there should now be a promising development in the matter. It is in your best interests, however, to think carefully before you speak or sign any legal document. If you are entirely noncommittal, however, suspicions could be aroused. On the other hand, if you say too much you could end up overextending yourself. If in doubt, consult your lawyer or other adviser first.

26. THURSDAY. Frustrating. You could end up tossing a coin in order to make a decision. There is likely to be as much available locally as there is a good distance away, particularly where social interests are concerned. However, you may be ready for a change of scene. If you have the time for travel, this is probably the best option. If you are worried about not being able to keep up with routine errands, see if you can get someone else to handle them for you. At work, get practical matters out of the way early in the day. Avoid spending too much time trying to weigh every option and solicit everyone's opinion. Act on the facts now available.

27. FRIDAY. Fair. You should be able to make sound progress in relation to professional interests. Keep a low profile, but assure co-workers and other people that specific jobs are being handled. Behind-the-scenes efforts are likely to be particularly profitable. If you are running short of time in relation to a particular project, ask for help; it is likely to be available if you need it. Be careful where all partnership matters are concerned. Your mate or other loved one is likely to be more sensitive than usual. It is best to think carefully before you speak, in case you end up pressing the wrong button. Pay special attention to the clues you get from body language.

28. SATURDAY. Fortunate. This is a busy and profitable day. You should have less trouble getting things done in both your professional and domestic life. If there are neglected tasks that have to be handled, attend to them early in the day to get them out of the way. There is every likelihood that you can catch up and possibly even get ahead. If you own a pet which has been sick for a while, it should now begin to show definite signs of improvement. Home life promises to be especially peaceful. This is a good time to start a new class, particularly in a subject intended to make your life fuller and less stressful.

29. SUNDAY. Challenging. Make a point of spending more time with friends you infrequently get to see but whose company you thoroughly enjoy. It is likely that you will end up having some inspiring conversations. This is a beneficial day for a trip relating to club activities and group interests. Activity with a common purpose ought to be particularly enjoyable because you are sharing the experience. You may be strongly drawn to spiritual involvements. This could be anything from learning to read Tarot cards to carrying out fund-raising in the name of an established religion. Follow your heart wherever it leads you.

30. MONDAY. Rewarding. Group and club activities should again be rewarding. If you do not have any real involvement in this respect, think about developing some. This is a propitious day for joining a club or for finding out more about a subject that you have been interested in for a long time. If you are short of money, look locally for entertainment options. These may be more affordable than traveling to well-known tourist sites. Your work is likely to be somewhat tricky. There may be a tense atmosphere because an important individual is visiting. Aim to relax more yourself so that you have a longer attention span. It is important to remember names and faces on first introduction.

31. TUESDAY. Useful. This is a key day for meeting new people and making new contacts, both in your social life and in the world of business. You may be invited to get involved in some networking which will be useful in putting you in touch with people who share your special hobby or interests. It may be possible for you to pass on useful tips to each other. This can be especially helpful if you are self-employed and the network relates to business interests. If you want to expand your business, consider making more use of mail-order markets. Someone you know socially could tip you off to a worthwhile new investment opportunity.

SEPTEMBER

1. WEDNESDAY. Unsettling. There are likely to be more than the usual number of changes of plan and other upsets to your routine. These are almost sure to interfere with your ability to get on with important matters. Unfortunately you are least able to cope with upheaval at the moment. Nevertheless, while you cannot turn back the clock or prevent changes from taking place, you can at least get yourself out of the line of fire. Aim to keep a low profile. Try to hide away somewhere more peaceful, preferably without a nearby phone. If you must stay on the scene out of a sense of duty, take charge the best you can. Do not let anyone make decisions on your behalf or use your name for any type of advertising.

2. THURSDAY. Disquieting. You will be kept on your toes this morning. There is likely to be more than the usual share of work to get through in a hurry. Expect to be rushing around constantly, chasing people down and trying to gather together the various resources and information you need. Burnout during the second half of the day is a distinct possibility due to the pace of the morning. Schedule tasks after lunch which require minimal concentration and little or no contact with other people. If you end up feeling exhausted, plan an utterly relaxing evening. Walking the dog at a leisurely clip, reading an engrossing novel, or taking a leisurely bubble bath can chase away the day's cares.

3. FRIDAY. Exciting. Spend time concentrating on your own private plans and affairs. There are a number of opportunities to expand your personal horizons. If someone issues an invitation which will involve an exciting trip, accept it without thinking twice; you are unlikely to be sorry. Important mental journeys are also foreseen. Learning a new subject is sure to be stimulating. A lecture on an unusual subject is likely to be mind-provoking. Friends and acquaintances may inspire you to break out of a rut. If you are involved in property negotiations of any kind, there should be some encouraging news concerning a recent offer. If you wait much longer, you are apt to lose out.

4. SATURDAY. Variable. Take it slow and easy. Do not worry if you have a cash shortage problem. An opportunity to earn extra money is likely to come your way. This is an especially helpful day for Gemini people working to raise funds for a good cause. In addition to collecting money, you may want to give more freely than usual to those in need, so long as you can afford to do so. Your efforts are apt to be repaid in full measure in a rather indirect way. If you are thinking about purchasing property, there is a good chance that you can negotiate a favorable deal for a site you view today. Be sure to work with a reputable agent who is skilled at bargaining.

5. SUNDAY. Rewarding. Get an early start. You should be able to make some solid financial and material gains. Once again there could be a new earning opportunity coming your way. This development should be especially encouraging if you have been temporarily out of work. If you recently went on an interview for a job, you can almost count on being offered the position. An investment made some time ago may begin to pay off now. News is also possible about an inheritance or a financial prize. If you have a special talent, you may be able to turn it into a money-making sideline by streamlining your methods and marketing aggressively.

6. MONDAY. Mixed. You may be quite perturbed this morning by worrying news which comes to you by word of mouth. This is one of those days when you cannot easily cast concerns aside and put on a brave face. Go over the facts with the individual who has informed you. It is possible that some of the news has been exaggerated or misstated. If the facts remain the same, you probably have to make some changes to your existing plans. Turn to your mate or partner for the advice or comfort you need. A loved one's intuitive sense of how best to help is bound to be reassuring to you. Try to focus on what is happening now; do not think too far ahead.

7. TUESDAY. Manageable. Spend more time making use of the various facilities available to you locally. The library can be especially helpful. The social scene should be quite enjoyable and exciting. Accept an invitation to a neighbor or relative's party. You may think that the get-together will be a bit boring, but you could be very pleasantly surprised. You and your mate or partner are likely to get along particularly well if you go out together. Be prepared for minor changes of plan. Do not dwell upon a disappointment in respect to your personal life. Chances are there are much better opportunities for you just around the corner. Do not neglect scheduling an appointment with your doctor or dentist for a checkup.

8. WEDNESDAY. Disconcerting. Expect ups and downs in relation to home and domestic matters. You and your partner may argue over a rather minor matter, probably because you are both under a lot of pressure from outside activities. Try to lighten up and not take life quite so seriously. It is vital to think before you speak, especially when you are angry. In this way you can avoid needless bickering. If you are thinking about moving, this is not the best day to view properties together. You and your loved one can expect to have difficulty seeing eye-to-eye about even little things, much less a major relocation. If you are trying to sell, you may be in for a piece of luck with a potential buyer.

9. THURSDAY. Useful. This should be a more peaceful day where family and domestic matters are concerned. Unlike yesterday, you can expect to have more success if viewing property for sale or rent. It is likely that you will come across a home which is a genuine bargain because the current owners need to sell in a hurry. If you are still trying to sell your own property, you may not make much progress today. A viewing may be canceled because the people have found another property to buy. Do not be disheartened; a buyer will come along soon. Guard against trusting someone who claims to be acting for your own good.

10. FRIDAY. Successful. Property or other negotiations are likely to take up a lot of your time. There is a good chance of a solid offer coming your way. If you are negotiating to buy someone else's property, your offer will probably be accepted so long as you are not trying to get the price dropped beyond a reasonable level. This is a favorable day for catching up on errands and for purchasing routine items. Spend as much time as necessary settling meeting arrangements and social plans. It is likely that you will meet someone from a distance who inspires you. Reassuring news in relation to behind-the-scenes developments is likely at long last, but do not bank on it quite yet.

11. SATURDAY. Enjoyable. Enjoy leisure pursuits which you do not have much time for during the workweek. Do not just rely on tried-and-true pastimes, though. This is a favorable day for trying something new and somewhat daring. If you are looking for an exciting and invigorating hobby to take up, consider water sports. A friend who is involved in boating or snorkeling should be able to give you some worthwhile advice and even a few beginner lessons. You may have an urge to get more involved in spiritual matters as you continue your search for the sense of life's meaning in general.

12. SUNDAY. Satisfactory. It is likely that a number of social invitations are coming your way. Make the most of whatever free time you have to spare. If you have children at home and they seem bored, introduce them to games you used to play as a child which do not need any special equipment. On a long journey, games can help break the tedium for adults as well as restless youngsters. If you leave your children with a relative or neighbor who does not have children at home, do not forget to provide them with toys. If you have the chance to include children in a social event, they will probably love the grown-up experience and make you proud of their behavior.

13. MONDAY. Confusing. If instructions, particularly those relating to work, are confused or unclear, double-check what is required and when it needs to be done. It is not a good idea to simply go ahead with information which may be incorrect or which you may have misconstrued. Busy Gemini people who are being presented with a whole new pile of work may find it difficult to know where to start. Take time before you start to establish just what is going to be involved. It is probably best to begin with the most difficult task and work your way down to the easiest, especially if you have a strict time commitment. Strive to do an adequate job in the time allotted rather than perfect work way past the deadline.

14. TUESDAY. Slow. You are likely to feel uncharacteristically tired and sluggish. This may be the result of your recent erratic workload, up to your eyeballs in work one day and sitting around twiddling your thumbs the next. Keep a low profile; do not volunteer for anything. Try to take life easy. You should make just as good progress in the long run if you plod through diligently rather than starting out in a rush and then fading fast and having to stop for a lengthy break. Although there is pleasant mail on the way, it may not contain the key information that you are waiting to hear. A phone call could ease any concerns you now have.

15. WEDNESDAY. Challenging. This is likely to be a particularly productive day where work and professional matters are concerned. For Gemini people who have been out of work, this is a key time for pushing ahead with plans to find a new job. Try another employment agency if the one you signed with has not been coming up with much. Make more of an effort to finalize social and business arrangements. Meetings which take place should be especially helpful, allowing you to bring key matters to an agreeable conclusion. Spend time exclusively with your mate or partner this evening. For single Geminis, someone new may just knock on the door unannounced.

16. THURSDAY. Changeable. For one reason or another, your partner or a co-worker is likely to be quite hard to get along with. It may be that this person is suddenly under more personal pressure and is taking it out on you. Whatever the reason, expect a temper outburst to be potentially explosive. The best thing to do is be very careful about what you say. Avoid talking about matters which you know can cause an eruption. Although you may be able to take a joke without a problem, keep in mind that some people lose their entire sense of humor when under stress. This is not a day for poking fun at anyone, and there is never a time for making any type of racial or ethnic joke.

17. FRIDAY. Easygoing. This should be a much more simple and straightforward day in your relationship with your partner and co-workers. The rapport between you is likely to be a lot smoother. Whatever pressures were interfering with your communication yesterday should have passed by now. It should be a lot easier to converse without worrying about what subject to discuss or how to phrase your thoughts. Spend some time out socially this evening if you can. There may be pleasant invitations from a neighbor or friend. Single Gemini people should also be open to an invitation that might lead to meeting a local person with whom the attraction is instant and mutual.

18. SATURDAY. Mixed. Avoid taking any type of wild risk. Avoiding gambling is vital. A lot of money could slip away from you before you know it if you make even a friendly wager. The line between borrowing in order to cover your expenses and getting into major debt is very fine. Important discussions relating to a loan are likely, although not necessarily for the wrong reasons. If you are hoping to convince your bank that you are in a strong enough position to take on a hefty loan, first be sure that you are convinced. Do some in-depth, long-term budgeting to see how much you can afford to repay on a monthly basis.

19. SUNDAY. Fortunate. A joint financial matter can be successfully settled. News you receive in relation to money matters should be generally reassuring. This is a favorable day for pooling resources with other people, which should add strength to everyone's position. Sharing what you buy in bulk can save everyone a lot of money. A kind and charitable offer may come your way. If it would help and you do not feel you would be taking advantage, accept it gratefully. It is unlikely that anyone who cares about you wants to see you go without life's necessities. If you have some money in the bank, offer a loan to a friend who you know is in financial straits right now.

20. MONDAY. Uncertain. There are likely to be some positive movements and developments in relation to property matters. You should feel quite encouraged by them and ready to move forward. An exchange of contracts should go though without a hitch. If you are looking for property to buy, there is a strong possibility that you will view somewhere ideal in terms of space and at the right price. If you are trying to sell, a buyer may appear even if you do not expect this to happen so soon. In all affairs, try to keep an open mind; much can and will change between now and the end of the week.

21. TUESDAY. Good. Take speedy advantage of an opportunity to broaden your horizons. You could do with more excitement in your everyday life. Do not be surprised, however, if excitement comes in bundles at the moment. After a while you could even start to feel overwhelmed by all the possibilities opening up to you. Try to pick and choose thoughtfully. There is probably time enough for all that you want to do. Much as it is in your Gemini nature to start by doing two things at once, a more focused approach is a better idea. If you are tired, take life easy tonight instead of going out or working late. Getting some decent rest should be your priority this evening, not entertaining or being entertained.

22. WEDNESDAY. Disquieting. Try to get out of making a long-distance trip if at all possible. It is likely that overnight travel will make you very tired for longer than you expect. If you must go, at least allow yourself some extra time to relax and unwind afterwards. It is best to keep specific arrangements to a minimum. If your boss or other higher-ups do not tend to follow this philosophy, it does not mean that you necessarily have to follow suit. Where future plans are concerned, focus on what is scheduled for the remainder of the week; put future plans out of mind for now. Much can change, and it may be difficult to imagine how things will actually turn out.

23. THURSDAY. Buoyant. It is likely that you can make excellent headway with a professional project. Focus on behind-the-scenes involvement. This is where you should be able to make your best progress. If cooperation from colleagues or clients is not easy to obtain at the moment, it may just be that they need more time to get used to the adjustments you are trying to make. It is also possible, however, that you have a genuine adversary in your midst at the moment. Professional jealousy is likely to be the cause of the problem. Do not allow this to deter you from trying to carry out your plans. If one idea does not work out, have another one ready to implement without delay.

24. FRIDAY. Exciting. Arguments can quite easily develop on the job. Do not worry too much about initial opposition to your ideas from a boss or colleague, however. It is likely that out of current conflict will come some form of creative resolution. A number of outstanding matters can be brought to a satisfactory conclusion today, probably rather unexpectedly. Where romantic matters are concerned, this evening is likely to be more passionate and magical if you and your loved one opt for a change of scene. The same is true for single Gemini men and women who are looking for love. It can pay to be a little more aggressive than usual in pursuing someone of the opposite sex.

25. SATURDAY. Pleasant. An opportunity arises for an outing with friends or acquaintances; the trip is likely to be inspiring.

Places of historical interest may be worth a visit if you have the time to go with an informed guide. Keep your guard up with an associate of the opposite sex whom you do not know all that well. Any unexpected invitation, particularly one made late at night, may not be as innocent as it first seems. Some people are unable to admit their true intentions. It is in your best interests to be a little more cynical and a little less trusting, at least for today. Do more listening than talking no matter who you are with this evening.

26. SUNDAY. Fair. This is a favorable day for hosting a social gathering in your home. Get your partner more involved, particularly if a new love has not met all of your friends. It is likely that they will get along extremely well. This is also a favorable time for getting to know a new neighbor. Try to get tedious chores done quickly and out of the way. Working as part of a team with the rest of the family can save time and make the work less boring. Ask people to help you out if you are preparing for a party. If you wait for them to volunteer, you may never get the help you need. It is important to enjoy your own party.

27. MONDAY. Mixed. Spend quiet time alone. Give yourself a chance to collect your thoughts before you start making any more plans. If solitude is hard to find in your usual surroundings, go off somewhere, where you know you will not be disturbed. A trip to the library could be just the ticket. If you are planning a long journey to visit a famous site, make a point of checking when it is open to the public. Seasonal variations may mean that some places have a reduced staff or have closed after the summer tourist season. Do not put off buying tickets for a plane or train trip later this year.

28. TUESDAY. Unpredictable. This is one of those days when it is difficult to feel entirely content with life because so much is changing around you. A series of upheavals all taking place at the same time can be a temporary burden. One of the best solutions is to spend more time with those people who make you feel particularly comfortable. Time spent with your parents or another older relative, if you get along well, is likely to help you to feel more secure and settled. It is also a good idea to do quiet things which you find relaxing and calming. Exercise, too, can be a good way to release stress and reduce anxiety. Be very selective in what you eat; avoid spicy food.

29. WEDNESDAY. Satisfactory. Be prepared to do a lot of chasing around, running errands and catching up with people from whom you need a favor or an explanation. Also take some time out to catch your breath or you are likely to end up wearing yourself out. Someone whose company you enjoy may pay a surprise visit. This should be a pleasant diversion from having to attend to routine work. Do not be tempted to get too wrapped up in conversation, however, if you have urgent matters demanding attention. It is possible that a well-meaning visitor may overstay their welcome unless you make it crystal clear that you really do not have much time to spare at the moment. Make a date to go out for lunch or dinner together at a more convenient time.

30. THURSDAY. Changeable. You need to attend to your more personal affairs, but be careful how you convey your intentions to other people. If they feel that you are not considering them, or are somehow neglecting the relationship, a cold or angry response is likely. If you are in the limelight socially, your partner could become quite jealous. Although none of these problems stem directly from you, you may nevertheless be blamed for creating disharmony. You may have to make a choice between being manipulated or asserting your independence. What you have to decide is what you stand to lose with each of those options, and which is best for you individually.

OCTOBER

1. FRIDAY. Fortunate. Concentrate on making progress with plans which are special to you personally. Where your social life is concerned, this promises to be an interesting and delightful day. A number of pleasant invitations are coming your way. Your only real dilemma is which to accept and which to regretfully turn down. A money-earning opportunity related to one of your special talents is likely to come along. Someone you know may encourage you in this respect out of respect for your abilities. If your mate or partner always does the cooking at home, take over this evening as chef and chief bottle-washer. You could turn out to be quite gifted and enjoy the creativity of cooking.

2. SATURDAY. Unsettling. This is one of those days when you may have some regrets about money that you have spent without much thought. Or you may have actually thought about it at the time but managed to convince yourself that it would not really matter. Now is the time to face the music. Cut back on luxury spending for a while in order to bolster up the family bank account. If you have debts to pay off, check exactly where you stand. Credit card bills which you are not paying in full each month could be costing you more interest than you realize. Look for a way to clear the debt as quickly as possible, perhaps by bringing your lunch to work instead of eating out.

3. SUNDAY. Variable. This is another potentially worrying day where financial matters are concerned. Various people, from sales assistants to friends, may try to talk you into spending more than you can afford. With friends it may be particularly difficult to say no, but you probably need to do so in your own best interests. If you have a tendency to get carried away after a few glasses of wine, or in the excitement of an auction, abstain. You should still be able to have a pleasant time socially. It does not have to cost a lot to have fun. Check today's newspaper for upcoming free events close to home.

4. MONDAY. Successful. This should be an active, sociable day because you are likely to be in a particularly outgoing mood. Spend as much time as possible with your mate or partner. There should be harmony at work and at home. You will probably shine at a social function. For single Gemini people, this is a day for expanding your social connections. If you are attracted to a friend of a friend, let someone know who may be able to drop a subtle hint or do some scouting on your behalf. Team efforts at work are the key to greater success. Many hands definitely make light work. Be willing to let someone else take charge for a change.

5. TUESDAY. Rewarding. You are likely to receive some interesting mail or even a gift through the mail. Be willing to change your plans on short notice. This is a favorable day for taking more initiative in contacting people in order to arrange a get-together. Get in touch with current or former work associates if you have a new business proposition in mind; you are likely to receive a positive response from them. You can excel at matchmaking on the social scene. Arrange to seat two compatible, single friends together at a party or even in a carpool. Once you become involved in a group activity with family members or friends you will soon be swept up by it.

6. WEDNESDAY. Mixed. Concentrate on getting things done around the house, particularly if you are falling behind with routine chores. This is a good time to initiate an important do-it-yourself project. As a Gemini you have an especially keen eye for unusual decorative features and clever color schemes. If you have a small room to decorate, you may be able to make it look larger through a careful balance of scale and light. Look through a few books or magazines on the subject. Make time for your private plans as well. Ideas for the future are better formulated when you are in a relaxed state of mind. Leave your mate or partner to their own devices this evening.

7. THURSDAY. Cautious. Your home life should be calm and peaceful since your mate or partner is likely to have sorted out a few problems and finally reached a decision. If overwork has been the problem, a decent night's sleep should solve it. There are likely to be positive developments in relation to property matters. If you have been patiently waiting for a buyer to come along, your patience may now be rewarded. This is also a starred time to buy a new home or the land on which to build. Ongoing negotiations which have dragged on for some time are now reaching a point of settlement. Be careful how you phrase your feelings to a sensitive love partner this evening.

8. FRIDAY. Easy. If you have the opportunity to take a trip, do so. You are particularly likely to enjoy a day spent on or near water and may even get involved in water sports. You are sure to benefit from a pleasant change of scene. For single Gemini men and women, there is a strong likelihood of meeting someone appealing if you socialize in relation to academic or sports interests. If you are ready to settle down in a permanent relationship, be the romantic pursuer. If you like the idea of being with someone with a clever intellect, go to a college function or attend a lecture and socialize afterwards.

9. SATURDAY. Enjoyable. Take advantage of an invitation to a pleasant and perhaps unusual social trip. Traveling as part of a group can help keep the costs lower. A day trip to a historical destination which is not too far away could be quite exciting. A friend may have complimentary tickets to a cultural event and invite you along. If you know someone who often has tickets to the hot event in town, it might be worth calling to see if they are looking for some company. If you are at loose ends, a night at the theater or opera could be quite inspiring even if you go alone. Do not stay home waiting for the phone to ring.

10. SUNDAY. Easygoing. Make room and time to add more romance and passion in your relationship with your love partner. Lessened tension because there has been a chance to recuperate from work pressures should create plenty of positive energy between you. Put off backbreaking tasks until a day when you have more stamina. You may find it difficult to concentrate on anything intricate as well. Your mind is apt to be more on the future than the present. This may not matter if you and your loved one are making plans together, but be careful not to drift into the realm of the impossible. For single Gemini people this is a day for worrying less about being unattached; enjoy the freedom.

11. MONDAY. Challenging. Expect a more industrious time on the work scene. It should be fairly easy to get a long-standing project finished. Communication with both colleagues and clients should be simpler and more harmonious thanks to your current optimistic frame of mind. The only trouble may be unexpected changes of plan. Fortunately, as a Gemini you are gifted at adapting at short notice. There should not be much that you cannot somehow work around or accommodate. However, be sure to avoid double booking yourself, which may be all too easy if you do not check your calendar before making a social or work commitment. The pieces of a puzzle are likely to start coming together, helping you clarify the way to proceed.

12. TUESDAY. Quiet. Take advantage of this quiet day to concentrate on organizing future plans. If there is room for improvement in a particular area, work at instigating changes. Where your health is concerned, this is an ideal time to improve your physical fitness. Consider changing the type of exercise you do if you have reached a plateau. If you are trying to lose weight, you may have more success if you increase your amount of exercise. Catch up on neglected matters in your work life. If temporarily out of work, contact previous colleagues in relation to possible job opportunities that they may know of. Also consider becoming self-employed.

13. WEDNESDAY. Happy. Your partner is likely to have some good fortune today, and you may be in receipt of a pleasant surprise as a result. There is opportunity to be closer than you have been lately. Dinner and dancing is the ideal outing for bringing you together. If your home looks cluttered, find time to clear away the piles and put things where they belong. If there is one area that you and your loved one are likely to argue about, it is lack of neatness and organization. Single Gemini people can make a strong emotional link with someone who is a friend of a friend, but guard against interfering in an ongoing relationship.

14. THURSDAY. Changeable. Extra kindness and generosity is present in your life thanks to other people. Individuals you have thought of as quite uncaring or self-centered may surprise you by their compassion. For them, it is probably related to a feeling of duty to help when someone is genuinely needy. There is good opportunity to expand your personal horizons through group or club connections. You may be drawn to taking a stronger personal interest in matters relating to the care of your local environment and community. Charitable work is apt to be more rewarding than you expect; do not hesitate to volunteer.

15. FRIDAY. Sensitive. Take advantage of the stronger position of your partner. Allow someone close to you to take more initiative and be more assertive in regard to joint decisions that count. If there is an item you have considered returning to the store because it is faulty, do not be dissuaded because the task irritates or embarrasses you. It is quite possible that your loved one or a friend is willing to accept the errand and will be successful at obtaining a refund. This is no time for playing games in a close relationship; you will tend to come out the loser unless you are honest and straightforward in expressing your needs.

16. SATURDAY. Slow. If you have something important to do this weekend, you are likely to make better progress if you arrange a joint effort. This is especially important where practical tasks are concerned. An opportunity may come your way to use a special talent to make some extra money. If this becomes a regular enterprise, you should be able to resolve any financial difficulties in a much shorter time than you expected. If you are considering part-time work, look into jobs related to beauty, health, and nutrition as well as food supply. Providing a needed service can be especially profitable.

17. SUNDAY. Sensitive. Be a little more careful than usual with money. Try to avoid impulse spending. It can be tempting in the supermarket to add a few magazines and other impulse items to your shopping cart, but you can probably get by quite happily without these. If you are tempted to squander your money in a bigger way, think twice. A pricey gift designed to impress the recipient may not be appreciated as much as something simple such as a bouquet of flowers or an invitation to a home-cooked dinner. Aim for a sincere and emotional expression of your feelings rather than a demonstration via material presents. Reserve the latter for big occasions such as birthdays or significant anniversaries. Get to bed early tonight.

18. MONDAY. Stressful. Having to drive a long time in order to complete a journey is likely to make you very tired. Stop for frequent breaks; a bite to eat and a glass of juice should help pep up your energy. People at or from a distance may not be as agreeable as you hope. If you have lately been missing out on sleep or sleeping fitfully, perhaps due to living it up more at the weekend, this may start to catch up with you now. Aim for another early night if possible. Sharing tasks with others should help reduce the burden. Your loved one will probably be more supportive without even being asked, but children may have to be prompted to help out at home.

19. TUESDAY. Disquieting. Sometimes life can seem like one big upheaval, and this is one of those days. It is a time for expecting the unexpected. You may be required to drop everything and make a long trip in order to help someone. If you have use of a portable telephone, you may start wishing that you were not so readily available. If called away from an important meeting, be sure to get someone to take notes for you or ask them to brief you fully later. What goes into the minutes of meetings does not always adequately express what actually took place. Focus on a minimum of tasks so that any disruption seems less bothersome. Avoid making any new commitments.

20. WEDNESDAY. Exciting. This is a propitious day for Gemini people involved in legal issues of any kind. In your personal life, a pleasant surprise is coming your way. Your loved one may have organized a trip for the two of you. An unexpected bottle of champagne for a minor celebration could be a nice bonus. For single Gemini people, this is a day for taking more initiative in romantic matters. In your professional life there is likely to be an increase in your workload and responsibility. If you are seeking to prove your suitability for a promotion, taking on additional work could be just what you need to impress higher-ups.

21. THURSDAY. Variable. You could be the subject of a certain degree of professional jealousy at work but not be aware of it. If you have been playing up to superiors and ignoring other staff members, your colleagues may start to wonder if a pending promotion has been earned. If your conscience is clear, you probably have nothing to worry about in the long term; the matter will eventually blow over. If this is not the case, however, question your own motives both in your personal and career life. Think about the future. Consider planning your next job move based on your special talents and pleasures rather than the monetary rewards.

22. FRIDAY. Rewarding. This should be a useful day for advancing your career. Discussions with higher-ups can lead to a greater appreciation of your skills and values by your superiors. Certain practical actions must be done now before you can be offered a promotion. For Gemini people who have been out of work, a temporary opportunity is likely which could lead to a more permanent position in the future. In this way you will have the chance to prove your capabilities right from the start. Spend this evening in the company of people you know and like. Avoid strangers or you could wind up feeling lonely even in a crowd.

23. SATURDAY. Disappointing. It is inadvisable to try to combine business with pleasure. If you are going to a party at a friend's home, keep a low profile. Do not discuss your work or any personal problem. A work associate may want to get you involved in a dubious business scheme. Fortunately, you are likely to know more about the matter than they do and will be able to advise them to back off. This is not a day for being overly generous with your time or money. Whatever problems you need to solve at the moment, your partner or an older family member can help if you are willing to seek their assistance.

24. SUNDAY. Changeable. Finding time alone should not be a problem. In fact, you could actually end up in the lurch if someone lets you down at the last minute. However, much that is useful can be done in your unexpected spare time. If your partner is having to spend time away from home, take advantage of the opportunity to focus on your own individual plans. If you do feel lonely at some point in the day, telephone people you do not often get a chance to chat with leisurely. This is also a good time for catching up with your correspondence. Stay in touch by letter or e-mail with a friend who recently moved. Make time to simply relax and unwind, too.

25. MONDAY. Demanding. You can make the most significant progress at work if you stay behind the scenes. Where business matters are concerned, a profitable option may come your way. Look into the matter in greater depth to ensure that everything is aboveboard. If you get involved in an underhanded deal, it could prove to be a problem later on. It is imprudent to commit yourself to a long-term proposition where you cannot openly declare your income or reveal the kind of work you do. Expect disruptions to your basic routine. Be gracious but firm with uninvited visitors. Time is too valuable to waste in idle chitchat.

26. TUESDAY. Mixed. Spend most of today catching up with neglected tasks. Be prepared, however, for a number of interruptions which are apt to delay your progress. This is likely to be a much busier day than you expect. There may be more meetings to attend, more telephone inquiries to answer, and more research to do than you scheduled. Certain individuals may try to push their way into your life by a personal appearance, uninvited and unannounced. However pressing their pleas for help may be, it is important to ensure that your more vital matters are not neglected, particularly critical correspondence. Also be certain to pay bills before the due date.

27. WEDNESDAY. Stressful. Your mate or partner may go overboard emotionally, perhaps due to jealously in regard to recent success you experienced. Do not allow this to detract from your own feelings of satisfaction with your efforts. If you are the center of attention in a social situation, your loved one may be irritable about this, too. In some ways, it is a no-win situation. If you deny yourself, you will feel frustrated; if you enjoy the attention, you will upset your partner. Do not fall prey to emotional blackmail. By yielding to manipulation even once, you could be setting yourself up for a repeat performance in the future.

28. THURSDAY. Frustrating. Be prepared to put in more effort in order to be able to finalize social arrangements. It could be difficult to pin other people down to a definite time or place. It is in your interests to have a number of different ideas to suggest. If you are not making much progress with one in particular, at least you can change tactics and switch to something else. Friends are likely to be extra supportive. If you need to discuss some of your more personal affairs, talk with someone who has gone through a similar dilemma in the past. Experience can make this person a wonderful adviser if you want specific help or just a good listener if you only need to unload your feelings.

29. FRIDAY. Fair. This should be a fortunate day where financial and occupational matters are concerned. Stay close to the phone. An offer of well paid work is apt to come your way. If you have been out of work, this offer could come just in the nick of time.

For Gemini people already working but struggling to make financial ends meet, a new offer could be a real answer to your problem. Use your initiative to create more opportunities for yourself, particularly if you are self-employed. Look into alternative marketing strategies in order to attract a different type of customer. Keep an eye on your wallet if you go out this evening; do not carry too much cash.

30. SATURDAY. Variable. This is a favorable day to shop for special items for your home. If you have saved up to buy with cash, so much the better. It should be thoroughly satisfying to spend your hard-earned money on something which will give you long-term pleasure. A time-saving gadget which will enable you to have more spare time is also a worthwhile investment. If you feel that you are squandering money on a certain hobby, consider cutting back in favor of something you value more. If you are susceptible to spending too much on mail order products, ask the companies to take you off their mailing list or just throw away the catalogs without glancing at them.

31. SUNDAY. Disquieting. On this fairly busy day you may be in the mood to get a lot done, particularly around the house. If domestic tasks had to go by the wayside lately, you are apt to feel less in control. While it is a good idea to try to catch up, do not overdo it. Basic rest and relaxation are also important for your well-being. An interesting invitation that comes your way today may involve extensive travel that could be so time consuming you decide not to accept. As an alternative, it may be possible to arrange a get-together for the future when you have less to deal with. A former neighbor may get in touch to discuss their plans to return to the community.

NOVEMBER

1. MONDAY. Calm. Spend some time sorting out correspondence and firming up arrangements relating to work matters. There should also be more opportunity to get organized in your social life. Catch up on news with friends and relatives. Do not neglect your car. This is the ideal time to get a routine maintenance check. If you have not had time for a while to wash and wax it, try to find time now. You may have to make a difficult choice later in the day that is sure to delight one person or group while disappointing another. In making up your mind, please yourself since you cannot possibly please everyone else.

2. TUESDAY. Variable. Increased contact from friends and acquaintances is likely. There may be an interesting invitation or offer. One particular person could need some particular help from you. Lend a listening ear; offer advice only if you are specifically asked. Sometimes people just need to talk, either because they are confused or because they are feeling on top of the world. It is all too easy to criticize others for their errors, but a more charitable approach is probably required now. Think back to occasions when friends have been kind in helping you out during a time of need. A personal relationship is reaching a new stage; gear up for some changes.

3. WEDNESDAY. Useful. An increased pace of developments is likely in property negotiations. If you are looking to buy, it is likely that more than one interesting property will be brought to your attention. What is offered is apt to be affordable for you. If you are renting and need to move in a hurry, pull out all the stops in order to find a new place. It is possible that a suitable home will become available through your association with friends or relatives. Check the local newspaper as well; renting or buying direct rather than through an agent can save you a lot.

4. THURSDAY. Excellent. Your home and family life should be particularly content and fulfilling. For restless Gemini people wanting to move, reassuring developments mean that you can relax and look forward to greater security. Where relationships are concerned, a romantic gesture is foreseen. For single Gemini men and women, a friend of a friend who you recently met a party may get in touch. This person may have gone to special trouble to obtain your telephone number. Married Gemini people need to speak openly about feelings, hopes, and wishes. Do not expect your partner to read your mind.

5. FRIDAY. Lively. Spend more time with your loved one to increase the level of understanding between you. Leisure activities are sure to be more enjoyable if you share them with someone you love. Today has the potential for being truly romantic thanks to a change of scene from your usual surroundings. Traveling could also bring love into the lives of single Gemini men and women. Where money matters are concerned, it is advisable to avoid making rash choices. Take the time to consider your overall budget and weigh your decisions carefully, then shop around for the best deal. Do not buy higher quality than you actually need.

6. SATURDAY. Difficult. Spend more time in the company of friends whose company you particularly enjoy. You are likely to have a mutually beneficial effect on each other, especially when it comes to seeing life from a less serious perspective. Be careful not to go overboard in any respect. As a Gemini you tend to overdo things when other people are around, perhaps due to their own tendencies toward excess. If you are planning on driving your vehicle, keep your alcohol intake to a minimum. Sports activities should be invigorating so long as every player manages to maintain a sense of humor about the outcome. Play for the fun of it; win or lose, you can have a good time.

7. SUNDAY. Uncertain. Expect a day of considerable upheaval for one reason or another. A chaotic or confused start on your part will not help your overall mood. Today should be slightly better if you have a number of alternative plans in mind. Be prepared for possible last-minute changes created by other people. You may have to begin adjusting your long-range plans as well. Avoid making many major decisions until and unless you are in full possession of the facts. It is likely that you need to know more about a particular situation before drawing any final conclusions or making any firm arrangements. Someone may question your motives or methods, then not believe your response. It is better to say as little as possible.

8. MONDAY. Sensitive. Get into work which you usually consider to be dull. Long, slow plodding along may be the only useful approach to take. It is better to make a start as early in the day as possible. Expect most of your progress to be gradual, especially where routine matters are concerned. A boss is likely to be more sensitive to your needs if you are both trying to get through a pile of work. It is vital, however, to get your timing right if you want to request a favor. If a few minor loose ends can be tied up another day, it is just as well to leave the matter until then. Go along to get along is the motto of the day.

9. TUESDAY. Exciting. You need to make time to sit down and have a talk with your mate or partner in regard to specific matters that are beginning to get on your nerves. Or it may simply be that you need to spend time together discussing your future plans. There is a strong possibility that this time with your loved one will lead to a romantic interlude, especially if you have not been in each other's company lately. For single Gemini people, this evening may bring a romantic encounter via a social event related to your academic interests or to a special hobby. Go out of your way to reassure a family member who recently made a dramatic decision; there is no turning back now.

10. WEDNESDAY. Happy. Increased intensity in each and every one of your closer relationships is likely. For married Gemini people who feel in a rut, now is the time to do something to improve the situation. A change of scene, even for a day, may be part of the answer. Being more broad-minded is likely to be helpful. Gemini men and women who have recently become involved in a new relationship can look forward to passion and romance. Even though you are in the early stage, it is possible that you will both want to discuss the possibility of a long-term commitment. This is also a starred day to buy or adopt a pet.

11. THURSDAY. Satisfactory. Somebody you have regarded as an enemy, or someone with whom you have had a major falling out, may now make an effort to be more charitable toward you. Although the approach is apt to be indirect, it should be clear that this person's heart is in the right place. Do something generous in return and the relationship is likely to be healed for good. Promising news is coming your way in relation to work matters. An advantageous promotion may be offered to you or a bonus for extra work. Your love life is likely to again be close and intimate. Show that special person just how much you care.

12. FRIDAY. Variable. You have to work hard to keep your money. It is not so much the risk of a pickpocket but the temptation of luxury goods and special offers which presents a problem. If you are shopping for a present for another person, however, you can take advantage of advertised bargains. Before finalizing a business proposition, it would be wise to look below the surface and find out more about your potential partners. It is likely that some key fact has not been openly revealed. Prepare to have to spend more money for an upcoming social occasion. It is important to keep up your appearance so that you feel good about yourself. Going out in a group is favored tonight rather than a twosome.

13. SATURDAY. Mixed. This is a fortunate day for money matters if you can manage to juggle your finances a bit. An investment made some time ago may start to pay off now. If you feel that adjustments need to be made to the family budget, go off somewhere quiet in order to concentrate on the details. Give some though to your current objectives and your long-term plans. If you are trying to save for a special purchase, shop around for the best return on your savings. Guard against using your credit card to the max; give yourself some leeway in case you have to use it in an emergency situation.

14. SUNDAY. Unsettling. This is a key day for discussions relating to joint financial and property matters. It is possible that there will be a delay in a contract being signed, but this does not necessarily mean that all is lost. A certain individual may just need more time to thoroughly read through the small print. If you have not already studied a legally binding document you have to sign, now is the time for it. If you are going to have to undertake a long-distance trip, expect to be on the road longer than you expect. Take some food and drink with you to keep your energy level high. Get to bed earlier than usual.

15. MONDAY. Fair. There may be an opportunity to obtain additional work-related education or training, perhaps paid for by your employer. Do not worry about being left behind in a new subject. Progress is likely to be easier if you are part of a team. Those with a faster capacity to handle a particular subject can help you, and at another stage you may be able to make a subject clear to them. Your working life is likely to be busy and active. There are apt to be a number of meetings to attend in order to make important decisions relating to the future. Be guided by your own good Gemini judgment. What seems complicated today may be commonplace tomorrow.

16. TUESDAY. Manageable. You are likely to be battling against time due to increased traffic delays and slow mail. It is best to allow yourself more time even for quite minor projects. If you are waiting for an important phone call, do not hold your breath. Mixups in relation to communications are also likely. It is in your best interests to do some checking up, however. An item which has been promised to you may not have even been sent yet. More patience is also required in relation to meetings, which will probably drag on longer than you expect. Patience should help you manage any situation.

17. WEDNESDAY. Challenging. New developments relating to your professional life are sure to keep you on your toes. It is likely that you have a lot of work to plod through. It may be quite difficult to bring negotiations to a simple, fast close. Instead, such matters have to be gone into in greater depth to satisfy all participants. New clients may wish to see more written evidence of your company's success or of your own prior achievements. It could take a while to track down all the information you need. For Gemini people who have been temporarily out of work, this is a favorable time for going back over old ground to be sure your application is still considered active.

18. THURSDAY. Favorable. This is a favorable day for negotiations of all kinds, but especially those relating to career development. This is also a key time for floating your ideas at work. You should be able to implement a number of new methods and strategies without too much resistance. Higher-ups are likely to back you in connection with promotion prospects and applications. An opportunity to become self-employed in a joint business enterprise could be quite advantageous. Take time, however, to consider just what you will be involved in changing the nature of your employment. Be sure to confer with family members, too, in order to gauge their feelings.

19. FRIDAY. Good. Certain members of your social circle are likely to be influential in helping you broaden your horizons in some special way. If you are planning to study a new subject, opt for a group class rather than individual tutoring. In a group learning should be easier and the cost will probably be less. If a problem has been troubling you for a while, consider getting some counseling. Group therapy is likely to be a useful option. If you cannot really afford to go out with friends this evening, come up with a reasonable excuse so that no one is embarrassed. If you reveal your true reason you could then be invited as someone's guest and become obligated to them.

20. SATURDAY. Disquieting. One of your friendships may develop some complications, perhaps because you or the other person is experiencing more romantic feelings than you care to admit. It is also likely that one of you only wants a platonic relationship. The whole issue is likely to come to a head now, giving you an opportunity to at least make some sort of a decision. An opportunity to travel to an exciting destination could come your way. A number of opportunities which will allow you to broaden your horizons are likely through a club or group association. If the price is right for you, sign up immediately.

21. SUNDAY. Enjoyable. Spend as much time as possible with your special friends. Their company is sure to be uplifting. If you need a favor, there are willing hands ready and eager to help out. Someone who cares about you a lot may go far out of their way on your behalf. If you are thinking about returning to school to study an educational subject, you may have to trim down your aspirations due to the cost involved. The same applies with opportunities to travel. This does not mean, however, that you have to abandon your plans entirely. Put matters in perspective. Reading about a foreign country or getting to know some natives of that land can be a good substitute for now.

22. MONDAY. Stressful. You may be feeling less than on top of the world because you are a little physically run-down. This can encourage negative feelings affecting all of your activities. Focus on something that will relax. If you ate and drank too much last night, make an effort to drink more water in order to rehydrate your system. Sleep is likely to be one of the best cures of all, so aim to get to bed early tonight. Try to maintain a low profile at work if you are not feeling your best. Delegate as many responsibilities as possible to other people. If you have to travel, make it as easy on yourself as possible by using public transportation instead of driving.

23. TUESDAY. Changeable. You should be feeling in better form today. Take advantage of the quiet start to the day to relax and prepare for work on your schedule. The easier you take it this morning, the easier things will tend to be. Spend some time sorting out financial matters. An interesting business proposition may come your way, but weigh the likelihood of it providing hard cash in the first year or so. It is best to find out more about any new opportunity where you will be making a long-term commitment. Be careful not to offer assurances if you are actually unsure yourself. Someone may be relying on you more than you think, and you do not want to mislead them.

24. WEDNESDAY. Fortunate. Focus on your personal goals and ambitions. This is a time for being a little more adventurous. You can take well-calculated risks without fear of a disappointing outcome. Look to the long-term future as you explore the many possibilities open to you. The social scene is likely to appeal, especially an activity that is a little out of the ordinary. A friend could come up with a good suggestion for a night out. Beware of doing anything close to home which may lead to your feeling embarrassed at a later date. A raffle chance or a lottery ticket could be lucky for you, but do not spend the cash until you win it.

25. THURSDAY. Easygoing. This Thanksgiving holiday is favorable for sharing hopes and aspirations with the people close to you. Friends and relatives will be supportive. Look into a new offer that could give you the opportunity to extend your business and work interests and increase your profit. A special talent that you have been practicing could be turned into a lucrative enterprise with a little clever marketing. Do not allow letters, bills, and other correspondence to pile up. Make a point of replying without delay. This is a favorable day for making preliminary inquiries among your family members. They may be willing to offer just the help you need.

26. FRIDAY. Mixed. A financial bonus is likely, probably in relation to an investment you made a while ago. Other past efforts should also start to pay off now. This is an important time for considering your future plans in depth. If you want to improve your overall financial situation, consider options geared to produce a good rate of return over a long period of time. It is important to establish a sense of greater financial security. Expect your working life to be quite hectic. It may be necessary to call a meeting on a particularly difficult or pressing matter in order to make a joint decision. Gemini salespeople can expect to be extremely tired by the end of the day.

27. SATURDAY. Variable. Spend more time getting your basic priorities in order. Much has changed recently, and it is now important to reassess your goals. Look to the future without losing sight of urgent immediate matters. Any area which has been neglected for a long time probably deserves more attention now. If you are having difficulty resolving a problem, turn to friends or family members for help. Colleagues at work or neighbors may also have some useful suggestions and insights. If you are single, get out and socialize. A magnetic mutual attraction with someone new is likely, but not if you sit at home and wait for the phone to ring. Dress to attract attention.

28. SUNDAY. Disquieting. This promises to be a particularly busy day. It is in your best interests to try to avoid getting to the point where you are frantic about everything you have to do. Sit down for a moment and gather your thoughts. Expect to be moving around more as the day progresses. There may be a lot of errands to run and people to see. Organize ahead of time so that you manage several tasks in one location before moving on. Otherwise you could waste time traveling in circles. Look forward to an exciting evening with friends or that special person in your life, but do not make any long-term commitments to them.

29. MONDAY. Confusing. There is a whole array of options to choose from where your social interests are concerned. Your only problem may be deciding exactly what you want to do. Do not place too much importance on making the right decision. It is possible that you can have the best of both worlds by spreading activities over a longer period of time. Home and family matters are apt to be quite tense. Friction may develop with your mate or partner if you spend too much time cooped up together. You both need to have some space and time apart. A change of scene is likely to ease the situation. News from someone at a distance may need to be clarified; do not jump to any conclusions.

30. TUESDAY. Fair. Expect life to be more chaotic and prone to change. Even the best laid plans can be upset at the last minute. There are likely to be more visitors to your home or office and urgent telephone calls. If you are busy, you must get your priorities in order. It is a good idea to go off somewhere quiet where you will be better able to concentrate. If you are getting tired and cannot see matters clearly, take a break. A change of environment could provide you with a better perspective. Be prepared for a temporary, though not serious, breakdown in ongoing negotiations. Give in a little and you should get a lot in return.

DECEMBER

1. WEDNESDAY. Enjoyable. Romance is in the air. It could be worthwhile to invest in a large bunch of mistletoe to hang in a strategic spot. For married Gemini people there is opportunity for a very relaxed evening at home. And for single Gemini men and women there is the possibility of meeting someone through your social connections who is quite different from the usual date. This person could be particularly creative and imaginative. If you have a date planned for this evening, wear a special outfit in order to create the right impression. Trust a hunch, and follow it to its logical conclusion. Gemini intuition will not steer you wrong.

2. THURSDAY. Buoyant. This promises to be another particularly loving and affectionate day. Make more time to be with that special person in your life. A passionate encounter is likely for single Gemini men and women. If you feel that a new relationship is moving too quickly, it is in your best interests to say so. Do not try to disguise your feelings. Greater intimacy, even in friendships, should not be avoided. You are likely to have deep, intense conversations with people you know superficially. Much of what you discuss may be quite thought provoking. If you are in love, do not expect to be able to concentrate very well on work and other routine matters.

3. FRIDAY. Changeable. Be discriminating in what you decide to do with your leisure time. There are a lot of different opportunities available. Friends may try to steer you into something that you are not especially interested in. At risk of being a wet blanket, make another suggestion. If you feel too tired for certain kinds of activities, it is probably best to back out even if you have a regular commitment. Friends ought to be quite understanding, although they may have to hide their disappointment. It is better to follow your own initiative and work on developing your creative potential. What has been an enjoyable hobby could be turned into a profitable sideline for you.

4. SATURDAY. Disconcerting. Make a point of pinning people down in order to firm up social plans and arrangements that you have in mind. Someone who refuses to be specific about their availability should probably be written off, at least this time around. In this way you are not letting yourself in for too much disappointment if they end up canceling out at the last minute. Expect to have to do a lot of telephoning in order to get any significant results. It is important to find time for rest and relaxation. This is the weekend, after all; avoid becoming stressed out. Pamper your pet with a bath or grooming followed by playtime.

5. SUNDAY. Frustrating. Expect to make rather slow progress with routine and home-based tasks. It may be necessary to take a step back and begin with tasks which have been neglected for some time. Do not depend on your mate or other family members to help. This is one of those days when they need to be left to their own devices. Do not arrange too much around other people; they are apt to end up making unpredictable, last-minute moves that let you down. It may be annoying not being able to get a firm commitment for social arrangements. Try to relax more and do your own thing, relying on yourself for entertainment and recreational activities.

6. MONDAY. Successful. This is a much more favorable day than yesterday where communications and negotiations are concerned. Friends and colleagues are cooperative. You should be able to finally get in touch with someone you have had problems contacting and make some firm arrangements. In your work life, be careful not to get too caught up in details. It is all too easy to lose sight of the larger picture if you begin nitpicking minor matters. Results are likely to be more important than your methods. Try to pick up speed on work which is falling behind schedule, perhaps by enlisting outside help to handle a portion of it.

7. TUESDAY. Satisfactory. This is a favorable day for making new starts. If a personal or business relationship has become stale and routine, come up with changes which will help revitalize it. Partners are likely to be willing to try a different set of rules geared to improve your quality of living. Plans which were abandoned a while ago may be taken off the shelf and tried once again. Single Gemini men and women may meet someone new at a social event with whom there is instant rapport. You could get quite involved very quickly. This is a fortunate day if you have been waiting for an answer; you will like what you are told.

8. WEDNESDAY. Pleasant. This is the ideal day for enjoying a social gathering with good friends or colleagues. If you are in the mood to entertain, invite a varied mix of people. There should be good rapport generally. Delegate some of the social responsibilities to your mate or partner, who may be of more help than you expect. Let guests take the initiative in bringing up conversational subjects. In this way you can ensure that they have an enjoyable time. It is possible that a hobby which a friend participates in regularly interests you more now. Arrange to go along to a meeting or class with them in order to learn more about it.

9. THURSDAY. Cautious. Be careful with your money. Work out the exact amount of your recent spending and intended future purchases. If you are spending a lot on shopping for other people, it can be easy to lose track of just how much and on whom. If you intend to make an important purchase, shop around. It may be possible to negotiate a more favorable deal going to a store where you are known because you have bought a lot in the past. The details of a joint financial arrangement should be discussed openly. With a little more give-and-take on both sides, you should be able to reach amicable agreements where joint endeavors are concerned. Avoid buying anything sight unseen.

10. FRIDAY. Mixed. Take the whole day at a slow, measured pace. Detailed matters need much more concentration than you may have planned. If you need to make an important decision affecting your financial position, it is especially vital to take time in deciding exactly what to do and when. Where joint financial interests are concerned, an investment made some time ago may begin to pay off now. Gemini people who have been out of work need to make an effort to get back in touch with previous contacts from the business world. It is likely that they will be able to steer some work your way or suggest an opening which has not yet been advertised.

11. SATURDAY. Deceptive. Avoid mixing business with pleasure. Certain friends of yours may think they have come up with a fail proof get-rich-quick scheme. However, if you can see obvious flaws in this enterprise, point them out, especially if you are being urged to get involved yourself. Trust your good Gemini instincts; they are sure to be an accurate guide. For single Gemini people anxious for a new love partner, it is possible that a meeting will occur via your academic interests. Just be wary of someone who is a complete stranger and may not be all that they pretend to be. Stay with a group rather than pairing up.

12. SUNDAY. Variable. Be firm about what you are willing to take on. You can get roped into running errands which were not on your agenda originally. If you are helping out a friend who is having problems, giving extra time and attention may not seem so annoying. If, however, they are imposing on you, be less willing to make personal sacrifices. Nobody can really blame you for wanting some time for yourself on the weekend. Where new interests are concerned, take your time learning the skill or technique involved. It could take a lot longer than you expect, but if you stick at it you will probably be quite pleased with yourself and your accomplishments.

13. MONDAY. Good. This is a favorable day for working to broaden your horizons in a significant way. Be more adventurous in your pursuit of leisure interests. Study of any kind, particularly on a new subject, is likely to be quite inspiring. Long-distance travel opportunities may appeal to you. If you are planning on doing some shopping, you may be able to combine this with a trip to see a friend or relative who lives a good distance away. Scan newspaper advertisements for expensive items which are being offered at a reasonable price, perhaps due to the lower overhead of certain stores or their ability to buy in bulk.

14. TUESDAY. Demanding. Expect a difficult day where professional matters are concerned. Conflict may erupt with your boss or with a colleague with whom you generally have trouble seeing eye-to-eye. Careful, tactful negotiation is your key to success in smoothing over difficulties. It may be tempting to stand your ground and argue your point just because you want to win, but you will not be doing yourself any great favor in the long run. In dealing with clients who may buy your products or services, your strength is in being totally convincing about the benefits you can offer over and above what a competitor offers.

15. WEDNESDAY. Manageable. This is a more favorable day than yesterday for moving forward with professional interests. Colleagues should be more cooperative and easygoing. If there has been a dispute over a contractual arrangement, it is in your best interests to go the extra mile to try to make up for any inconvenience that has been caused to the other person. In this way you can leave a sweeter taste in the person's mouth and expect future business from them. Be very careful in the way that you phrase delicate issues at the moment. It is difficult to predict other people's overall responses because they are apt to mask their true feelings and intentions.

16. THURSDAY. Mixed. Although yesterday's tactfulness should have helped you considerably, today you may have less success in gaining cooperation from various business associates. The basic problem could be that they have other matters to attend to which are demanding top priority. As a consequence you simply have to be more patient. It may start to seem that you and those you work with have quite different basic aims. If you foresee this causing a lot of problems in the future, it might be advisable to discuss the matter with your boss. For now, try to find areas of possible compromise. Do not take on anything new unless you know who you will be working with.

17. FRIDAY. Productive. You can get a great deal done if you are mentally and emotionally alert. If you have a specific issue to resolve, talk it through with a good friend or an insightful business associate. Verbalizing the details of a dilemma should make it easier to find the best solution. Your partner is likely to be especially helpful, better than you at seeing the heart of a tricky problem. Invitations to celebrations are on the way. Try to include your mate or partner more than you have been able to do on other occasions. Avoid a get-together geared solely for work colleagues. Public transportation is a better choice than driving tonight.

18. SATURDAY. Misleading. Expect this to be a busy and vibrant day for all social matters. If you feel that your schedule is a little too hectic, however, trim it down. It may be possible to postpone a couple of errands or chores until a more suitable time. An evening event is likely to be more drawn out than you anticipate. Particularly with friends that you have not seen in a long time, there is a tendency to keep on talking and talking until it is way past your bedtime. Consider suggesting another gathering soon and cutting this one short, especially if you have important plans for tomorrow.

19. SUNDAY. Routine. You should be able to make good progress in catching up with matters which have been neglected for one reason or another. You should also have the opportunity to get back to a hobby or pastime which had to be put aside temporarily. Expect to make gradual, sound progress rather than zipping through a lot of work carelessly. If you need to study, concentrate on in-depth reading instead of skimming the text. There could be a number of minor distractions to contend with, which may temporarily blur your concentration. If telephone calls come through and you are busy, try to make the conversation brief and to the point, or turn on the answering machine and call back at a more convenient time for you.

20. MONDAY. Exciting. This is a favorable day for concentrating on personal affairs and plans. Be prepared to be more adventurous than usual in both what you do and where you go. You are sure to discover something new which pleases you. If there is a special function to attend soon, perhaps a formal Christmas party, you will probably feel better about yourself if you turn up in a new outfit. This is especially important if you go to this same event every year. However, if you need to save money, consider alternatives to buying new; check a secondhand store selling designer clothes, or look into the possibility of borrowing what you need from a friend who is your size.

21. TUESDAY. Disquieting. Do not expect a great deal of co-operation from your mate or partner. For reasons of their own, it is likely that they oppose your plans and initiatives. It is probably best just to do your own thing. If your partner is nursing a major grudge, however, the two of you need to talk about the matter at some time. Try to have such a discussion later rather than sooner, as you could end up getting yourself into a stew of complex emotions. If someone wants to discuss a personal problem and you are short of time, encourage them to work out the solution on their own, promising that you will support whatever they decide.

22. WEDNESDAY. Variable. There is a good chance of making significant progress with your personal aims and ambitions. An opportunity may come your way which allows you to broaden your social circle and your general horizons. A number of last-minute social invitations are likely by mail or phone. Accept at least one which offers something a little out of the ordinary. You are likely to start feeling the pinch now if you have been spending a lot on holiday celebrations and gifts. It is advisable to start tightening your belt and thinking about the bills to come rather than continuing to use your credit until it reaches the limit.

23. THURSDAY. Satisfactory. Expect encouraging news regarding current money matters. If you have been expecting a check or payment by mail, it is likely to be delivered today. If you made a resolve yesterday to improve your overall financial situation, stick to it today. You can probably think of plenty of reasons for spending, but try to avoid temptation. This is one of those days when you may start to wonder if you will ever be able to get away in order to enjoy the holiday. Stay busy tying up last-minute deals and loose ends; do not start anything new or make any commitments for the new year.

24. FRIDAY. Stressful. Do not bank on some big social event being all that you hope it will be. If you set your expectations quite low you are less open to possible disappointment. You may end up spending more money than you budgeted, but probably this cannot really be avoided due to the expense associated with buying gifts and with partying. Unless you keep your distance from associates who are renowned for turning up with insufficient funds, you may end up having to cover their bill as well as your own. If a long-distance journey seems too much for you late in the day, cancel out of the trip with sincere apologies.

25. SATURDAY. Merry Christmas! This promises to be a particularly enjoyable Christmas. People with whom you are sharing the day are generally more talkative and sociable, making them enjoyable company. Today's events should more than make up for any disappointment you experienced yesterday. Your only real problem is a tendency to tire as the day goes on. Everyone else may be ready to party, while you are close to falling asleep. It might help to make time for a nap this afternoon. Loved ones are likely to be good at reigniting your energy and enthusiasm, knowing just how to treat you. Be sure to show appreciation for each and every gift you receive, even those that are way out of the ordinary.

26. SUNDAY. Enjoyable. This is likely to be a particularly enjoyable part of the holiday. The major celebration is now over, and the hassles associated with Christmas preparation are mostly out of the way. You should have more opportunity to relax and enjoy yourself. Being able to spend a lot of time with family and relatives is sure to be a pleasure. With neighbors, too, there should be a chance to catch up on their news. Do not hesitate to discuss quite important plans for the future with your nearest and dearest. If you have no reason to travel or keep busy, avoid inventing a reason to do so. Take advantage of the opportunity to rest, relax, and unwind.

27. MONDAY. Pleasant. Time spent with family members and friends should once again be particularly pleasant. You may feel like doing some entertaining at home. Make it a team effort, getting the whole family involved rather than overburdening yourself. In this way you can join in the conversation and general fun of the party. For Gemini professionals who are already back at work, this is a favorable day for tying up loose ends left over from before the holiday break. Concentrate on clearing up what has been neglected before starting anything new. Eat light and right throughout the day; keep meals simple and not too spicy.

28. TUESDAY. Tricky. Get out and about. Too much time spent cooped up with your thoughts is a bad idea. If there are important matters to discuss, arrange to have the conversation in a different environment. Walk and talking might be the best option and should also be quite refreshing. Good rapport is likely with friends. If you want to improve matters between you and your partner, go out together with friends in a group. People generally are ready and willing to discuss future plans, making it easier for you to bring up a subject that has been on your mind or conscience for a while.

29. WEDNESDAY. Fair. This is potentially a very creative day. You are likely to get good ideas and inspirations if you opt for a change of scene. Even if it is bitter cold outside, a short walk should be invigorating. For single Gemini men and women there is opportunity for romance in a social setting that is new for you. Travel is likely to provide the right setting for romance between Gemini spouses. It may be tempting to spend a lot at the post-Christmas sales, but first consider if you can really afford to do so. Paying off your credit card in full should be your first priority.

30. THURSDAY. Excellent. Expect the unexpected, in the nicest possible way. This is a day full of pleasant surprises. A romantic interlude is more likely if you are out of town. A journey to an unusual place is sure to inspire you. Start making some resolutions for the new year. This might be the right time to take up a new hobby or interest. If Christmas overeating is starting to show on your waistline, start planning a diet and exercise program. For single Gemini men and women, a magnetic and instant attraction could occur with someone you meet this evening. Be more aggressive in getting to know a person who appeals to you as a potential partner.

31. FRIDAY. Sensitive. Try to take life easy where social activities are concerned. Keep your eating and drinking to a minimum. You have the willpower now to say no when you would prefer to say yes. You are likely to do something which later embarrasses you if you are under the influence. Start preparing for any major new year resolutions. Think how good you will feel when you succeed. You may not feel so enthusiastic about a journey you have been thinking of making if it involves getting up early tomorrow morning. If you intend to travel, consider going to bed early tonight if you do not mind missing ringing in the new year.

GEMINI
NOVEMBER–DECEMBER 1998

November 1998

1. SUNDAY. Mixed. You might want to start the new month with a trip to spend the day with relatives or friends you have not seen for a while. Traveling should be easygoing on the whole, but have a map available if you are driving a new route. If you are meeting someone for the first time you are sure to make a good impression by just being yourself. This allows others to feel relaxed in your company. You may also want to browse around antique shops and could pick up some bargains. A painting can be a good investment. This evening is a favorable time for returning telephone calls, writing letters, or paying bills.

2. MONDAY. Quiet. Avoid attempting to repair a relationship with someone who has become a source of constant trouble or worry to you. This is a time to think seriously about clearing the deadwood out of your personal life. There is no point continuing a friendship just for the sake of it. You can be much happier at the moment if you spend time with people who share your outside interests as well as your general philosophy on life. A romance may come to an end when you discover that you no longer have much trust in one another. As a Gemini you are not usually short of social invitations, but you may want to turn down a night out in favor of staying home this evening.

3. TUESDAY. Uncertain. Although teamwork can be tricky, you need to call upon others if there is a lot to be done. What would take hours to accomplish alone can be dispatched quickly and easily with the help of friends or colleagues. Even though you are under a lot of pressure, try to be patient with someone who is naturally slower than you. If you work in a managerial capacity, spend more time training and supporting your staff. Keeping your finger on the pulse is the best way of nipping problems in the bud. If you do not have much money in your wallet, keep in mind that you do not have to spend a lot in order to have a good time.

4. WEDNESDAY. Good. You are right to feel that life is going your way. Friends will be there for you without your having to ask. Someone is ready and willing to return a favor and put themselves out for you. If you want to celebrate a friend's special occasion, send flowers or a bouquet of balloons. A colleague who has been difficult to work with is likely to respond now to your friendly overtures. This is not a time for bearing a grudge or withdrawing from people. Keep in mind that every relationship is a two-way street. This evening favors sorting through old photographs or rereading old letters; enjoy the memories. If you keep a diary, hide it away from prying eyes.

5. THURSDAY. Disquieting. You could become involved in confidential discussions at work. Do not be tempted to repeat information which you are asked to keep to yourself; you risk damaging your professional reputation. Private notes and other backup material of all kinds should be filed away for future reference. This is a good time for bringing your records up to date. If you can put your hands on the right documents at a moment's notice you can save yourself a lot of time and worry. A relative may want to talk about issues from the past which continue to be painful for them. Love means being there for support when someone needs a shoulder to lean on.

6. FRIDAY. Unsettling. Morning hours favor working alone. A project which requires close concentration can be time consuming; do not let less pressing matters distract you. Take other people's advice with a healthy grain of skepticism; what they have to say could be self-serving. However, heed those who have already shown that they have your best interests at heart. If you want to heal a broken romance, prepare for some honest conversation; you may have to tell, and hear, some home truths. This day gets busier as it goes on. A social arrangement which you are looking forward to could be canceled on short notice. Follow a hunch and you may soon have second thoughts.

7. SATURDAY. Difficult. Faith in your own abilities and decisions could be somewhat shaky at the moment. If your self-esteem is at a low ebb, you should ask yourself why. You may have been dealing lately with too much criticism or disapproval from someone you admire. Remind yourself of your strong points; refuse to be judged by others. Nobody is perfect, no matter what they would have you believe. In your personal relationships let it be clear that you practice what you preach. In this way you can win the trust of someone special and impress someone new. Keep a close eye on your belongings; there is a risk of loss or theft.

8. SUNDAY. Excellent. Even if you normally sleep late on Sunday mornings you might decide to get up early today. You should have lots of energy this morning; it is the best time of day for getting your domestic chores out of the way. This is a propitious time for celebrating a special occasion such as an anniversary or an engagement. The general atmosphere should be happy and positive. If you are in a strong financial position, you can get a lot of pleasure from helping a loved one who is just starting out. Make a gift rather than a loan, although you are sure to be repaid in one way or another. A telephone call from someone special can be the highlight of the day.

9. MONDAY. Changeable. The new workweek may not get off to the best of starts, but any problems can probably be solved by lunchtime. Do not waste time worrying over any matter which is ultimately beyond your control. Trust other people to do their best, just as you are doing. For Gemini business people this is a good day for taking a client out for lunch. You are more likely to strike a deal in a restaurant than from behind a desk. This is a fruitful day if you are looking for new business premises of any kind or new living accommodations for yourself. If you have a spare room at home, consider renting it out, perhaps to someone you know.

10. TUESDAY. Challenging. It can be hard to whip up any real enthusiasm for work in the early part of the day. You will probably just be going through the motions. Keep in mind that what does not get done today still has to be done tomorrow. Your best approach is to set achievable targets, including at least one job which you dislike or which you have been putting off for too long. This can do wonders for your motivation, and you should finish the day in a much better frame of mind. Someone who is not doing their fair share cannot escape your notice for long. Find out what the underlying problem is before complaining.

11. WEDNESDAY. Starred. It is safe to take on any new commitment which requires you to be in sparkling form; you should have no trouble rising to the occasion. In the workplace find time to put your own affairs in order. Deal with outstanding filing and letter writing, and return telephone calls as promptly as possible. If you have a heavy workload at the moment, carefully plan a detailed schedule for the rest of the week so that you have a more realistic view of how much you can expect to achieve. You are apt to feel in a sociable mood this evening. If you have not made definite plans, call a few of your friends and arrange an impromptu gathering.

12. THURSDAY. Confusing. A state of confusion concerning a personal relationship is unlikely to ease up now. Make a point of distinguishing between fantasy and fact. Your own active imagination could soon lead you to believe something that has no relation to the real situation. To sort out just how you feel, stand back and try to be less emotional. Only when you do this can you hope for a successful heart-to-heart discussion to clear the air. This is not a good day for making final decisions of any kind. There is a greater chance that you do not have all pertinent facts. Do not rely on someone who has been untrustworthy in the past, no matter what assurances they give you.

13. FRIDAY. Fair. If your work involves serving the public you may have to tap into your extra reserves of patience and good humor. Someone is likely to waste a lot of your time with endless questions or complaints which seem unnecessary. Try to compromise with your work colleagues, even if you think that your way of doing things is by far the best. In this way you should avoid accusations of being overbearing. Keep in mind that your own success and efficiency ultimately speak for themselves. Let someone else draw attention to a recent achievement of yours rather than blowing your own horn. Spend the evening with your family; togetherness may be long overdue.

14. SATURDAY. Satisfactory. The weekend gets off to a cheerful start. Find time to enjoy a special hobby or an academic interest. Sports of all kinds are also favored. Keep your timetable flexible. It is wise not to make any specific arrangements for today, which you may have to cancel. In your personal relationships be prepared to give in regarding certain small details in order to keep everyone happy. A night out can be fun; you might decide to attend a concert or a dinner theater. Single Geminis could be introduced to someone who soon becomes important on an everyday basis. Romance is in the air.

15. SUNDAY. Good. Gemini parents could find that children are calmer and better behaved than usual. Youngsters are likely to be happier to amuse themselves rather than constantly looking to you for attention or stimulation. This is a good time for the generations to be together at home. Children's games can be as much fun for adults if you play for the joy of it rather than just to win. If you are playing an individual or team sport there is a greater chance of coming out on top. You can breathe new life into a romance if you set aside the day to be alone together. Put off other social engagements until another time.

16. MONDAY. Deceptive. This is a busy start to the working week. If you are a manager, be careful not to delegate too much. You could put someone under more pressure than they can cope with effectively. Creative work is not especially favored; you are likely to feel blocked. It may be best to put aside any project which has you stumped at the moment; you should have fresh insights when you return to it at a later date. Children can cause extra expense. You may have to sacrifice some desires of your own in order to meet their needs. If a social invitation is too expensive to accept, make up an excuse.

17. TUESDAY. Variable. A colleague may become ill or have an accident at work. This can be a timely reminder to keep a well-stocked first-aid kit available at all times. If someone close to you is hospitalized, there may be some encouraging news of the prognosis not as serious as you had feared. As a Gemini you have a tendency to worry a lot about the little things. Try to relax about matters which are beyond your immediate control. You may have to arrange a trip on short notice. Make sure that your luggage is well identified and not too heavy for you to handle alone. The offer of a pet can be tempting, but think carefully about the long-term responsibility involved.

18. WEDNESDAY. Easygoing. You are unlikely to be under any particular pressure. In fact, you may have to hunt around for things to do in order to keep boredom from setting in. If you are unemployed at the moment, there is a greater possibility of being offered some part-time work. Your personal job hunting efforts could be more fruitful than those of an agency supposedly working on your behalf. This can be a good time for taking on an evening job if you need to earn some extra cash. For Geminis who are weight conscious, this is a favorable time for starting a sensible diet. It should be easy to shed a few pounds if you give up a few of your favorite snacks. Make a point of getting some exercise, perhaps walking when you would normally drive.

19. THURSDAY. Fair. If you are thinking of becoming self-employed, a friend or colleague may express an interest in joining you. Discuss what you both want from a business venture so that you can find out in advance if you are professionally compatible. Get-rich-quick schemes are not likely to work out for you. Something which seems convincing on paper may have many hidden flaws. Some unexpected changes may be foisted on you. Although these can be disruptive in the short term, you could soon see that they make good sense; do not be too quick to object to them. Tension in romance seems inevitable at the moment.

20. FRIDAY. Unsettling. You can get the most out of the day by being as flexible as possible. Cooperating with colleagues is essential if a job is to be completed satisfactorily and on time. This is a good time for pooling resources and ideas. Try not to offer advice unless you are specifically asked for it. People are usually happier doing things their own way; they might mistake any of your well-intentioned suggestions for interference or bossiness. For single Geminis a new relationship could start up unexpectedly. The attention being paid to you can be flattering, but guard against being swept along too fast for your liking.

21. SATURDAY. Variable. Someone close to you may be in an unusually difficult mood. It may not be easy to figure out how to handle them; try to read the signs. If they clearly need extra sympathy or support, give as much as you can spare. If you ignore someone's plea for help you could alienate them, maybe permanently. Your spouse or partner may be preoccupied with personal matters. This is not a good time to be too demanding; try not to take their neglect personally. Make your own social arrangements to show that you can be independent. This should strengthen your relationship and put you back on an even keel.

22. SUNDAY. Fortunate. Joint finances may require some discussion. If you or the person you live with has recently had a pay raise, you may want to adjust the sharing of bills accordingly. Make sure, however, that you both fully agree to any changes. You can afford to celebrate if you have recently paid off a loan in full; your quality of life should be on the upswing. You may decide to dip into your savings for a special purchase, but do not be tempted to fritter away hard-saved cash on casual spending. You could regret being impulsive. A social gathering may exceed your expectations. A fear that you could be overdressed or could become tongue-tied is likely to be groundless.

23. MONDAY. Disquieting. A friend or colleague who is normally very reliable may let you down, leaving you feeling unsettled. You may wonder if your trust has been misplaced, but keep in mind that there is usually a good reason when someone acts out of character. This is a time to give them the benefit of the doubt. If you are involved in a new relationship or a new job, make sure that you are not neglecting a friend. Make an extra effort to stay in touch; arrange a get-together for later in the week. Discussions about spiritual matters can be intriguing, although arguing with a total skeptic is probably pointless.

24. TUESDAY. Manageable. This promises to be a productive morning for Geminis who work directly with the general public. A new customer can steer a lot of new business your way. Geminis who are full-time students may be tempted to give up on a course which is difficult, but a seminar or lecture today can be an eye-opener. Small discussion groups provide the ideal setting for delving into a subject in more depth. With the holidays coming up, you may be thinking of spending your vacation away from home. This is a good time to visit a travel agent to find out about special vacation package deals. Rent a video or go to the movies this evening.

25. WEDNESDAY. Good. If you are involved in legal action of any kind this is a good time to push for a settlement. Put some pressure on people who are acting on your behalf. Keep in mind that it is often the people who make the most noise who get the quickest attention; do not allow your case to be ignored or constantly delayed. Business transactions of all kinds can be finalized more quickly than you expect. Be ready to think on your feet if you are taken by surprise. Single Geminis could be asked out by a newcomer. You have nothing to lose by agreeing to a date even if the person is not your usual type.

26. THURSDAY. Mixed. Geminis are known for curious minds. You may want to read up on a subject in more depth for your own satisfaction and understanding. It is important to be around people who share your interests. Avoid discussing serious subjects with those who are clearly not interested; you will only end up feeling frustrated. Steer clear of a family member who is clearly not in the best of moods. Because an older relative's concern may come across as criticism, be careful not to overreact to their well-meaning comments or advice. Be sure to include children in your free-time activities on this Thanksgiving holiday.

27. FRIDAY. Frustrating. This can be a testing end to the working week for Gemini business people. A transaction which has taken up a lot of your time and energy may come to nothing after all. It is important now not to dwell on negative developments. Try to learn from the experience, and let it spur you on to greater things. A problem in a personal relationship which surfaces today may be puzzling. It could be an old issue in a different form. Do not wait any longer to address the source of the problem. Self-examination can be painful, but it is probably the only way of gaining deeper self-awareness in making plans for the future.

28. SATURDAY. Fair. This is likely to be an active start to the weekend. If you have young children they may wake much earlier than usual, giving you no choice but to get an early start. When you are out and about you may run into an old friend. Exchanging news and gossip with them can be fun, but information about someone from your past could give you cause for concern. Find out their current telephone number or address so that you can get back in touch. This evening favors hosting a party. To avoid complaints about late-night noise, invite the neighbors. Stay alert for signs that a guest has had too much to drink.

29. SUNDAY. Exciting. This is a propitious time for making renewed efforts in your social life if you feel somewhat isolated or have just broken up a relationship. Fresh starts with old friends are likely to be successful. Accept any invitation even if you may not know many of the other guests. You are apt to have a lot of fun if you are adventurous. You can afford to put pleasure first. If you get involved in a political discussion, listen with an open mind even if the views being expressed do not represent a party you would not normally vote for. Be willing to take part in a sponsored event aimed at raising money for a charity.

30. MONDAY. Pressured. This is unlikely to be an easy start to the workweek. You may have to take on more responsibility than normal. A meeting with a superior can make you feel nervous. If you are called upon to justify certain actions or decisions, just stick to the facts. Do not fall into the trap of being apologetic or of explaining yourself in too much detail. If a problem at work is clearly beyond your expertise, be willing to admit that fact and hand it over to someone else. A new romance may be more like hard work than fun. Consider whether you really want to be paired with someone who makes you feel tense or inadequate.

December 1998

1. TUESDAY. Changeable. Although you may start the day suffering from low energy, being in the company of other people can soon get you going. This is a good time for beginning a new project. You should be at your best when working closely as part of a team. If you use your Gemini creativity to earn a living, this can be a productive day. You should find it easy to produce well above your average and could be offered an exciting one-time opportunity, perhaps involving visiting a celebrity. You may be able to secure a good price for original work. On the job there is the chance of a promotion or pay raise. Someone in authority is busy behind the scenes pulling some strings on your behalf.

2. WEDNESDAY. Unsettling. If you had a hectic day yesterday you might not feel you have had sufficient time to recover. Because your mental processes are probably not up to your usual standards, stick to routine tasks. A recent misunderstanding with a loved one can leave you feeling angry. Consider whether you are holding on to your resentment rather than trying to set the record straight. Personal dilemmas of any kind should be thought through alone. If you solicit other people's opinions you are apt to end up with a lot of conflicting advice, which will get you nowhere. A restful evening and an early night are the best plan for tonight.

3. THURSDAY. Variable. This is a demanding day for Geminis. Get an earlier start than usual. If you are feeling anxious about a certain meeting or appointment, try to relax and get a grip on your nerves. When the time comes, you should be able to think brilliantly on your feet. Do not hesitate to engage an adversary in a debate; others are sure to admire your fighting spirit and cleverness with words. Although anxiety about a loved one could be preying on your mind, your best policy is to stay in the background while offering moral support rather than trying to take on their battles. Avoid discussions at home concerning any sensitive subject; wait for a better opportunity to bring it up.

4. FRIDAY. Slow. The Gemini nature usually considers all sides of a situation. Someone who trusts you to be frank may seek your opinion about a personal matter, but this does not mean that you should be too upfront with criticism. By all means say what you think, putting it in such a way that the other person can easily accept it. Check your calendar before saying yes to an invitation; there is a greater risk of double booking. In the workplace you may not be in the right frame of mind for pushing yourself and your ideas forward. Be content to let others take center stage. Arrangements for this evening should be confirmed in advance.

5. SATURDAY. Mixed. This is a fun start to the weekend on the whole. You are high in the popularity stakes at the moment. There is unlikely to be any shortage of choices when it comes to social events; the festive season may already be getting into full stride. All you really need to guard against is careless spending. If you plan to start your Christmas shopping today, work out a budget in advance. If you have a lot of people to buy for, agree among yourselves how much you will spend. Children's gifts can be the most expensive; be prepared to shop around and compare prices. A handmade gift is likely to be especially appreciated.

6. SUNDAY. Disquieting. You may not be in the best mood. Even the smallest task can seem to require too much effort. If you usually do the cooking at home, you might want to let someone else take over in the kitchen for a change. You may feel in the mood to be looked after rather than tending to other people's needs. You might also suggest going out for a meal so that everyone gets a break. Geminis who are unattached at the moment may be thinking about someone new on the scene. If it appears that this person is unwilling to take the initiative, it is probably useless waiting for the telephone to ring. Instead, enlist the help of a third party or arrange to attend the same social get-together.

7. MONDAY. Fair. This is a busy start to the working week. You may have to deal with more than the usual amount of administrative tasks. Written work of all kinds can be time consuming. Be extra meticulous if preparing a document for a client or a superior; slapdash work is almost certain to be returned to you to be redone. If you have not yet made any definite plans for the Christmas vacation, there may be an offer to visit friends or relatives at a distance. If you want to break with tradition, make sure that other family members will not be too disappointed or feel let down. If you are married your plans should include both families.

8. TUESDAY. Excellent. By making a list of the people to whom you want to send Christmas cards this year you are less likely to overlook someone. Gemini business people should make a separate list for clients and work associates. Vintage wine could be the perfect gift for a particularly valued customer. It can be difficult to get out of a social engagement which does not appeal to you, especially if someone is putting you under a lot of pressure to accept. The occasion could turn out to be far more fun than you expect. This is a good day for office reorganization. A romance which has so far been carried on in secret could now come out into the open.

9. WEDNESDAY. Happy. Your mail is likely to include several cards from friends, both old and new. A message from someone in your past may not be so welcome. If you do not want to revive the relationship, there is no need to return greetings just out of politeness; doing so could be just asking for trouble. Your workload is apt to be heavier than usual, but there are several tasks which could easily be delegated. This evening is a sociable time. You may be invited to a function connected with your or your partner's work. Be a little wary of saying too much to someone in a position of authority.

10. THURSDAY. Disquieting. If you do not have as much free time as you would like, carefully plan ahead. Consider ordering gifts through a catalog or sending money, which is always welcome. Do not miss a child's play or concert, no matter how tired or busy you may be. This is a good day for putting up decorations at home or at your place of work; a festive atmosphere can do a lot to lift the general mood. Family squabbles are more likely at this time. Although you may wish to stay neutral, someone could be pushing you to take sides. Try to arrange a truce if you cannot arbitrate a settlement.

11. FRIDAY. Cautious. This entire month is a notoriously bad time for break-ins. If you are at work all day, make sure that your home is secure. Do not leave valuables in the open, especially if they can be seen by a passerby. Single Geminis are unlikely to be short of offers for the Christmas vacation. Take your time accepting; avoid committing yourself to any arrangement which you might later want to break for any reason. Time is at a premium at the moment. Make an extra effort to plan ahead so that you can squeeze everything in. Try not to overcommit yourself socially. Burning the candle at both ends for too long can be exhausting and drain the fun out of any gathering.

12. SATURDAY. Successful. If you are shopping you may be dismayed at how much everything costs. You might have to re-think some of your purchases. You can make a little money go a long way if you use your imagination. Make sure that gifts are hidden away at home so that they cannot be found beforehand. If you have cards or parcels to send abroad, get them in the mail as soon as possible in order to guarantee that they arrive in time. A romance which has been a struggle for a while could now take a turn for the better. There is a greater chance of heartfelt commitments being made on both sides.

13. SUNDAY. Mixed. If you have children at home, make arrangements in advance for when you will be out during the festive season. Write a list of presents you still have to buy. You may be able to share more expensive items with another member of your family. If you are throwing a party you may end up with fewer guests than you had planned for, but a small gathering can be just as much fun. You may get confirmation that you have successfully played matchmaker between two of your friends. Their actions are all you need to see. Make extra time for a friend who is going through a difficult period. Your moral support counts for a lot at this time in their life.

14. MONDAY. Changeable. You may have been expending too much energy on other people's problems lately. A former colleague or a friend who always expects you to be available at the drop of a hat could turn up unannounced If you are busy or just not in the mood to entertain, it is up to you to say so. Do not let them take over your day. In the workplace you may have to deal with some disruptions to your usual routine. Try to take these in stride. If you are unemployed at the moment, this is a favorable time for taking a seasonable job. Although it may not last more than a couple of weeks, there is a good chance that you could earn a considerable amount and get valuable experience.

15. TUESDAY. Exciting. This promises to be a successful day at work. You should be feeling enthusiastic about a new project. Learning a new skill can be stimulating. Gemini students should be in the right frame of mind for settling down to studying; you can clear a lot of work out of the way before breaking for Christmas vacation. When it comes to decision making of all kinds you can afford to place more faith in your hunches; they are unlikely to let you down. A party this evening should go with a swing. In an informal setting you get the chance to know a neighbor or a co-worker a lot better. Romance is in the cards for single Geminis currently unattached.

16. WEDNESDAY. Manageable. Do not agree to take on extra work unless you are sure that you can fit it into your schedule. Spending extra time at work at this time of the year is unlikely to be well accepted by your loved ones. This is a time when your personal life should take priority as much as possible over your work. Today's mail may include cards from all sorts of people. If you hear from someone you missed on your own list, it is not too late to send a card. If you are shopping, perfume or jewelry could be bargain buys. Give special thought to a gift for the most important person in your life; make it something personal rather than merely useful.

17. THURSDAY. Fair. This is a busy day for Geminis dealing directly with the public. Profits are likely to be up compared with this time last year. If your work involves personal service, expect to be rushed off your feet. Do not let a customer's difficult behavior rattle you; being calm and polite can defuse a potentially awkward scene. If you still have Christmas presents to buy but have run out of ideas, it might be more sensible just to ask the recipient what they really would like. Gift certificates are perfectly acceptable for teenagers or friends who live at a distance. You could pick up some extra work for the festive season.

18. FRIDAY. Tricky. Although charity appeals are always numerous at this time of year, realize that you probably cannot afford to respond to every request. Make a donation to the charity whose cause is closest to your heart. If you are unemployed, this is a good time for doing some volunteer work; it may lead to other opportunities in the new year. If you want to attend a certain play or concert over the festive season, buy tickets today for the best seats you can afford. You are likely to be feeling the pressure building. It can be hard to imagine having everything finished before your vacation. You can keep on top of things as long as you prioritize the jobs still to be done.

19. SATURDAY. Calm. Shopping malls may not be as busy as you fear. You should be able to finish off your Christmas shopping long before closing time. Your active social life at the moment could be making a big dent in your finances. You may have to turn down an invitation to an event which is sure to prove expensive. Guard against paying more than your fair share when you go out in a group. Someone who never seems to pay their way can be irritating; keep in mind that it is not up to you to bail them out. If Christmas is a rather sad time of year for you, do not hesitate to opt out of the party scene. Spending a night at home can be more relaxing than forced merrymaking.

20. SUNDAY. Mixed. The effects of the past hectic week can be hard to shake off. Some gentle exercise could help get your system going again. However, avoid very active or dangerous sport; there is a greater risk of an injury. Young children can be harder to handle than usual. The excitement of the upcoming holiday can make them hyperactive. Try to be extra inventive when it comes to keeping them quietly occupied. Finalizing a social arrangement for next week can be a headache. If you suspect that someone is likely to let you down, now is the time to come up with alternative arrangements. Try not to get caught in the middle of a dispute between family members or friends.

21. MONDAY. Confusing. Geminis who have to work right up to Christmas are in for a demanding start to the workweek. You may have to cover for a colleague who has already started their vacation. A certain problem may have to wait for their return if it has you stumped; do not waste too much energy on it. This evening is a good time for wrapping gifts or putting the finishing touches to your Christmas decorations at home. An invitation to a friend's home may conflict with family duties, but with some clever juggling you should be able to make time for both. Caroling can be an enjoyable experience, whether you sing along or just enjoy the performance.

22. TUESDAY. Demanding. This is a hectic day for Gemini workers. Extra responsibilities may be imposed on you although you could easily do without them. Even Geminis who are already on a break could be in for a busy day. The key to finishing all your preparations is to be well organized and then rope in some help. If you are leaving on a trip, be prepared for highway delays or long lines at the airport. In the rush to get away you might end up leaving something behind. Double-check that you have the essentials, especially gifts that you hid away. Do not forget to cancel the newspaper or other deliveries if you will be away for a while.

23. WEDNESDAY. Good. If you have been very busy at work the festive mood may not creep up on you until today. Now, however, you are ready to enter into the spirit of the season. Pressure in the workplace is likely to ease off. A sense of urgency about some tasks is probably unnecessary. Lunch with colleagues or friends could go on well into the afternoon. If you are shopping for last-minute gifts, you should find inspiration when you need it. Packages may arrive today, but resist the temptation to open them. This can be a good day for traveling out of town if you are spending the vacation with friends or distant family members.

24. THURSDAY. Fair. If this is your last day at work you may have a lot to do. Get down to tasks as quickly as possible and you should be able to leave a little early. Even if you are not working you still have to be well organized to get through the list of things which need to be done at home. If you expect guests to arrive today, make sure that you are well stocked with their favorite food and beverages. Have extra supplies in reserve in the likely event of unexpected visitors. A Christmas Eve party should be memorable. Make sure that you look your best; someone could be paying more attention to you than you realize.

25. FRIDAY. Merry Christmas! Christmas is usually a day of excess, and this is unlikely to be an exception. Enjoy the chance to indulge. Exchanging gifts is apt to go on for some time. You may be overwhelmed by the amount you receive. Someone special is set on spoiling you with their generosity. A carefully worked out schedule for the day might get ignored when high spirits and festive goodwill take over. Make dinner a leisurely occasion with sufficient time between courses. This holiday can be especially memorable for Gemini parents of young children. New lovers may end up talking late into the night. Personal relationships can be strengthened on all levels.

26. SATURDAY. Variable. If you are sharing the Christmas vacation with friends or relatives, this morning is a good time for a leisurely breakfast, or brunch if you get up late. There is probably still lots of news to catch up on. Restlessness later in the day may lure you out of the house, maybe just for a walk. You may also want to break away from family activities in order to visit some friends. Some stores may already be starting their sales, giving you an opportunity to spend some money or a gift certificate which you received as a present. There could be a choice of social gatherings choose the one where you will know the most people.

27. SUNDAY. Buoyant. Even the usually sociable Gemini could have less energy than usual. However, you are unlikely to get much time to yourself. Friends may telephone or just drop by unannounced; spontaneous get-togethers can be the best. A late exchange of gifts with loved ones who have been away could be on the agenda. Make a point of dropping in on an elderly neighbor or someone who you suspect may be lonely; you are sure to cheer them up. Young children could be feeling a sense of anticlimax. Be willing to play games or take them out for the day. If you sorely miss loved ones who is away, plan something special for the day of their return.

28. MONDAY. Demanding. If you are back at work any hope of an easy start is likely to be dashed. Work may have piled up in your absence, but at least that should make the day go quickly. If you have been hosting Christmas in your own home you may relish putting everything back in order. A certain guest could be outstaying their welcome; it may be hard to feel continuing good-will toward them. For single Geminis, a friend's party can be the perfect place for meeting someone new. If you have someone special in mind whom you would like to get to know, do not hesitate to invite them to an occasion of your own; this could get the social ball rolling.

29. TUESDAY. Pleasant. Working Geminis are likely to have an easier time today. It can be fun to exchange news and stories with your colleagues. Someone who has not had a particularly happy Christmas is sure to benefit from your cheerfulness. Strive to lift their mood rather than letting them bring you down. If you are at home there should be time for just relaxing or spending time with someone special. Old friends who are visiting for a short while may call. If you argued with anyone over the Christmas vacation, this is the perfect time for healing the rift. Lend your support to a charity occasion this evening, or write a check in response to a mailed appeal.

30. WEDNESDAY. Sensitive. You may feel sluggish and not up to par. Although it will probably require a lot of effort to get some exercise, you should feel a lot better for it. If you have to go to work do not expect too much of yourself; be satisfied with attending to the essentials. Someone you expect to hear from may not get in touch. Try not to jump to conclusions even if you feel that you have been forgotten or ignored. Trust that you will hear from them soon, and that their explanation will make good sense. It is smart to confirm arrangements for tomorrow evening; there is a greater danger of having your wires crossed with someone who has been out of touch.

31. THURSDAY. Enjoyable. You should be able to shake off any morning tiredness or apathy. The prospect of welcoming in the new year should fill you with optimism and renewed energy. Review your achievements of this year, both in your personal and professional life. You may be surprised to realize how many things have changed for you. Focus your resolutions for 1999 on your personal aims and goals. This evening favors a party which includes people you know well. Wear flashy jewelry and enjoy dressing up to the nines; you could easily win new admirers. Be with your favorite person when the clock strikes twelve.

Having A Good Psychic Is like Having A Guardian Angel!

Love, Romance, Money & Success
May Be In Your Stars....

Get a **FREE** Sample
Psychic Reading Today!!!

1-800-799-6582

Must be 18+. For entertainment purposes only! First 3 minutes FREE.

Let The Stars Guide You To The Future...
Where Love, Money and Success are waiting for you!
Find Out How to Get A FREE Sample Psychic Reading Today!!!
1-800-841-7648
For entertainment purposes only. Must be 18+. First 3 minutes FREE.

Find Love & Happiness

The Professional
Psychic Loveline ®

Talk live to our genuinely talented Psychics in matters of the heart. They have helped thousands of people just like you find true love, wealth and lasting happiness. Call anytime and get the answers you need from psychic who care.

NUMEROLOGY · TAROT ASTROLOGY · CLAIRVOYANT

FREE 2 MIN!

AS LOW AS $1.93/MIN

1-800-472-9015

CREDIT CARD OR CHECK

1-900-420-6500

FIRST 2 MIN FREE $3.99/MIN. AFTER

24 HOURS. 18+. ENTERTAINMENT PURPOSES ONLY.

AMERICA'S BEST PSYCHIC SOURCE

Astrology · Clairvoyants · Tarot Numerology

Have the life you always dreamed of with amazing insights from gifted psychics

AS LOW AS $1.93/MIN

1-800-472-4966

CREDIT CARD OR CHECK

1-900-420-0033

FIRST 2 MIN FREE $3.99/MIN. AFTER

24 HOURS. 18+. ENTERTAINMENT PURPOSES ONLY.

The PSYCHIC Romance SPECIALISTS

Try our elite group of gifted Psychics specializing in your personal questions about romance, love and mysteries of your heart. Our Specialists will empower and help guide you to the true happiness you deserve.

FREE 2 MINUTES! $3.99/MIN. AFTER

1-900-740-4466

1-800-784-9758

AS LOW AS $1.93/min.

CREDIT CARD OR CHECK ONLY
24 HOURS. 18+. ENTERTAINMENT PURPOSES ONLY.

FREE
Love
Advice

Does he really love me?

Will I ever get married?

Is he being faithful?

Call To Find Out How To Get Your

FREE Sample
Psychic Reading!

1-800-869-2879

18+. For entertainment purposes only. First 3 minutes FREE.

AMERICA'S MOST TRUSTED PSYCHIC NETWORKS

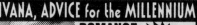

IVANA, ADVICE for the MILLENNIUM

ROMANCE MONEY HAPPINESS

MONEY BACK GUARANTEE

LIVE 24 HOURS

1-900-378-5959 $3.99 PER MIN.

USE YOUR CREDIT CARD & SAVE 50¢ PER MINUTE

1-800-449-7679 $3.49 PER MIN.

your Guardian ANGEL

Knows ∞ Protects ∞ Guides

10 MINUTES FREE!

CALL NOW TO HEAR WHAT SHE NEEDS TO TELL YOU!

1-900-378-6277 $3.99 per min.

Use Your Credit Card & Save 50¢ per min.

1-800-781-7865 $3.49 per min.

SERVING YOU 24 HOURS A DAY!

10 MIN FREE

Is It... **TRUE LOVE?** OR IS YOUR LOVER USING YOU?

Our PSYCHICS have ANSWERS to MARRIAGE & ROMANCE problems

1-900-378-6661 $3.99 PER MIN.

1-800-277-6661 $3.49 PER MIN.

USE YOUR CREDIT CARD & SAVE 50¢ PER MINUTE

Call NOW!

connie francis

"Where the Love is..." 9 minutes FREE

FOR YOU!

MY AUTHENTIC *Love Psychics* WILL HELP YOU FIND THE *Love of Your Life* AND MAKE YOUR *Dreams Come True*

1-900-378-5858 $3.99 PER MIN.

1-800-781-7865 $3.49 PER MIN.

Use Your Credit Card & Save 50¢ Per Min.

PAST LIFE READINGS

YOU MUST LEARN ABOUT THE PAST IN ORDER TO SAVE YOUR FUTURE

1-900-378-6161 $3.99 PER MIN.

Use Your Credit Card & Save 50¢ Per Minute

1-800-781-7836 $3.49 PER MIN.

PSYCHIC ANSWERS

Love
Health
Money

12 FREE MIN

1-900-378-6464 $3.99 PER MIN.

Use Your Credit Card & Save 50¢ Per Min.

1-800-781-7836 $3.49 PER MIN.

TALK TO YOUR PETS

through our animal loving psychics

Call for the LOVE of Your PET

1-900-378-6468 $3.99 PER MIN.

Use Your Credit Card & Save 50¢ Per Min.

1-800-781-7865 $3.49 PER MIN.

Affection Connection

SINGLES LINE

CONNECT NOW!

Call Now To Meet Someone Interesting & Exciting In Your Area

1-800-993-2722

ANCIENT ACCURATE ANSWERS

from Authentic Psychics

LUCK - LOVE

10 MINUTES FREE

TRUE CHANGE

24 HRS LIVE! Incredible Readings

1-900-378-6262 $3.99 PER MIN.

1-800-781-7865 $3.49 PER MIN.

Use Your Credit Card & Save 50¢ Per Min.

NOSTRADAMUS has FORECAST the FUTURE for more than SIX CENTURIES!

NINA NOSTRADAMUS PREDICTED THE 1989 SAN FRANCISCO QUAKE WITHIN 11 MINUTES!

6 FREE MIN

1-900-378-6386 $3.99 PER MIN.

1-800-781-7896 $3.49 PER MIN.

Use Your Credit Card & Save 50¢ Per Min.

Make The Most Important Call Of YOUR LIFE!

ISABEL "WEEZY" SANFORD Star of "The Jeffersons"

RUSSEL TODD Known as "Dr. Jamie Frame" Another World

SUSAN BROWN Known as "Dr. Gail Baldwin" General Hospital

AS SEEN ON TV

MASTER PSYCHIC READINGS

1-900-378-6225 $3.99 PER MINUTE

USE YOUR CREDIT CARD & SAVE 50¢ PER MIN.

1-800-988-6785 $3.49 PER MIN.

PSYCHIC BELIEVERS NETWORK • BOCA RATON, FL • MUST BE 18 YEARS OR OLDER TO CALL • FOR ENTERTAINMENT ONLY.

CURIOUS? TRY A PSYCHIC FREE

You've heard how psychics have changed the lives of others, and you want to try a psychic reading. Call the Psychic Readings Line first - **1-800-549-4736** - try it free. If you have personal questions about romance, love or relationships, sample the Master Psychics on **1-800-282-6711** for free advice and more. And, if you want to hear our most gifted psychics speak and interpret before you choose, call for Free Samples on **1-800-709-2224**. Adults over 18; optional paid services available. Entertainment only. 24 hours a day, 7 days a week.

FREE SAMPLES ON EVERY CALL

Sample the power of a gifted live psychic. Dial **1-800-569-6902** - listen free, then decide. Call to sample and choose from a hand-picked panel of renowned readers, seers, and advisors. And, for urgent matters of fortune or fate, dial and sample **1-800-803-5477** - FREE! Curious about what Cupid has in store for you? Dial **1-800-295-3012**, you'll find a psychic who may change your romantic future - plus, now you can try it free. Entertainment only. Optional paid services offered for use by adults over 18 only.

TROUBLE WITH LOVE, MONEY OR LUCK?

Dial **1-800-865-5925** for free samples with amazing psychics who speak what they see and feel. Or, sample the Psychic Power Line **1-800-955-8677**, where gifted psychics share visions and dreams to help you open your future and change your fate. And, if you want to find a top psychic for confidential readings, try **1-800-695-7364**, our special private line for free samples and more. No credit card required. Samples for entertainment only. All paid service optional. Adults over 18 only.

PY-905

STRAIGHT TALK

The LaToya Jackson Psychic Network

Pay By **CHECK** or **CREDIT CARD** and **SAVE** More Than a **DOLLAR A MINUTE**

TV 1-800-994-1800
OR CALL!
1-900-737-2442 $3.99 PER MIN.

"MY PSYCHICS TELL IT LIKE IT IS... JUST LIKE I DO!"

The **Amazing** JAMISON TWINS

TV **The WORLDS most Celebrated Psychic Twins**

WILL DOUBLE YOUR CHANCES FOR FINDING LOVE AND HAPPINESS

Listed in "100 Top Psychics in America"

The First 3 Minutes are FREE You Can Call 5 Times for a Total of 15 MIN. FREE!

15 MINUTES FREE 1-800-240-7007

The Witches of Salem

TV NETWORK℠

Pay By **CHECK** or **CREDIT CARD** and **SAVE** More Than a **DOLLAR A MINUTE**

1-800-799-5959
OR CALL!
1-900-370-1586
only $3.99 per minute

BRIGITTE NIELSEN

MOTHER LOVE

Is Love In Your Tarot? • Is Love In Your Stars?

LOVE IS IN THE AIR!

TV

Pay By **CHECK** or **CREDIT CARD** and **SAVE** More Than a **DOLLAR A MINUTE**

1-800-218-2442
OR CALL!
1-900-370-5330
only $3.99 per minute

MOTHER LOVE

Past Life Readings

To know where you're going you must know where you've been

Let us take you back in time.
CALL NOW!

1-800-564-8668

BARBARA NORCROSS

THE PALM BEACH PSYCHIC

PALM BEACH PSYCHIC TV

Psychic Advisor to the Rich and Famous. Trusted & Respected by Law Enforcement Agencies

Listed in "100 Top Psychics in America"

1-888-461-3663 TOLL FREE

---

6 MINUTES FREE

PSYCHIC READINGS

The First 3 Minutes are FREE...You Can Call 2 times for a total of 6 Minutes FREE!

LAURA BRYAN BIRN   *Soap Opera Star*

TV **1-800-737-2226**

FREE TAROT CARDS

with every call!

Tarot Card Readings

Call Now! Toll Free
1-888-732-4733

Spiritual Answers from Authentic Psychics

Let the ancient spirits guide you towards love and happiness. *CALL NOW* for an authentic **Native American Reading!**

Pay By **CHECK** or **CREDIT CARD** and **SAVE** More Than a **DOLLAR A MINUTE!**

1-800-923-3444 or 1-900-454-1156
only $3.99 per minute

12 MINUTES FREE NOSTRADAMUS

His Predictions Changed the World!

1-800-965-3663

 The Zodiac Group, Inc. • Boca Raton, Fl. • Must be 18 years or older • For Entertainment Only

HAVE YOU EVER NEEDED
SOMEONE TO TURN TO FOR ADVICE ON LOVE, MARRIAGE, ROMANCE?

LET OUR LIVE PSYCHICS BE THERE FOR YOU!

24 HOURS A DAY 7 DAYS A WEEK THEY'LL NEVER LET YOU DOWN! CALL NOW!

1-800-873-8327

OR

1-900-745-5601

The answers to your problems are only a phone call away!

Just $3.99per min. Billed to you Visa/Mc/Amex or directly to your phone you must be 18+

AS SEEN ON TV

KENNY KINGSTON PSYCHIC HOTLINE

THE MOST IMPORTANT PHONE CALL YOU'LL EVER MAKE

Kenny Kingston is the most sought after psychic in modern times. World famous celebrities and stars seek his guidance. Now you too can know what lies ahead. Take control of your own destiny. Talk to your own personal and confidential psychic today.

Stephanie Williams   William Katt   Sharron Farrel

Don't be afraid. Call now.

1-900-737-0802
7 days, 24 hours.
Only $3.99 per minute

Use your credit card and SAVE $1.00 per minute. Only $2.99 per minute

1-800-498-6614

www.kennykingston.com

Must be 18 years or older • Gold Coast Media, (305) 576-1358
3050 Biscayne Blvd., Miami, FL 33137

SHAN0802

Our Friendly Psychic Astrologers
Want To Give You A

FREE SAMPLE READING!

Get up to 24 FREE* Minutes!

1-900-VIP-FREE

1-900-847-4733

Great Psychics Just For You!

1-800-756-4SEE

1-800-756-4733

LIVE CANADIAN PSYCHICS!

FOR CANADIAN CALLERS ONLY!

1-900-451-3885

Blocked from 900 Numbers?
No Problem!
Just call this easy direct dial number
FROM ONLY .69¢ PER MIN.

THE MAGIC TAROT 011-592-580-322

SH99 Be 18+. First two minutes free, from $2.99/min. thereafter.*24free minutes offer includes two free minutes per monthbased on annual use for 900-847# only! 900-451# $3.99/min. 011# L..D. rates apply. Entertainment only.